HOLOCAUST AND HUMAN RIGHTS EDUCATION

HOLOCAUST AND HUMAN RIGHTS EDUCATION: GOOD CHOICES AND SOCIOLOGICAL PERSPECTIVES

BY

MICHAEL POLGAR
Penn State Hazleton, USA

United Kingdom – North America – Japan – India – Malaysia – China

Emerald Publishing Limited
Howard House, Wagon Lane, Bingley BD16 1WA, UK

First edition 2019

© 2019 Michael Polgar
Published under exclusive licence by Emerald Publishing Limited.

Reprints and permissions service
Contact: permissions@emeraldinsight.com

No part of this book may be reproduced, stored in a retrieval system, transmitted in any form or by any means electronic, mechanical, photocopying, recording or otherwise without either the prior written permission of the publisher or a licence permitting restricted copying issued in the UK by The Copyright Licensing Agency and in the USA by The Copyright Clearance Center. Any opinions expressed in the chapters are those of the authors. Whilst Emerald makes every effort to ensure the quality and accuracy of its content, Emerald makes no representation implied or otherwise, as to the chapters' suitability and application and disclaims any warranties, express or implied, to their use.

British Library Cataloguing in Publication Data
A catalogue record for this book is available from the British Library

ISBN: 978-1-78754-499-4 (Print)
ISBN: 978-1-78754-498-7 (Online)
ISBN: 978-1-78756-000-0 (Epub)
ISBN: 978-1-78756-001-7 (Paperback)

INVESTOR IN PEOPLE

Table of Contents

On Terminology ... *vii*

Preface ... *ix*

Chapter 1 **Introduction** ... *1*

Chapter 2 **Why We Teach Holocaust Education** ... *11*

Chapter 3 **How We Teach Holocaust Education** ... *31*

Chapter 4 **Realizing Our Responsibilities** ... *55*

Chapter 5 **Teaching Strong Cultures** ... *73*

Chapter 6 **Survivors Share Resilience** ... *95*

Chapter 7 **Global Holocaust Education for the Twenty-First Century** ... *111*

References ... *129*

Index ... *147*

On Terminology

The Holocaust was a 12-year historical event that is defined by the international community and the United State Holocaust Museum as "the systematic, bureaucratic, state-sponsored persecution and murder of 6 million Jews by the Nazi regime and its collaborators (United States Holocaust Memorial Museum 2018)." "Holocaust" literally means a sacrifice by fire. The Holocaust is also well described in other terms as a catastrophic event ("Shoah" or "Kurban"). In this text, therefore, *catastrophe* and **Shoah** are used in this text synonymously with "the Holocaust." In this text, the term "Holocaust" will not, and many believe *should not, be* used or *misused as a metaphor* for other destructive, violent, or catastrophic events, since doing so can dilute, distract from, or confuse learning about historical truths and consequences of *the* Holocaust (Novick, 1999).

Genocide is a general term for intentional efforts to destroy, in whole or in part, a national, ethnic, racial or religious group of people. After the Holocaust, the United Nations agreed that genocide is an international crime marked by mass violence (Lemkin, 1947). The Holocaust was the first, but certainly not the last or only, event that has been classified as a genocide. Therefore we will explore how Holocaust education can be (but is not always) part of genocide education.

The term *Holocaust survivor* is often used for those Holocaust protagonists who were directly harmed by the Holocaust, but more specifically those who were defined as such by official agencies after being held in ghettos or/and interned in concentration camps and in lands under Nazi occupation (Stein, 2014). More expansive definitions of this term include people who were harmed in other ways, including those who were forced to flee and become homeless or refugees, people robbed of possessions, and people who were deprived of ways to live or earn a living. Thus we may classify or specify *survivors* according to their experiences during the Holocaust, sometimes by including the names and types of camps experienced (e.g., Auschwitz survivor and author Primo Levi). "Genocide survivors" more generally describes people who endure persecution during any of many different genocides. Other important Holocaust-era protagonists include perpetrators, bystanders or onlookers, resistors, and also many groups of refugees displaced by war and conflict (Hayes & Roth, 2010).

Testimonies from Holocaust *witnesses* are spoken, written, and other accounts from survivors and others who lived through the Holocaust. What gets called "testimony" can and will also be called *narratives, accounts*, or more fully described with the verb *recounting*, which more fully describes the processual nature of sharing and then *retelling* experiences, rather than a more formal and completed "*witness* testimonial" which is more like a response to inquiry where the narrator is reporting on a contested or uncertain situation, often in a legal setting (Greenspan, 2010a). Challenging accounts by survivors may further harm those who may already have difficulties with anguished or humiliated memories (Langer, 1991).

Survivors recount experiences in many contexts. Some narratives are simply given as presentations while others are drawn out through interviews, sometimes creating **oral histories**. Witness accounts can also be treated as "oral philosophies" and "oral psychologies" that help us understand the difficult consequences and sometimes traumatic memories (Greenspan, 2010a). These distinctions matter since not all narratives are simply or strictly reports on past events and also since many authors and observers seek more from survivors than a descriptive accounting of the past. With the exception of fictional accounts, survivor narratives are *not* often well described as *stories*, even though many do use this term in this context, since these are most often true. Clearly, the ugly truth of some deep, anguished, and even unheroic aspects of testimonials can be difficult for survivors to share, drudging up "the ruins of memory" (Langer, 1986, 1991). Narrative recounting of the Holocaust can also be difficult for some audiences to stomach or even to accept as real experiences.

Many other terms, particularly those for status groups, may require clarifications during Holocaust education and discussion, reinforcing the fact that educational standards promote political literacies and civic education. These include "Nazi," "Jew," and "Roma," along with "Camp" and "Ghetto" (Cowan & Maitles, 2017). "Nazi" is a political (not strictly national) status, reflecting membership in a (German) National Socialist Party or governmental role; Nazi should and will not be used synonymously for a person who is nationally, ethnically, or culturally "German."

Educators can help students by discussing the varying definitions of "Jewish" and "Roma" in classes where these terms are not well understood. "Ghettos" during the Holocaust should and will be distinguished from this term's modern use to describe certain impoverished urban areas, while "camps" should be prefaced by a (sometimes overlapping or evolving) type or types (transit, detention, concentration, forced labor, death, POW, and DP camps). It's not easy to simply or exactly describe all of these prisons, however, since all *concentrate* people and many served multiple functions (Cowan & Maitles, 2017).

Thank you for your patience with these linguistic details and specifics! While I genuinely appreciate and work to use inclusive language in general, I do not consider only one vocabulary to be "correct." At the same time, I do want my or our uses of terms and language to effectively communicate exactly what I mean. These are sensitive topics and much more oppressive and false uses of terminology were previously dictated by criminal Nazi persecutors. We communicate more effectively through best uses of key concepts and terms and best usage of our languages. *We*, kind readers and this author, are each both educators and learners, people welcome to explore Holocaust studies, and fellow human beings.

Preface

This book is written to encourage all of us to learn and teach about the Holocaust. I hope it will encourage and help Holocaust educators develop our skills and insights. We continue to learn about, share, and develop engaging educational resources and curricular materials that inspire learning about the Holocaust and human rights. As colleagues, we all can help one another to make good choices in this process. We learn from each other as we learn from the past and extend chains of memory into the future. Teaching and learning about the Holocaust, genocides, and human rights, we can discover inspirational examples of resilience, including Nechama Tec, a child-survivor of the Holocaust and scholar of women in the Holocaust. Tec began 10 years of careful interviews with fellow survivors with the reasonable assumption that compassion, cooperation, and self-sacrifice were somewhat rare during times of upheaval and in contexts of oppression and coercion. She then discovered evidence to the contrary (Tec, 2003).

I hope that this text, along with many others, helps us to sustain a pedagogy of hope which supports our individual and cultural resilience. There are many good ways to learn about and from the Holocaust. Even when the truth is tragic or grim, we can humanize the Holocaust and find resilient role models. We can learn to teach about the Holocaust from a position of strength. We can find heroes in historical reflection and gain courage for the times we face powerful challenges in our own lives, even while we recognize that our world remains vulnerable to oppressive and harmful human and social forces.

Holocaust and genocide education can be challenging. As present or future Holocaust educators, and as lifelong learners ourselves, we are often challenged by detailed or distressing information. While teaching and learning about the Holocaust can and should lead to educational discussions, it requires participants who are open to interpreting difficult and complex subjects (Novis Deutsch, Perkis, & Granot-Bein, 2018). We may hesitate to bring these difficult subjects into our educational contexts in the first place. But these challenges need not prevent or dissuade us from learning and teaching about the Holocaust, human rights, and genocide. I hope that this text helps us to affirm our responsibilities to remember past injustices and to create a brighter and enlightening future for ourselves, our students, and our coworkers. I am confident that we can and should continue to construct an ethical and responsible pedagogy of hope within Holocaust education.

We are fortunate to live in the twenty-first century. Modern and contemporary generations have learned about oppression and about genocides including the

Holocaust as historical facts experienced by earlier generations. We appreciate that the *catastrophic* and *destructive* impact of the Holocaust (as described in Hebrew: *Shoah, Kurban*) has disturbed billions of people since its initiation by Nazi authorities in 1933. It was so upsetting that Theodor Adorno famously wrote that poetry was impossible after Auschwitz (Adorno & Tiedemann, 2003). Thankfully he appears to have recanted this statement, noting that suffering has the right to expression (Horowitz, 2010).

As this catastrophe sticks in our collective memories and echoes through subsequent generations, including our own, we become reluctant witnesses to history (Stein, 2009, 2014). Nations and citizens have constructed Holocaust memorials, supported survivors, and amassed impressive scholarship on this topic. We agree that we will remember, not forget, and so we build cultural continuities, appropriate and enduring representations, and shared resilience. We do not allow the Holocaust to become obscured or lost in time. Now, with greatly improved resources for and support of Holocaust and human rights education, entryways to teaching and learning seem less like obstacles and more like entrances. Please come in and join the communities of Holocaust and human rights educators; we need you.

There are many among us, and many more new generations in our future, who have not yet found opportunities, time, or reasons to learn about the Holocaust and other genocides. Many generations will soon be arriving at the point where these topics are a part of cultural studies of world history, social studies, literature, or the arts. We can help educate all kinds of students using all kinds of materials and methods, adapting strong curricula and lesson plans that can promote dynamic and transformative educational moments. It is our privilege as educators; it is also our responsibility.

As Holocaust educators, we are fully aware that twenty-first-century learners and teachers bring a variety of important and diverse concerns and contexts for comparison to each educational process (Cowan & Maitles, 2017). Many students and teachers around the world understand far too well the sting of past or recent prejudice, injustice, and discrimination. Microaggressions, social injustices, and enduring inequalities can and do affect our lives, our families, and our public health, making our communities sicker, less safe, less productive, and more difficult (Colen, Ramey, Cooksey, & Williams, 2018; Williams, 2012). Racism and racial privileges are with us still, not relics of the past (Bonilla-Silva, 2014). Modern life is still and too often challenged by illegal discrimination, hate crimes, and racialized violence (United States Federal Bureau of Investigation (FBI), 2017).

While the Holocaust may appear to some distant or less relevant than other forms of persecution or genocides, we can find common understanding among our students and ourselves. We can link and compare past and present global and cosmopolitan examples of injustice, discrimination, racialization, and violence without forgetting to remember and provide particular details of the Holocaust (Levy & Sznaider, 2006). The Holocaust was not entirely different from modern racism; antisemitic racism was enacted through Nazi law by racializing definitions of Jews and Roma (Sinti) (Bazyler, 2016). We must educate and cooperate to eliminate oppressive social forces across national, racial, and ethnic inequalities, in order to improve society for all cultural groups (Collins, 2016).

We believe that resilience is an important aspect of education and that challenges to educational inclusion remain (Duckworth, 2016; Goodman, 2018). As educators promoting student success, we share stories of resilience to inspire and engage one another. We illustrate our curricula and our classes with facts, statistics, and by example. In Holocaust education, and when discussing other examples of genocide, we can humanize even the most horrific statistics. We can access survival narratives and listen to surviving voices who endured genocide, thanks to digital technologies. Survivors-as-witnesses to the Holocaust and other genocides share profound truths; we need only and first to listen or read (USC Shoah Foundation, 2018). Once we read, see, or hear survival testimonies, the narrators are educational ambassadors, with human experiences carrying us into monumental historical tragedies, reinforcing historical knowledge and also a sociological imagination (Kushner, 2017; Mills, 1966). We can sometimes apply consequential lessons learned about resilience to our own lives. Holocaust education can inspire, not just shock, sadden, or evoke pity. As Holocaust educators, we can be part of this inspirational process. Yes we can—we can do this.

I myself have an unusual family history that similarly inspired me to write this text. I am a child and grandchild of Holocaust survivors. I first learned of my family experiences in the Holocaust while doing research for a family history project. I was taking a history course in a Quaker-inspired North Carolinian high school, Carolina Friends School. My father, Dr. Steven Polgar (born in Budapest, Hungary, in 1931), was a Holocaust survivor who was born of Jewish parents. He had been a refugee, educated in the United States, earning a PhD in anthropology at the University of Chicago. He worked as professor until his early passing in 1978. As a teen, I could not imagine or fathom the difficulties that he had faced as a young person. I did not ask him to describe or record his experiences until it was too late to do so. As an adult, I later learned some information about the historical context he endured: the Holocaust in Hungary was one tragic chapter of the Shoah, arriving late in the history of genocide in Central Europe (Vági, Csősz, & Kádár, 2013). Along with his elder sister Vera and his parents, my father was (I learned from relatives when I was a young man) unusually fortunate to have survived "the camps."

All four of my nearest paternal relatives, along with a few of our extended family members, survived confinement in a prison camp. My father, aunt, and their parents survived a concentration camp in Bergen-Belsen, in northern Germany. Even after US President Ronald Regan visited Bergen-Belsen (Jensen, 2007), this "camp" was, in my mind, a terrible and faraway place in which I had little interest. I had a clearer view of Auschwitz, where I knew many Jewish people were murdered, and I knew that few had been as "lucky" as my paternal relatives. I also knew, as a young adult, that many survivors had immigrated to the United States. But I did not know more than one or two, outside my family. Now I know that there are entire communities of people with survivor lineages (Epstein, 1979), and I have a collection of books that teach us about the Holocaust. When I can, I ride the tumultuous tides of history that swept my paternal family across continents and later across the Atlantic Ocean (Bardgett & Cesarani, 2006; Reilly, 1997). I am one of a specific type of second generation immigrant in the United States; perhaps 200,000 of us were born to more than 100,000 postwar immigrants (Stein, 2014). We share the experience that at least one of our parents was pushed out of Europe by a catastrophe and then was able to move to the United States to make a new life. We tend to be curious about our family history, but we also have less extensive kinship networks (Bukiet, 2002).

My father and his immediate (nuclear) family were all survivors and thus unusual in comparison to the majority of Jews who were sent to concentration camps during the Holocaust. As I learned from my aunt and grandmother, all four of my nearest paternal kin were released from Bergen-Belsen and taken to Geneva, Switzerland, on one of the "Kasztner trains," aided by the Red Cross in late 1944 (Bauer & Keren, 2001; Vági et al., 2013). They were able to live as refugees in Geneva and then migrate to the United States in 1948 because my medically trained grandfather got invited to work at a medical laboratory in New Haven, Connecticut. My grandmother, Sophie Fonagy Polgar (1908–1988), was already an educated woman before her deportation from Hungary; as an immigrant to the United States, she became (in the United States) a teacher of French language at Oakwood School in Poughkeepsie, New York. She was a loving presence for all her grandchildren, becoming a widow at an early age, and working to educate everyone around her. She inspired us all; she was a resilient and caring teacher, and also a grandmother whom everyone both respected and loved.

Grandmother Sophie (we called her "Anyu") was the first to share my family's Holocaust experiences with me. Her words reinforced the fact that she was resilient and strong, not visibly sad or resentful, and she was always proud of our family and its continuity. She spoke warmly of wonderful family past, lives in Budapest, with riverside boating and comforts of urban life. She was multilingual, as were my father and aunt, a skill which aided her in their survival and careers. In addition to her native Hungarian language, Sophie taught French in the United States and English as a second language. She spoke English fluently, along with some German and Italian. She was respected and loved by all who knew her.

For Sophie F. Polgar and for her husband and children, survival meant release from Bergen-Belsen on two different and successive trains to Geneva. Her mother Frieda Fonagy had a separate experience; she was said to have hidden in a convent. We learned of a miraculous moment where, as children, my father Steven and his elder sister Vera were reunited with their parents (Sophie and Ferenc) in Geneva. A first transport (a kind of "freedom train," which I have learned since carried refugees from Bergen-Belsen to Geneva in September 1944) brought out my father and aunt. A second train in December later carried out my paternal grandparents, resulting in this wonderful moment of nuclear family reunification. Grandma Sophie gave partial credit to the (International) Red Cross for this liberation, though it appears international Jewish relief groups (including the JRC) were also involved (Favez 1999). This privilege, first release from Bergen-Belsen for "the children" (including my father) and later for their parents, was a rare gift that shortened their persecution and led to familial survival. I lament that my grandfather died before I was born and my father died when I was a teen, limiting my chances of hearing his recounting of these events. Vera and Sophie shared these experiences, but they have also passed, leaving some historical questions without answers. I have reconstructed this difficult and partial family history, with help from historical materials, precious family interviews, discussions with a few relatives, and some shared recollections.

My father and his family were deprived of their property and most possessions, like most Jewish camp survivors. They were starved, shamed, and shaved. I was told by surviving kin that our family experienced painful mistreatment before, during, and after their imprisonment in the Belsen concentration camp. When released, as noted, they were reunited and then housed in a Geneva "home for intellectual refugees." They were able to slowly regain health and weight, though their lives were interrupted and forever changed. Like many others, they slowly recovered and continued life as displaced people who lived as refugees, first in Geneva and then (I think by ship from France) as migrants to the United States. As a later chapter will describe, these were difficult experiences, and these narratives were sometimes left to fade into the past, while at other times recounted as anguished memories that could upset those family members learning about their difficulties, creating burdens of memory (Langer, 1991). We carefully but rarely received these narratives from our family members, sometimes reluctant witnesses, who were perhaps protecting their kin from the harms of sometimes painful and potentially humiliating memories (Stein, 2014).

My aunt, survivor and scholar Dr. Vera John-Steiner, was the eldest, daughter of Sophie Fonagy Polgar and Ferenc Polgar, born with our family surname (Vera Polgar). She earned higher educational degrees (including a doctorate) in the United States, married and divorced, and was until very recently a respected professor of linguistics and psychology. Her life and scholarship remain influential (John-Steiner, 1985, 2000; Lake & Connery, 2013). Vera told us that the camps were difficult and hardest for the male members of the family. She was an elder sibling who helped my father endure ongoing challenges, both during and after the Holocaust. It is still hard for me to imagine my relatives in the camps; the image of gaunt figures during and after imprisonment, which my grandfather sketched in a drawing, haunts my ideas of our family's Holocaust experiences.

Like many children of survivors, my life has been comparatively privileged, far less disrupted, and not as remarkable. I happily grew up in North Carolina as a kid whose parents had "moved south" from New York City. I attended our rural Quaker school and, while always happily identifying as Jewish, I had limited Jewish cultural education or experience of Jewish rituals. As an adult, sometime after my father had passed away, I learned that my immigrant kin had assimilated by necessity. They believed in science over religion and were resilient but not entirely unique in many respects. Like others, my paternal kin were pushed by the Holocaust into a forced relocation, what academics like to call a form of exile or diaspora, traveling among emigrant European waves toward many different shores beyond the European continent (Dwork & Pelt, 2009).

I eventually learned that I am a "second generation" Hungarian-American and one of many children of Holocaust survivors who may also have been impacted, even harmed, by the lingering effects of a catastrophe (Stein, 2009, 2014). As part of modern generations who learn that our cultural identities require development and preservation, not just adaptive assimilation, I learned about and am proud of my Hungarian and Jewish heritage. The Internet and social media now allow me, among many others, to find online community with family and other people around the globe who have also experienced such complicated histories. These problems continue for many transnational families to this day.

My paternal grandfather was a Holocaust survivor named Ferenc Polgar, an assimilated Hungarian physician and radiologist who suffered greatly during and after his mistreatment in the Holocaust. Ferenc died in the 1950s when my father was still a young man, prior to my birth; we retained only limited knowledge of his life and difficult experiences. As an eldest son, my middle name is a limited but poignant memorial to his importance and survival. I was comforted to learn that fragmented families and second generation concerns were and are common in the wake of the Holocaust (Epstein, 1979). One author reflects on growing up with survivor-parents and summarizes this well: "Other people's parents had parents" (Bukiet, 2002).

I am thankful to have learned from the work of sociologist Arlene Stein (2003) that my father's silence on the subject of the Holocaust may have been protective toward. Silence in response to anguished or unheroic memories was not unusual (Langer, 1991); many other survivors remained, some for decades, relatively quiet or silent about their experiences. Some may have been trying to spare their own spouses and children from the pains of traumatic memories. After all, who can fully appreciate the suffering and difficult adjustments required by traumatic experiences, including those in concentration camps (Frankl, 1992)? In the United States and elsewhere, during the early postwar years, many Americans preferred to focus on the heroism of militaries, not the harsh worlds that harmed millions of victims (Stein, 2014). Even so, we had some comprehensive social responses during postwar periods. Good people helped and associations arose to generate a 1950s war on prejudice, aligning Jewish and Christian values, to create more inclusive society, in the wake of the Holocaust (Svonkin, 1997).

My father, among many others, heroically endured the Holocaust, along with immigration, and variable degrees of antisemitism. He chose to become an academic, worked hard as a student of cultures, became a scholar and then a teacher. While my paternal grandfather struggled with assimilation after immigration, my father became an American teacher and scholar, and thus followed the lead of his mother. My father worked in leading institutions, became a professor, and showed great respect for cultural resilience and human diversity. In April 1978, he passed far too early in life from a heart attack. I regret that he did not speak to me about his survival, but I respect his (not uncommon) decision to spare us (his children and family of choice) the terror and humiliations of the Holocaust (Stein, 2014).

I have slowly come to realize that my father and aunt were not just impressively academic family elders but a sort of unexpected global representatives. They were in a generation of refugee-survivors who came to the United States, having experienced the same European catastrophe as Anne Frank (also a teen who was imprisoned at Bergen-Belsen, though later during the Holocaust), and of the same nationality as Elie Wiesel, author and Nobel Prize winner, a fellow-Hungarian survivor. It is not surprising to me now that my aunt became a professor of linguistics and psychology. My father became a student and teacher of human cultures, an anthropologist, and he worked cross-culturally with many different groups, including Native Americans and West Africans. Both were more secular than religious, for different reasons, and both participated in multicultural education and multicultural research, along with gender studies, before such topics were widely understood or even accepted in their academic circles. Now, I am blessed to learn more fully about the Holocaust from the many organizations that preserve Holocaust memory for us all. I hope you can and will join me in this process.

I've researched and written this book in part as a tribute to my family members who survived the Holocaust. I should also note that my late mother, Dr. Sylvia K. Polgar, was herself a resilient woman, and I never forget that I owe her my life. I was relatively slow to arrive to my present responsibilities that I consider part of a post-Shoah procession which I now understand as a chain of Holocaust memory. I am honored to have the chance to share my family history and other insights with you as readers. I owe my own Holocaust education to the memories of my father and his sister, and especially to my grandmother ("Anyu") Sophie F. Polgar. I am proud to recall that she expressed great joy in many aspects of life and that I never heard her digress into anger or self-pity, even after all that she (and her family) had endured.

Sophie Polgar's description of her Holocaust survival remains my founding model of resilience and caring. I will never forget what she told me as a teen: she helped others in her barrack; she offered dignity and respect to her elders during the ordeal, and she continued as a caregiver for her disabled mother (Frieda Fonagy) for years after her survival and immigration to the United States. Her compassion for others was emulated and continued by her children, my father Steven Polgar and my Aunt Vera (born Polgar) John-Steiner. Resilience and human compassion are the themes in this text that I learned from my family members. Subsequent chapters will elaborate this theme. I hope that you too, kind readers, will find examples and models of such qualities in your work as Holocaust educators.

I owe a special thanks to Dr. Vera John-Steiner, my paternal aunt, who helped our family endure many challenges, aiding my father when they were refugees in Europe and when new to the United States, and later helping those of us in our second generation to endure more modern challenges. Like her mother Sophie, Vera John-Steiner was an inspiring teacher and a scholar (Lake & Connery, 2013), a resilient and caring role model to many, collaborating and helping us appreciate collaboration well beyond our extended families (John-Steiner, 2000). Vera was a humanist who passed away while I was writing this book, a psychologist and linguist whose books and writings on linguistics and collaboration show us the best of human and social capacities. She provides inspiration through observation, much like her fellow scholar Patricia Carini, both associated with Columbia Teacher's College. Thanks to scholars like Dr. John-Steiner,

Dr. Sondra Perl, and Patricia Carini, we continue to learn that respect for others is both the center and the driving force of our educational work. We cannot practice a pedagogy of hope without writing, including, and teaching about all people, first and foremost.

Dr. Arlene Stein's work *Reluctant Witness* also inspired me to write this book (Stein, 2014). Stein reminds us that there were roughly 125,000 European Holocaust survivors who immigrated to the United States after the war. As Stein shares her work, including such simple demographic insights, many of us feel that our complex lives have good company. We, as children of refugees and immigrants, are truly privileged to be part of the United States (Alba & Foner, 2015; Kasinitz, 2008). We in the second generation who are children of Holocaust survivors, comprise about 250,000 people in the United States. We each have unique and important lives and stories to share and compare.

Good ideas about any subject begin with inspiration, hope, and respect for humanity. Certain types of scholarship should add to compassion for our subjects and for one another. Both scholarship and education can show that we are all valued as human beings, regardless of our demographics, affiliations, or statistical profiles (Carini, 2001). Education and scholarship is for people, not just about people; this is a critical lesson that I have learned from the women and teachers in my family: my mother Dr. Sylvia K. Polgar, my grandmother Sophie F. Polgar, and my aunt Dr. Vera John-Steiner. I see their work and lives as an enduring form of support for human dignity; we are lucky that strong women grace our lives and our families.

I have other kin who are engaged in the process of creating culture and preserving memory. My cousin Dr. Suki John is a leader in this respect; she works and inspires as a dance professor and choreographer. My brother Christopher Polgar reminds us that we can reflect on our own Jewish cultural traditions just as well as we can reflect on others. My cousin Sandor John works to improve life for immigrants still, and this reinforces a point shared by Dr. Martin Luther King in his final speech in 1968: All work has dignity (King & Honey, 2011; Miller, 2012). Likewise, every person who survives violence or catastrophe is an inspiration to us all. Thank you for helping us dignify these inspirational experiences through Holocaust and human rights education. Perpetrators were found responsible for the horrific and criminal injustices of the Holocaust (Bazyler, 2016); we now find ourselves responsible to carry lessons of the Holocaust forward to improve future generations.

Chapter 1

Introduction

During the years 1933–1945, the Holocaust grew from a series of unjust laws and practices within Germany into an unparalleled catastrophe in Europe that shook the world (Bauer & Keren, 2001; Berenbaum & United States Holocaust Memorial, 1993; Cesarani, 2016; Hayes, 2017). Discriminatory laws developed by the Nazi German governmental systems were combined with violent industrial military forces and used to fuel persecution and the mass murder of Jewish and several other populations throughout central Europe (Bazyler, 2016). Never again will our international communities allow such brutality and barbarism. To this end, the term and the crime of genocide were coined in the wake of the Holocaust (Lemkin, 1944, 1947). International law has developed ever since. The abuses of power and national policies that enabled mass violence were profoundly unjust. Nazis came to power through both violence and law; the global community has worked ever since to ensure human rights and to make sure that the Holocaust was a warning, not a precedent (Bazyler, 2016).

As the Holocaust grew in Europe, some in the international community were incredulous or even doubtful about the true extent or nature of this crime. Some were uninformed, and some were resistant to accepting the growing evidence for this evolving atrocity (Feingold, 1995). Prior to German occupation of neighboring nations and subsequent declarations of war, democracy was eliminated, antisemitic and eugenic laws were established, and a Nazi police state created a growing system of concentration camps (Bergen, 2016). The international community nonetheless attended the Berlin Olympics. International public protest was limited, though there was a rabbinical march on Washington by Jewish leaders in the United States designed to spur assistance (Sarna & ebrary, 2004). Military efforts, starting in 1939, were the most powerful and ultimately successful response to escalating Nazi German aggressions and totalitarian state violence. Only after the war, when the scope of the carnage was visible to all, was the Holocaust fully revealed, named, and recognized as a central tragedy of the twentieth century. Once revealed, it became a symbol of human suffering and moral evil, the first internationally recognized case of genocide, the symbol of our need for nations to establish and preserve human rights.

During the Holocaust, atrocity "stories" in the press were at times viewed by some people as a kind of Jewish moral panic. Some who learned of atrocities considered them unbelievable, exaggerated reports similar to discredited stories from the World War I and met with some degree of public doubt (Alexander, 2009). International assistance was initiated and sometimes coordinated but not always successful in slowing the rapid genocide that took place from 1933 to 1945. Immigration policies, including those in the United States, were not open or particularly helpful during wartime attempts to escape the Shoah; Wyman calls this an "abandonment" of Jewish people (Wyman, 1998). In the spring of 1945, with the end of the war in Europe and the public revelation of systematic and genocidal mass murders, the scope and truth of the Holocaust was revealed to all (Gilbert, 2000). Doubts and uncertainties were replaced by shock, horror, and recognition. A collective and corrective public sentiment developed as postwar reconstruction took place; the perpetration of the Holocaust became fully revealed as an absolute evil, and then it became a benchmark for state-sanctioned immorality, a lesson in moral education, and a symbol of a collective trauma that has cast a shadow on modern culture (Alexander, 2009).

After 1945, a "surviving remnant" of beleaguered European and Jewish refugees became known as displaced persons. Some remained in camps for a time, and all traveled, some east or west, to places including Palestine and America (Dwork & Pelt, 2009). Some, little more than stories, filtering out of camps that were hidden by Nazis as "secret operations," some returning home, and others wandering out into a disbelieving world (Wyman, 1989). Anne Frank's father Otto was among those seeking refuge and recovery, having lost both his children and his wife. Fortunately, Anne's diary was returned to him and he helped the diary to become published and performed as an iconic representation of resilience. Otto's younger sister also survived, living in Bern, Germany, allowing part of his extended family to live on (Jacobson, Colón, and Anne Frank, 2010; Prose, 2009).

The United Nations and the Zionist promise of a Jewish state (Israel) were each established and constructed in the years just after the Holocaust. The Holocaust spurred both of these important developments. And the Holocaust has provided a variety of lessons for the world ever since. In Holocaust education, this history demands that we learn both about and from this catastrophic historical chapter (Cowan & Maitles, 2017). We cannot and will not forget. In doing so, we "face history and ourselves" (Anti-Defamation League, USC Shoah Foundation, & Yad Vashem, 2014). What will we learn?

I write as a son and grandson of Holocaust survivors. Like many descendants of Holocaust survivors, I am privileged in ways that our elder kin were not. Most of us did not experience oppression or suffering in any way comparable to the experiences of our elders (Epstein, 1979). We may have been spared some of our parents' anguished and traumatic memories, but we have experienced our own challenges as we have sought to learn about our family histories and to promote compassion and Holocaust consciousness (Bukiet, 2002; Stein, 2014). In the United States, we had an immediate family connection to history: our parents (and other elders) were among over 100,000 refugees and immigrants who came to the United States after enduring the Holocaust (Stein, 2014).

Unlike some of our elders and survivor-relatives, most of us in post-Shoah generations have had the benefit of hindsight and freedom, along with memorials and museums in our communities or nations. It was not always so; New York

City rejected its first application for a Holocaust museum in the 1960s. We experienced both the rise of Holocaust consciousness and the establishment of Holocaust memory. These resources help reinforce our cultural and personal resilience. Thanks to organizations like the US Holocaust Memorial Museum (USHMM) and the Olga Lengel Institute (TOLI), I am one of many teachers now educated and trained to teach the subject of the Holocaust. I cannot ignore this privilege and responsibility because I now understand that we descendants of survivors, along with many others, are *links in a chain* of Holocaust survival and memory (The Olga Lengyel Institute for Holocaust Education and Human Rights (TOLI), 2017).

Through Holocaust education, we will remember and not succumb to Holocaust amnesia. Even though we are not now as exposed to the harsh forces of antisemitism, we are among peers and in a society that is learning to respect all cultures and our shared human rights. We appreciate that our very lives, and the lives of our family members, are part of cultural continuity and resilience. Like others in a second generation of Holocaust survivors, we have grown to understand and appreciate many Holocaust-related complexities, including silences and trauma-related difficulties (Monroe, Lampros-Monroe, & Pellecchia, 2015; North & Pfefferbaum, 2013; Stein, 2009). Stein finds that some descendants learned to play up heroic survival (as found in ghetto resistance organizations) while others muted memories of difficulties, keeping past trauma from present family, unless they were also in the Holocaust. We are learning to see and represent our lives and our families as part of history, albeit a difficult and bloody history that is not always so easy to share (Spiegelman, 1997).

Some postwar silences, quieting Holocaust survivors as well as heroic military veterans, have been at times rather difficult to understand and to overcome. Research shows that it is not easy for people to endure, live as, or even live *with* survivors of trauma (Monroe et al., 2015; North & Pfefferbaum, 2013). Among wounded "storytellers," memory fragments from the past haunt the present (Frank, 2013). Trauma, both individual and cultural, remains both a major consequence of the Holocaust. "Survivor syndrome" is an early description of a disruption in both humans and cultures that followed the Holocaust, among other episodes of mass violence (Epstein, 1979). Like too many other victims of violence, Holocaust survivors and their families have become "reluctant witnesses" to the Holocaust (Stein, 2014), even as the truth of the Shoah has been more fully recognized and respected.

In the United States and in other nations, throughout our cultures and in our education systems, it has taken decades to come to terms with the Holocaust (Carrier, Fuchs, & Messinger, 2015; Fallace, 2008; Levy & Sznaider, 2006; Stevick & Gross, 2014). International law and justice were first brought to bear after the Holocaust (Bazyler, 2016), but even Nazi war crime trials were only partial justice because they were incomplete and limited by limitations of jurisdiction and by strategic excuses. We are now fortunate to have a more complete picture of the catastrophe, thanks to historians and educators. We can use these lessons as we aspire to prevent further harm to the world, as did Rafael Lemkin, the lawyer and linguist named and criminalized genocide (Lemkin & Jacobs, 2012).

The term "Holocaust," now fundamental to our historical conceptions and our curricula, was not initially available or used to describe the disastrous Nazi attempt at cultural genocide. Holocaust education was also limited, only gaining foothold within our national education systems in the late 1970s (Fallace, 2006; Fracapane & Hass, 2014; Levy & Sznaider, 2006). In the United Kingdom, more and more secondary students have been introduced to Holocaust education, thanks to recent but still incomplete efforts (Foster et al., 2016; Pearce, 2014). Around the world, Holocaust education is varied; in some nations it still remains limited, partial, or an indirect consequence of education in other topics (Carrier et al., 2015; Fracapane & Hass, 2014).

Acceptance of the Holocaust also required "seeing through" deceptive and Orwellian communications and representations created by Nazi ministries. Antisemitic and other propaganda were used to gain power in 1933, to scapegoat Jewish people and communists, and to expand state power thereafter (Luckert, Bachrach, & United States Holocaust Memorial Museum, 2009). Racialized antisemitism was not only spread by media campaigns but also established by Nazi Germany in the 1930s through a system of discriminatory and ultimately eugenic national laws and enforcement practices (Bazyler, 2016). Jewish people, communists, and other groups were blamed for a myriad of social problems, while systems of autocratic authority facilitated the development of a planned system of discrimination and segregation that was later adapted to carry out genocidal mass murder. False narratives and multiple forms of prejudice also slowed national and international responses, though timely help did arrive for some (Favez, 1999).

Leading scholars seek to explain why the Holocaust happened (Hayes, 2017). The Holocaust was accelerated by fascism, nationalism, antisemitism, colonialism, world wars, and the false science of eugenics. With hindsight, historians and others describe multiple groups of Holocaust protagonists, including Nazi perpetrators, bystanders, rescuers, and multiple groups of people who were persecuted (Dwork, 2002). Perpetrator actions were facilitated by the tacit acceptance of bystanders or onlookers, along with the compliance of national and fascist governments in neighboring occupied territories. Jewish people were primary among many persecuted groups. Persecuted populations (who became known somewhat judgmentally as "victims" of the Holocaust) included multiple cultural, national, and political groups; these groups were subject to systematic mistreatment, discrimination, and harm, and sometimes aligned with allies to resist the powerful and brutal Nazi German government (Hayes & Roth, 2010).

The Holocaust was carried out during what was called a *Third Reich* in Germany; Nazi leaders worked to expand their rule, occupying adjacent nations to realize the perceived need for "more living space." This expansion of the German state was designated for and limited to people and groups eugenically defined as Aryans by a false ideology of "racial science." German aggression and later occupation took place at the immediate and ongoing expense of many oppressed groups, primarily Jewish Europeans, and also Roma, people with disabilities, and any groups designated as political or national enemies (Bauer, 2010; Bergen, 2016). People not privileged by racial heritage were subject to legalized discrimination and persecution, including segregation in employment, education, and housing. Under Nazi rule, Jewish and others targeted groups were segregated and put into ghettos, deprived of human rights. As the Holocaust progressed, billions of people were shot, gassed, and/or incinerated, creating the mass murder that has come to define the Holocaust. Concentration camps across Europe were established to segregate these persecuted populations. Some camps were used for detention, some for work, and ultimately six camp locations were designed for mass murder through gassing and incineration. Imprisoned people who were selected to work or aggregate in labor sites could get a tattooed number on their arm and perhaps survive by working; often prisoners worked for the German war effort (Levi, 1978), and sometimes these forced laborers worked for the camp system itself (Lengyel, 1995).

The Holocaust has been recognized as a series of mass crimes that ultimately were addressed through criminal prosecution. International law flourished in the wake of the Holocaust, despite the fact that few crimes (including few war crimes) were successfully prosecuted (Bazyler, 2016). We are still able to access many primary documents that attest to these crimes, including German administrative documents, along with Jewish diaries and chronicles ("salvaged pages") and survivor accounts (Hayes & Roth, 2010). The Holocaust and related film, music, art, and literature also continue to develop, raising questions about what constitutes respectful memory and what should be representative of the Holocaust in our curricular content (Cowan & Maitles, 2017).

In the wake of extensive false propaganda and misinformation, many of us struggle to find the correct vocabulary to describe the Holocaust. British and American allies, concurrently with Soviet forces in the east, fought against Nazi axis perpetrators, focusing on winning the war. After victory in the first part of 1945, militaries then discovered the disastrous conditions in concentration camps, creating systems of care for displaced people and refugees. International legal tribunals were set up to prosecute enemy leadership, starting with a core group of perpetrators, who claimed to be following orders simply as "problem-solvers" (Browning, 2000). Many diplomatic and institutional efforts to rescue Jewish and other endangered populations had been attempted and most failed (Bauer & Keren, 2001). Persecution was documented nonetheless; the Holocaust was perpetuated by institutionalizing authoritarian, eugenic, and antisemitic policies. Tragically and importantly, some persecution during the Holocaust was often legally sanctioned under German laws and often outside the jurisdiction of what was at the time the very limited reach of international law (Bazyler, 2016). Jewish and other groups were forced out of their homes and robbed, giving new meaning to "grand larceny." This is one reason why restitution claims were later brought and why some reparations were later paid by the government of West Germany.

"Solutions" through mass murder required the treatment of Jewish and other groups of people as "problems." Planning and carrying out mass murders was considered state secrets that were "finalized" at the Wannsee conference in Munich Germany, which authorized chemical gassing centers in newly annexed Reich territories in "the east" (six locations in Poland) (Dwork, 2002). Jews and others were transported to the east by rail in cattle cars (again, nominally to free up more necessary "space" for "folks" or Aryan population expansions). Nazis reduced human populations to corpses and ashes, nightmares based on the industrialization of violence. Perpetrating killers were empowered; onlookers stood by; resisters and rescuers were brave but rarely successful (Yahil, 1990). Antisemitism and violent Nazi actions muted greater support for resistance. Allies, confederates and supporters of persecuted Jewish and other populations in Nazi-occupied nations, risked losing their own freedom, property, families, and lives. In this context, resistance and righteous upstander narratives remain important and notable (Rohrlich, 1998).

After the war and the Holocaust, we can explore the histories of liberation, displacement, and dispersal of refugee populations (Rice, 2017). Plunder was widespread, in the context of chaos and famines. Some refugees returning to European homes found their former residences occupied by others. Many sought new lives in the United States or Israel, though transit and permission to immigrate was often and still limited. In time, diplomats and others established restitution from West Germany (Bazyler & Alford, 2006). Efforts to establish and institute human rights law grew. Education, documentation, and research were initiated in multiple disciplinary contacts. Judeo-Christian interpretations struggled to find meaning in the events that the world witnessed. Jewry helped build Israel. Holocaust denial also found expression (Lipstadt, 1993).

In the United States and elsewhere, we searched for common interpretations of the unimaginable catastrophe (Alexander, 2009). Proud and well-deserved heroic military narratives sometimes overshadowed difficult and sometimes anguished survivor narratives (Stein, 2014). Jewish and Roma cultures had been dehumanized and shamed, not only in the wake of Nazi propaganda and law but also by popular cultural tropes. Jews in the Holocaust were and are sometimes unfairly described as "sheep" (animals, not humans) who "went to slaughter" (without resistance). This stereotype was not applied to other groups who suffered at the hands of the Nazis (Russians, Poles, Roma, etc.), only to Jews (Bauer, 1989). The murderers, only some of whom were found guilty years later, were simultaneously portrayed as butchers, brutal but nonetheless product producers, and not as organized criminals. Such representations did not help survivors recover and integrate. In addition, international work to fully understand and represent the Holocaust was complicated by conflicts and secrecy that characterized the postwar cold war period (Lewy, 2017; Longerich, 2010).

Why did we fail to prevent this genocidal persecution? Why do we now sometimes hesitate to describe these histories? Perhaps education alone is insufficient to prevent injustice. We know that there are challenges to ongoing initiatives for Holocaust education (Cowan & Maitles, 2017). But still, we are not sure if children and youth can or should be exposed to such horrors. We may worry, reasonably, that we will not fairly represent the subject or perhaps we might upset our audiences (Totten, 2002; Totten, Bartrop, & Jacobs, 2004; Totten & Feinberg, 2001). It's not a simple or easy subject to teach or to learn about. We may confuse people by presenting historical novels or period fiction that misrepresents history; no boys in pajamas could have ever gotten close to a fence with a commander's child, and commanders were not paid to be sympathetic to the plight of prisoners (Cowan & Maitles, 2017). History, while sometimes dry, is not always fairly represented by fictional or semifictional stories and movies, though historical fiction does inspire many of us to learn more.

In teaching about the Holocaust and genocide, we should not privilege a perpetrator perspective. Instead, we need to find and highlight the many groups of people affected by Holocaust persecution. We can show how, despite cruel perpetrators, individuals and groups were heroic, helpful, and certainly worth learning about. Many showed purpose and resilience in the context of ongoing catastrophe and tragedy. We can be inspired by Historical figures like Janusz Korczak (born Heinrich Goldschmidt), a Warsaw-born educator who devoted his life to children-in-need (Cohen, 1994). We can find dignity in the fact that the "final solution" was neither final for Jews nor a solution to any of the real problems in our shared world. While we learn that the world will never be the same, that people of faith questioned God, we learn that even the darkest experiences and the depths of despair did not cause our people to abandon all faith (Wiesel, 1995). We see that human rights were clearly and universally defined and internationally established after the Shoah. We can respect those who brought genocide into our vocabulary (Power, 2002) and give due respect to all those who made improvements in our international laws (Bazyler, 2016).

While it helps to use respectful terms for social groups, we do not need to get caught in unnecessary debates over who suffered most among those persecuted. There are statistics to summarize the comparative demography of "victim groups" but we are obligated to find humanity in *all* of these statistics. The Holocaust's harm to humanity was *both* particular and universal. We do and will remember and memorialize *both* Jewish *and* all other people who have experienced genocidal crimes (Levy & Sznaider, 2002, 2006). Industrialized mass murder by Nazis targeted *multiple* cultures and the disabled, nationalist civilians, and political dissidents. Large percentages of Jewish *and* other populations were murdered or forced into exile. West Germany, to its credit, took responsibilities to repair some of what was lost (Zweig, 2001). Still, it was a catastrophe of epic proportions.

There is a lot to see and a lot to learn about as we are studying and teaching about the Holocaust and genocide. Let's open our eyes, using a pedagogy of hope to help us through the difficult historical accounts and records (Perl, 2004; Simon, 2006). Let's not get distracted by propagandistic or perpetrator perspectives. "The world must know" (Berenbaum and United States Holocaust Memorial, 1993). We must not be hesitant to show the world this important period of history.

The remainder of this text focuses on our motives and methods for Holocaust education, asking *why* and *how* we share Holocaust education. In answering the question of "why we teach," our second chapter explores rationales for teaching about the Holocaust. We find multiple and inspirational reasons to continue this important work. In our third chapter, we consider how best we can make choices as we teach about and learn from the Holocaust. We see the Holocaust education involves teaching *about* events, sharing historical content, and helping us all learn *from* the Holocaust, gleaning lessons from the abundant and amazing details in history and its reflections.

In the fourth chapter, we focus on dignifying and humanizing the subjects of Holocaust education. This was a mass crime, after all. Can't we give those persecuted the dignity of being subjects of our narrative? Why should a perpetrator perspective be the first or more powerful way that we present the Holocaust? Didn't Nazi misrepresentations and crimes harm enough of us already? While there are "sides" to most conflicts, we hope history will "side" with the righteous, who respected human dignity and thus condemned, fought, and prosecuted genocidal criminals.

Holocaust education does not need to be limited to the period from 1933–1945. Exploring cultures and lives *before, during, and after* the Holocaust, we better represent and remember those persecuted and affected, creating chains of memory that can reinforce cultural resilience and counter the corrosive effects of genocide. Respectful memory is ethical and responsible, but law can also be preventive, so the fourth chapter concludes with a discussion of the Holocaust and human rights law. This is an important topic by itself; the Holocaust has opened both a window into human rights and set a precedent that helps international organizations to prevent and prosecute subsequent and future genocide and mass violence.

In the fifth chapter, we expand our scope to understand how Holocaust education and Holocaust studies are becoming part of multicultural education and cultural studies. Even so, educators should not refute the truth; we condemn Holocaust denial as a form of antisemitic cultural misrepresentation. We nonetheless appreciate the many groups harmed by injustice, violence, and genocide.

The sixth chapter explores important topics related to choosing and interpreting Holocaust and survivor narratives. To humanize the Holocaust, teaching the topic from the perspective of people who were harmed by eugenic discrimination, these textual and recorded narratives remain invaluable. We can learn both from and about Holocaust survivors themselves, even when their accounts are partial, anguished, and sometimes difficult to hear or share.

The final chapter concludes with an array of reasons to be optimistic about global Holocaust education in the twenty-first century. We find online technologies and museums that allow us unparalleled access to Holocaust histories and resources. We have global perspectives and opportunities, thanks to international studies by UNESCO and other initiatives. We can learn from diverse national and local initiatives, improving our work through creative collaborations. We can appreciate cosmopolitan variations, leaving behind arguments between particularistic and universalistic forms of education or memory. Descendants of Holocaust survivors, like myself, can help us to continue the traditions of Holocaust education, leaving behind "Holocaust hesitation" and finding strong cultures of Holocaust education where there were once only silences and anguished memories.

In our work as Holocaust educators, we can and should remain optimistic as we realize the ongoing responsibilities that come with providing Holocaust education. We can continue to treat humans and history with respect, emphasizing humanity, dignity, and resilience in recounting history. In sharing and representing historical memory, we focus on teaching respectfully about groups that were harmed, while also recognizing the power of perpetrator perspectives and the complexity of bystander situations. We reject Holocaust denial and push past any attempts to rationalize or tolerate genocide. We receive and respect the narrative accounts of survivors; survivors help us to appreciate human and cultural resilience. We do not forget or neglect the fact that many large and small acts of resistance and bravery were also part of the Holocaust, as they were part of the allied war efforts. We encourage one another to collaborate with prevention and memorialization projects that started even before the war ended (Waxman, 2006). Since the Holocaust ended and genocide became an international crime, we embrace the principles of human rights. We remember and we are working together to never again endure such injustice. Thank you for your work in Holocaust education.

Chapter 2

Why We Teach Holocaust Education

Holocaust education starts with a set of purposes. *Why* should we raise this subject? Why should we teach about the Holocaust *in particular*? There are many good answers to this question, but some are related to a second question: Why not teach about more universal or global concerns, using many or other examples of persecution or genocides? A simple and useful answer is that many of us *do* teach about *both* Holocaust *and* genocide, supporting Holocaust education with human rights education. The combination of Holocaust and human rights education has grown since the 1990s. While curricula and context do and must vary depending on our educational contexts, many of us need not select *either* one *or* another topic and purpose. As we will elaborate in our next chapter, learning from the Holocaust involves finding and applying its lessons to other abuses of human rights, particularly genocides. Educators need not rank one goal or one group over or above others; we can and often do teach about the interrelated topics of the Holocaust, human rights, and genocide (Levy & Sznaider, 2006).

We also need to consider the question of *what* we teach. Which specific content should we teach when we teach about the Holocaust? At which historical point in time should we begin our educational narrative? Which historical narratives do we bring into focus? Which protagonists, which groups of people, which events, and which years do we share in and through our classes? While these questions are addressed well by fully developed and flexible curricula that are widely available (ADL, USC Shoah Foundation, & Yad Vashem, 2014), they remain salient. Educational choices can fall to individual teachers or groups of educators. Do we lead, work with, or follow the lead of our educational organizations? How much detail is helpful or required? Making such choices can also be linked to our own perspectives and identities. A recent empirical study suggests that narrative identity, the meanings of our content, and our teaching perspectives are interconnected factors that affect teaching choices in Holocaust education. Simply, what we teach may be related to our own personal and professional perspectives and our educational audiences. Holocaust educators convey content, guide learners in developing knowledge, nurture students, and help society (Novis Deutsch, Perkis, & Granot-Bein, 2018).

We also reflect on *how* we teach about the Holocaust. This question is the basis of our next chapter, which explores ways that people can learn both specifically *about* the Holocaust (conveying mostly historical facts) and what we can learn *from* the Holocaust. Learning about the Holocaust is a historical project or exercise which involves review of primary source material that takes us back at least to Central Europe between 1933 and 1945. Learning *from* the Holocaust is a more interpretive exercise that applies this history to examine ethical or moral issues and other "lessons" from history. In applying the Holocaust to wider contexts and to our contemporary concerns, we discover important ideas and institutions that have been developed in the aftermath of the Holocaust, including genocide prevention and international law, which both reinforce global standards for human rights.

Why We Teach

Why do we teach about the Holocaust? When we can confidently respond to this question, we can more energetically continue our work Holocaust and human rights educators. Our educational goals, our job descriptions, our organizational roles and goals, and our shared values can all provide good reasons for our work as Holocaust educators. We can then develop these reasons to make choices of subject matter and to create rationale statements (Totten, 2002). Rationales help us select educational content. If necessary, we can formalize or adapt these statements into our learning objectives. Learning objectives drive the content of our curricula. Informed choices must be made with respect to time management; we do not have enough time to teach all topics or every subject. So, we may hone or refine our rationale for teaching, but not too much. If and when our responsibilities include Holocaust education, we should not minimize or provide an alternative for this topic.

The question of *why* we teach this subject arises even before we must face the central historical question of *why the Holocaust happened* (Hayes & Roth, 2010). Offering plural explanations for complex historical events allows teachers and students to incorporate multiple perspectives. And just as there are no singular or simple reasons for complex historical events like the Holocaust, there are multiple rationales that we can use to justify or explain our pedagogical approaches to the subject. We need not select *only* one of many good answers to the question of why we teach about the Holocaust and genocides. Holocaust education is provided for many reasons in many different schools and nations (Schweber, 2010, 2011). Holocaust education continues to grow and grow in importance, both in American schools (Fallace, 2008) and internationally (Carrier, Fuchs, & Messinger, 2015; Cowan & Maitles, 2007, 2017). While there are standards for Holocaust education, there is no standard Holocaust education.

We appreciate that each educator, each educational institution, and each curricular or educational policy group may develop different motives and reasons to offer and deliver Holocaust education. It seems natural that different motives can and *should* inspire many different curricular forms. Sometimes these motives will develop or change, as they are changing at broader national and international levels. This is natural since the very nature of Holocaust memory is itself evolving with both time and globalization (Levy & Sznaider, 2002).

Prevention and Reparation

We begin with two major reasons which justify our work in Holocaust education: *prevention* and *reparation*. First, we teach about the Holocaust and human rights as a part of larger efforts to *prevent* future genocides and related injustices (as reinforced with the respected slogan "never again"). Second, we teach about the Holocaust and human rights to respond, repair, and at times even redeem our modern world, working constructively to counteract the destructive and catastrophic injustices that we have witnessed and recounted. Once we recognize the many moral, legal, and political lapses that were perpetrated during and since the Holocaust, we want simply to do something to "make it right." To repair our sense of justice and to provide or restore dignity to all people, we are compelled to some sort of positive social action. We also can dignify and humanize the Holocaust and its victims by realizing our responsibilities as educators and teaching from a position of strength, allowing survivors to share resilience, as we will explore in future chapters.

Prevention of genocide is a shared and global objective, not just an abstract or academic idea. The concept and definition of genocide was established by the pioneering work of Raphael Lemkin (Lemkin & Jacobs, 2012). Genocide prevention is further established by subsequent international law (Bazyler, 2016). Prevention and justice are globally promoted through the United Nations Declaration of Human Rights (United Nations 2017 (Enacted 1948); Wronka, 1998), the Convention against Genocide (Power, 2002), and other international legal agreements. While not all nations understand the concept in the same way, and there is debate over which historical events meet the definition of genocide, establishing the concept gives us a standard from which we can discuss catastrophic events (Fein, 1990, 2000). Some measure of justice for crimes committed during the Holocaust was established through the Nuremberg and subsequent trials, but legal and other constraints, especially of jurisdiction, limited justice to a significant degree (Bazyler, 2016).

Some forms of economic reparations and restitution have been court-ordered, initially through negotiations between West Germany and World Jewish Congress representatives (including Israel), which arrived at the Luxembourg Accords of 1952 and empowered the New York-based "claims conference." This reparations process has evolved during subsequent decades (Bazyler & Alford, 2006). While a restitution or reparations model has not been successful in other or all cases of mass violence or genocide, the Holocaust remains a strong catalyst for modern national and international criminal justice, now based on a case law of genocide, adjudicated through the modern International Criminal Court (ICC) and through international military tribunals (Bazyler, 2016).

In this historical and legal context, we promote and provide education as prevention. Education as prevention has worked, to some extent, through many modern initiatives against a variety of public health and social problems. In public health, evidence shows that prevention campaigns in the United States and in other nations do work, especially to reduce the incidence and prevalence of problems such as smoking, drug abuse, drunk driving, and sexual assault

(Herzberg, Guarino, Mateu-Gelabert, & Bennett, 2016; Potter, 2016; Warner, 2014). In Holocaust education, we can focus first on the goal of preventing future genocide, but there are many other potential and related benefits, such as reduction of prejudice, reduction of hate crime, inclusion of refugees, and civic engagement; these benefits that can be and have been promoted and measured in many educational and general populations (Krysan, 2000; Stefaniak & Bilewicz, 2016; Svonkin, 1997).

Since the barbarity and destructive impact of the Holocaust was revealed in the 1940s, authors have described at least four time periods with respect to Holocaust education and memory. At first, from the 1940s until the early 1960s, there was a period of marked and tragic silence concerning the destruction of European Jewry, broken only occasionally by events such as the publication and dramatization of Anne Frank's diary. A second period, from the 1960s into the mid-1970s, saw the beginning of a more developed and public Holocaust consciousness (Fermaglich & Koret, 2006; Stein, 2014). Starting in the late 1970s, television and "Americanization" of the Holocaust brought both particular themes (such as Jewish persecution) and more general themes (particularly human rights) into the public sphere, raising the urgency of Holocaust memory and building international support for Holocaust education (Napolitano et al., 2007; Totten, 2003). Once globalization accelerated in the 1990s, a fourth period of Holocaust education and memory grew to create more and diverse cosmopolitan perspectives on the meanings of human rights and all forms of genocide (Levy & Sznaider, 2006).

The Holocaust has often been represented by shocking and discomforting images of starved prisoners, crematoria, or mass graves (Buettner, 2009). *Never again* was an important remark initially offered by US General (later President) Dwight D. Eisenhower, an understandable reaction to the shock and anger of first seeing horrors and mass graves at concentration camps (Ambrose, 1990). "Never again" is also and literally written in stone on an exterior wall of the United States Holocaust Memorial and Museum (USHMM). Linking memory with a resolve for social justice, it has evolved into a prevention-slogan that motivates the Holocaust and human rights education. As educators, we work toward genocide prevention starting at a middle-school level, where teachers and students can start to explore and discuss preventive interventions to injustices like bullying, and when we can start to apply problems of intolerance to larger problems of society, helping even younger children to realize that prejudice and intolerance have been requisite to stages of genocide (Kelleway, Spillane, & Haydn, 2013).

While not all students or global citizens awaken to the importance of the Holocaust and genocide in similar ways, reactions may be strong and our responses must be supportive and serious. Creating a supporting environment is one of the several principles of the Echoes and Reflections curriculum (ADL et al., 2014). We agree to prevent future barbarity and potential genocides; we share in the moral outrage that humans could do, allow, or ignore such atrocities. We do not want to forget this dark chapter in our global past. If those who forget history are condemned to repeat it (Santayana, Wokeck, Coleman, & Gouinlock, 2011), then we must work to reduce this risk and prevent the widespread "forgetting" condition that may be called "Holocaust amnesia."

To elaborate our second purpose, we offer and develop a full range of Holocaust and Human Rights Education (HHRE) because education is an accepted form of *reparation* for a variety of transgressions against humanity. Many educational and social movements work to increase education as a corrective response to past injustices related to social problems. While social problems rise and fall, educational responses remain useful (Hilgartner & Bosk, 1988). Holocaust education continues a tradition of responsive social justice. When injustice harms us, education begins to heal our world. As noted, reparation has also involved specific and targeted economic reparations by the nation-state perpetrating the Holocaust as a crime (Bazyler & Alford, 2006; Zweig, 2001).

We repair both through education and through building better international law. In the late 1940s, when global authorities first identified and prosecuted Holocaust-related war crimes during the Nuremberg trials (Power, 2002), the list of criminal charges did not (and could not, at the time) include the crime that we now know as genocide (Lemkin & Jacobs, 2012). Subsequently, based on Lemkin's formulation of the concept of genocide (Cooper, 2008), the United Nations created and member states accepted a convention that made genocide illegal (Frieze, 2013; Power, 2002). Thereafter, all United Nations have agreed that genocide is an ethical and legal transgression in need of international response. The nature and scope of these responses are subject for international law and adjudication (Bazyler, 2016).

Our needs for repair and for justice apply to both the Holocaust specifically and to genocide more generally. Preventing and redressing ethical and legal violations offers hope that most populations and cultural groups will less often, if ever, be subject to leaders or forces that commit mass violence and mass crimes such as genocide. We stand against injustices; we do not persecute or prosecute people based on culture. We seek to repair our moral transgression through our shared cultural response. We are both traumatized by and ashamed of the fact that the Holocaust happened (Alexander, 2009). Education is one type of first response; developing law and policies are another. Having learned about the Holocaust, we are civically educated and less likely to stand by when we see modern injustices.

In the wake of war crimes and trials, many educators and scholars continue to provide factual history, teaching about the Holocaust so student can learn about (and from) the Holocaust. As this chapter will elaborate, learning from the Holocaust turns our curricula toward sometimes controversial topics in social justice or moral education, creating tensions that arise and arguments that flare at different points in the history of Holocaust education (Fallace, 2008). Regardless of our justifications for and interpretations of Holocaust education, we remain ethically compelled to educate learners about historical and modern genocide in order to correct what is considered the tragedy of the twentieth century, the "trauma drama" that has come to define our modern era (Alexander, 2009).

Redemption through education is a motivation whether or not we focus on social justice and whether or not we use a universal perspective that finds parallels between Nazi antisemitism and related problems, including religious intolerance or racism. Some critics of the Holocaust and Human Rights education have debated the blending of particular and universal perspectives (Novick, 1999), but there are many inspiring forms of Holocaust education which need not provoke or offend, as we see in a growing literature. Questions of redemption, reconstruction, or reparations after the Holocaust and other genocides are historically and ethically appropriate, whether or not we promote a focus on Christian or Jewish topics, and whether we take a religious or secular perspective. We simply cannot ignore injustices at this scale. We can also humanize the victims of the Holocaust, we can affirm human rights and sanction genocide prevention, and we can learn from the resilient examples of people and groups who stood against injustice, both during the Holocaust and since.

Holocaust Consciousness

Historically, public awareness or *consciousness* of the Holocaust was limited in all nations, especially in the early postwar years (Ben-Bassat, 2000; Fallace, 2006; Pearce, 2014; Stein, 2014). In the United States, as in many nations, the Holocaust was not often taught as a subject in schools, no less taught well or in detail (Fallace, 2008; Napolitano et al., 2007; Totten, 2002). In contrast, many (though not all) modern and twenty-first century nations are now working toward widespread education for high school (secondary) students around the world, often linking the Holocaust with genocide and human rights (Bokova, 2014; Carrier et al., 2015; Fracapane & Hass, 2014; Stevick & Gross, 2014).

The first generations that became conscious of the need for Holocaust education were somewhat hampered by limited and variable choices in Holocaust awareness and curricula. Public awareness and public interest were relatively muted among general populations in many nations, including in the United States and in Germany (Kaiser, 2014; Levy & Sznaider, 2006). Earlier and more involved study of the Holocaust took place in Israel and among Jewish groups, writing and representing those harmed in "memory books" (Magilow & Silverman, 2015; Waxman, 2006). Israeli Holocaust education was and has remained more particularly focused on the Jewish experience of the Holocaust, while US Holocaust education has been more universalistic; Germany's curricula has, in the past, fallen in between (Levy & Sznaider, 2006).

After the war, the terms and concepts of "Holocaust" and "genocide" were newly invented and applied, debated, and complicated political and social concerns. "Genocide" was a term invented only in the 1930s by legal scholar Raphael Lemkin (Docker, 2010; Power, 2002). The term "Holocaust" was itself applied only after the war, but it remains a standard term. The use of "Holocaust" can itself be debated for good reasons, and it is even replaced with other more descriptive terms by some authors and observers. "Shoah" or "Kurban," representing (respectively) a catastrophe or destruction, are sometimes preferred terms, since "Holocaust" literally means a form of "sacrifice," thus potentially misattributing a higher meaning to what were in fact Nazi crimes, including mass murders. Are Nazi actions best described as human sacrifice? (ADL et al., 2013).

In the United States, postwar media campaigns against prejudice and discrimination constructively responded to the Holocaust. Interfaith collaborations created a lesser known social movement that was called "a war on prejudice." These events are well described by historian Stuart Svonkin in his book *Jews Against Prejudice*. Led by the Anti-Defamation League (ADL), the war on prejudice was the work of a collaboration which included military, media, and academic organizations. To reduce prejudice, organizations worked to create and promote anti-bias education through a broad coalition of faith-based groups and national councils (Svonkin, 1997). Frank Sinatra and many others created anti-prejudice educational advertising campaigns for the army, radio, and TV. As educators and as citizens of many nations, we would be wise to revisit and continue to be part of this tradition, in my opinion.

With greater Holocaust consciousness in the late twentieth century, scholars document significant growth in Holocaust education and curricula, in the United States and in many other nations (Fallace, 2008; Napolitano et al., 2007). The Holocaust first attracted public attention in the United States and internationally after publication and dramatization of Anne Frank's diary, first on Broadway in 1953 and later in films. Holocaust consciousness grew to become a part of public American cultural life, especially in the 1960s (Fermaglich & Koret, 2006; Stein, 2014), and then education and part of public education in the 1970s and 1980s.

In the late 1950s and early 1960s, especially in the United States, nightmarish representations of Nazis and Holocaust were used (some might say misused) freely by authors and artists as a metaphor to help liberate Americans dreaming of freedom during the early stages of the social transformations of the 1960s (Fermaglich & Koret, 2006). In 1961, the Eichmann trial in Jerusalem was televised for the world to see, creating a new, popular, and visual reminder that Nazis has perpetrated genocide through "evil" and industrialized mass murders, and that some criminal perpetrators remained to be prosecuted or still "at large" (Arendt, 1965; Cesarani, 2006). In fact, as will be elaborated, very few perpetrators received trials at all, and many trials were delayed or limited due to narrow statutes of limitations (Bazyler, 2016).

During the 1970s, social movements promoted greater awareness of cultures and heritage among many cultural and ethnic groups. With the help of journalism and other forms of public discussion (Epstein, 1979), cultural heritage became more salient for groups of Jewish decedents of Holocaust survivors (Stein, 2014). General public attention to the Holocaust increased during and after the US television miniseries ("Holocaust") was shown in the spring of 1978 on NBC. Also in 1978, the 30th anniversary celebration of the Universal Declaration of Human Rights (UDHR) was celebrated (Belzberg, 2016). That same year, a presidential commission on the Holocaust was initiated by the US President and human rights champion Jimmy Carter, who is said to have watched this NBC program (Magilow & Silverman, 2015, President's Commission on the Holocaust. Elie Wiesel—Chairman, 1979). The commission delivered its report in 1979 and the US Holocaust Memorial Council then grew out of this Commission. Both the national Holocaust Commission and the Council were (until 1986) headed by respected writer, survivor, and Nobel laureate Ellie Weisel (Kolbert, 2001).

Holocaust education matters a great deal, especially for Jewish people since (in the words of Elie Wiesel's introduction to the 1979 Commission report) "while not all victims were Jews, all Jews were victims." (President's Commission on the Holocaust. Elie Wiesel—Chairman, 1979). Initiated by the Holocaust council, the USHMM was subsequently designed and built; it opened to the world in Washington, D.C., in 1993 and remains a cornerstone of Holocaust education for the world (Berenbaum and United States Holocaust Memorial, 1993). Effective education about the Holocaust became a national project with the USHMM.

National and international events and initiatives fueled growth in Holocaust consciousness and encouraged more systematic, public, and widespread Holocaust memorialization and education (Fallace, 2008). National and international memorials and educational museums remembering the Holocaust and other genocides have been firmly established around the world, though it is worth noting that some efforts at memorialization during the 1960s in New York City were not successful, due in part to a failure to receive local (city) permission (Saidel, 1996). Many memorial efforts that succeeded have grown since the late twentieth century, including a fine museum of Jewish heritage in New York City that was ultimately built with cooperation from the State of New York, among others. Holocaust education and curricular developments followed the growing development of museums, promoting public consciousness of this important chapter in world history (Napolitano et al., 2007; Totten & Feinberg, 2016).

Documentary and feature films have also helped to popularize greater public understanding of the Holocaust and Holocaust education. Nazi propagandists used films effectively too, but soon film was also used to satirize the Nazis, most famously with Chaplin's *Great Dictator* (1940). People more fully imagine and realize conflicting protagonists and Holocaust themes through film genres, including news reels, realistic documentaries, and more recent dramatic films. The Diary of Anne Frank was an early dramatization in this genre, adapted from Broadway to film, providing an innocent victim's perspective and becoming the prototype for representing the Holocaust as a topic for universal concern (Baron, 2010).

While not all films present entirely accurate historical accounts from primarily educational perspectives, and while concerns about cultural representations and stereotypes reasonably apply to some films, *Sophie's Choice* (1982) and *Schindler's List* (1993), among many other films, have boosted growing Holocaust awareness with visual representations of the extreme challenges and horrors of persecution and conflict, moving beyond formulaic stories and making use of a range of cinematic styles. A large proportion of the public knows the Holocaust, thanks to narratives from films. Holocaust film scholarship has grown as well (Baron, 2010). Popular cultures also now depict the Holocaust through gaming cultures (Grever, 2018).

As films illustrate, we continue to struggle with the challenges of finding good perspectives on the Holocaust. Even in groups as important as the United States Holocaust Council, debates arise about how best to portray or represent the Holocaust. People argue over which mortality statistics should represent the Holocaust, as if we need to choose to recognize only some among the many groups of victims and casualties. People debate because there has been a false choice put before us: is the Holocaust a particularly *antisemitic* tragedy or a more *universal* moral lesson? Why not agree that it is both at the same time? Certainly, the mass murder of Jews was most egregious and motivated by eugenic and discriminatory policies and practices during "a state of deception." National Socialist (Nazi) government inflamed German and other publics to systematically target Jews through extensive, misrepresentative, and offensive propaganda (Luckert, Bachrach, and United States Holocaust Memorial Museum, 2009). But many other groups were also targeted and harmed, including other cultural groups (particularly the Roma), as well as people with disabilities and very large numbers of people who were enemy military or political opponents, including communists and Poles, among others (Arad, Gutman, & Margaliot, 1999; Bergen, 2016). Such debates frustrated many, including Holocaust educators, but did not prevent growth in public education and culture.

In hindsight, it seems that the extent of debate may have been unnecessary. Is it fair that curricular focus on the Holocaust or human rights should be limited to only one (universal or particular) perspective? Does presentation of a particular or exceptional narrative preclude the presentation of multiple or universal narratives? Is there only one best way to teach history? Is there only one best perspective on history that precludes comparison? If and when we can take a longer historical view, and as we can now also include other examples of genocide, we need not diminish, minimize, deny, or forget the importance of the Holocaust as a central event in modern history. The Holocaust was a particularly antisemitic *as well as* a universally abhorrent chapter in history. Even so, each school, organization, and each nation still selects somewhat different emphases and perhaps different lessons (Fracapane & Hass, 2014). In the end, we still share common understandings and concerns: all nations agree that the Holocaust was a tragic injustice and all forms of genocide are illegal.

In studying and passing on lessons from Holocaust history, students and teachers learn that this subject helps us appreciate and nurture democratic values and institutions that can become vulnerable to abuses of power and other oppressive forces (United States Holocaust Memorial Museum, 2018). Students can and often do learn that silence and indifference to human or civil rights violations is tolerance of injustice that can perpetuate these problems. Therefore we choose to offer Holocaust and human rights education; we can continue educating inclusively and taking moral actions. Individuals have made and will always make choices that affect the course of history. So too do responsible organizations, including industries and corporations (Hayes, 2017). We teach and learn as individuals, groups of teachers and learners, and as people in organizations. We educate using our curricula and our narrative identities (Novis Deutsch et al., 2018).

Improving Students

As educators, our actions and curricula, including our choices of words and our attitudes, do influence others. We are reminded that our human conscience and social responsibilities are sensitive to education; our attitudes and values are reflected by how we respond to examples of persecution and injustices. Research shows that Holocaust education can have lasting impact on learner values, exemplifying the important concepts of prejudice and discrimination (Cowan & Maitles, 2007, 2017). Inclusive and supportive pedagogy can welcome and encourage learning; accepting or cynically repeating exclusive perspectives risks reproduction of potentially harmful social divisions. Dehumanization is a painful subject but it was an intended aspect of the Holocaust; humanizing Holocaust victims brings compassion into the classroom (ADL et al., 2014). Teaching and learning inclusively through multicultural education has become central to how educators stand against harmful, exclusive, hateful, or otherwise corrosive social forces (Appelbaum, 2002; Southern Poverty Law Center, 2017).

Humanizing the people and groups harmed by the Holocaust is easier with survival narratives but it is still not a simple task. We recognize that Nazi laws, policies, and practices reduced many groups and individuals to less-than-human social and legal statuses (Bazyler, 2016). Laws and policies, starting in the city of Nuremberg Germany, officially discriminated against and stigmatized all Jews and many others (Bergen, 2016; Levin, 1968). Eugenic Nazi policies, both national and local, labeled people with yellow stars and pink triangles. Forced laborers, rather than being murdered, were identified and managed through tattooed numbers on their arms (Roth, 2016). Millions of people were terrorized, herded like cattle, and often reduced to mortality statistics. A majority (approximately two thirds) of Jews were eventually murdered (Bauer & Keren, 2001; Dawidowicz, 1976; Yahil, 1990). This grave injustice rested on intentional and elaborate cruelty and systemic dehumanization.

Carini's educational philosophy addresses problems of dehumanization and reminds us to work for fundamental human rights, starting with human dignity, that are established by the United Nations in the articles of the Declaration of Human Rights (United Nations 2017 (Enacted 1948)). All students and educators, along with people who were subject to persecution, deserve dignity, rights, and equal recognition as a person under the law:

> To deny the status of self or person to anyone, to categorize them as not having, or not being capable of having, selves, of being persons, differs them so fundamentally as to separate them at the root from humanness. That done, and it has been done, there is nothing that cannot be done to them–and justified by some others of us on the grounds that they are less than human... it takes vigilance, hard, recursive work, and educating ourselves in the largest sense of that word to keep alive awareness of human complexity (Carini, 2001).

Holocaust educators recognize that persecution of populations was intended but not inevitable. The Holocaust harmed millions through abuses of prejudice, hatred, xenophobia, and scapegoating. The Holocaust involved fellow humans committing horrible crimes including genocidal mass murder. While Nazi

Germans and others used antisemitism to target Jewish people and cultures, the Holocaust *also and simultaneously* targeted and harmed many other groups. While all educational moments are limited, students can seek and learn from multiple perspectives. Therefore we do not need to choose only one tragic perspective from among the many narratives or crimes that comprise the Holocaust or any genocide. We can therefore appreciate Holocaust education is and can remain part of multicultural and antiracist education (Short, 1999).

Holocaust education is also, nationally as well as globally, advancing global citizenship education (Stevick, 2018). Modern scholars and many educators recognize that the Holocaust can and should be taught as a specific historical event of great importance as well as an example of genocide that spurs us toward genocide prevention. Citizenship education, affirming the human rights of all citizens, promotes a positive power of state authority, in contrast to all violations of human rights that are exemplified by atrocities like genocide. Positive rights (sometimes defined narrowly to include social and economic rights) can also include civil and political rights that were denied by Nazi decree during the Holocaust (Bazyler, 2016; Fein, 2007). "Human wrongs," including killings, torture, and slavery, threaten the integrity of human life, which is a basis for all human rights (Wronka, 1998).

Global citizenship education is and can be designed to help create a "world which is more just, peaceful, tolerant, inclusive, secure and sustainable" (Stevick, 2018). It weaves together knowledge, a sense of belonging within diverse communities, and responsible social behavior. Holocaust education applies well to citizenship education goals that call for global knowledge and critical thinking. We develop empathy and respect for diversities through Holocaust studies. And we encourage students to share responsibilities for both justice and prevention of injustice.

Given the importance of Holocaust education, how should we proceed? We may be able to blend the Holocaust, human rights, and genocide studies into our curricula, lesson plans, and pedagogy. We are not simply or newly constructing or standardizing Holocaust curricula, as has been done in the past (Fallace, 2006, 2008). Nor must we work alone. We can and should first use and adapt improved and accessible content and guidance, thanks to both curricular leaders social justice organizations and our national and international memorials and museums (ADL et al., 2014, Imber, 2016, United States Holocaust Memorial Museum, 2018).

Curricular resources on the Holocaust and human rights have become more widely available, improving in quality and quantity, extending easily to educators through a variety of respected organizations, collaborations, and online resources (ADL et al., 2017, USC Shoah Foundation, 2018). Even so, recent research shows that national curricula and resources vary a great deal (Carrier et al., 2015; Fracapane & Hass, 2014; Pingel, 2014; Stevick & Gross, 2014). Research in the United Kingdom shows that most secondary students receive and appreciate only a minimal exposure to Holocaust education; few learn or know detailed historical facts (Foster et al., 2016). Holocaust knowledge and education gaps have been documented around the world and in most countries, including the United States (Schoen Consulting, 2018; Smith, 1995). Student learning and depth of understanding is also affected by attitudes and perceptions; Holocaust knowledge can be complicated by national and local contexts; educators and student in any nation can have complex concerns about a group's or a nation's role in historical conflicts (Gray, 2014). We appreciate that the design and delivery of Holocaust education, along with its effects, vary over time, by context, and by nation.

A variety of studies of Holocaust education span many nations over many years (Schweber, 2010). Some find significant gaps in knowledge across multiple dimensions (Schoen Consulting, 2018). The Holocaust has been fading from the real-time memories of the living, creating a greater need for knowledge and education in more recent (younger) age cohorts (Foster et al., 2016). Despite knowledge gaps, the public in the United States supports Holocaust education as part of prevention. Even so, most people in the United States (80%) have not visited a Holocaust museum nor do most (66%) know or know of a Holocaust survivor (Schoen Consulting, 2018).

It's challenging to measure change and compare across groups in assessing Holocaust-related knowledge and attitudes, especially since it is done in so many different ways and places, but this should not prevent us from using and designing new research to improve our pedagogies (Chapman & Hale, 2017; Jedwab, 2010; Lawson, 2017; Pettigrew, 2017). Still, knowledge gaps are not the only reason to educate; many of us agree that Holocaust education remains our ethical responsibility, regardless of how much people know or learn about the Holocaust, human, rights, or genocide.

Holocaust education can serve many ethical purposes, illustrating the human costs of racism, ethnocentrism, xenophobia, and antisemitism. We recognize that genocide is immoral and thus requires a moral response, as it has required for many years (Alexander, 2009). The scope of moral responses to the Holocaust was at times incomplete and limited, but many organized, ethical, and ongoing reactions to the Holocaust did take place at collective, group, and individual levels. Collectively, allied world nations bravely responded to Nazi aggression and violence through allied military interventions. Neutral nations including Sweden and Switzerland offered refuge and support. Many nations continued to assist through postwar global support, as well. At the individual and group levels, organizations including the World Jewish Congress, the War Refugee Board, and the American Jewish Joint Distribution committee supported resistance, rescue, hiding, and escape (Yahil, 1990). Some may pessimistically presume humanity was callous, antisemitic, or inconsiderate during the Holocaust, recognizing that some were self-serving and not altruistic, but we will still can find examples to the contrary even during the Holocaust (Monroe, Lampros-Monroe, & Pellecchia, 2015).

Ethical or moral lessons have been central themes in the cultural construction of Holocaust history, especially when we consider people who stood up and served as rescuers (Block & Drucker, 1992). Iconic writings remind us to stand up to injustice before it consumes all of us (Niemoller, 2007). As educators, we can ask why rescuers risked their lives to help, rather than bend toward what we commonly assume would be natural self-preservation or self-interest (Monroe et al., 2015). Focusing on moral actions, undertaken by heroes and victims of genocidal crimes, helps provide a pedagogy that reinforces our values, despite feelings of hopelessness and helplessness that may come with recognizing the horrifying circumstances that surround genocide and related crimes (Simon, 2006).

The singular horror of the Holocaust can act as a "bridging metaphor" across multiple catastrophes, genocides, and global tragedies (Alexander, 2009, 2016). On the other hand, many have misused the *idea* of "holocaust" as a metaphor for evil or mass violence, diluting our abilities to learn about and describe the *actual* Holocaust as a series of true historical facts (Novick, 1999). We must use care and find distinctions between the actual Holocaust and those tragedies that some may describe comparatively as their own (small h) "holocausts." This is an important point, because while historical facts can and should sometimes be presented *without* moralizing, students are nonetheless encouraged to use critical thinking and comparative evaluation to interpret history individually and independently. "Reading" or interpreting the Holocaust (learning *from* the Shoah) can be a required aspect of Holocaust education, so we do not want to "shut down" all forms of comparison. We can also remember that development of moral citizens by educational institutions is an old and venerated principle; ethical or moral education has long been the basis for a variety of both theories and practices in education (Dewey, 1909) and in sociology (Durkheim & Pickering, 1979).

Remembrance, Respect, and Resilience

Holocaust education can focus on *remembrance, respect,* and *resilience,* the three R's that establish and reinforce some of our most important pedagogical goals and learning objectives. As we *remember* those who were murdered in a time and place of injustice, we are also encouraged to *respect* one another, learning to find the *resilience* in those exemplary people, like Holocaust and genocide narrators, who have suffered and hopefully survived to endure persecution. Through collective and individual memories, with respect for human dignity even in the worst of times, and appreciating our capacities for strength and resilience, we find greater motivations for Holocaust education. These three R's can help simplify, structure, and support our rationale statements, reinforcing effective objectives in Holocaust education.

Holocaust education helps us to *remember* our histories. We are often reminded to remember, so we do not forget, and we do not to fall prey to "Holocaust amnesia." The USHMM offers extensive guidance in this process. The Holocaust was a tremendously consequential global disaster, involving criminal mass murders and genocide. It has been an enduring and tragic lesson for the world. In the wake of this tragedy our representatives generated shared global principles (human rights) that were and are established in our international (UN) declaration for human rights and convention against genocide (Lemkin, 1948, United Nations 2017 (Enacted 1948)).

Holocaust education improves our strengths and skills to serve as links in chains of historical memory. In the United States, our work to remember the Holocaust was advanced by President Jimmy Carter's 1978 initiation of a presidential commission. This Presidential Commission on the Holocaust, later adapted and renamed the United States Holocaust Memorial Council, was first led by author and survivor Elie Weisel. It issued a 1979 report to the president and later recommended the construction of the USHMM. The creation of this commission was announced on the May 1 commemoration of Israel's 30th Anniversary in the presence of Israeli president Menachem Begin and 1000 Rabbis (Magid, 2012). As we know, Israel itself was developed to realize the biblical promise of a Jewish homeland, and this vision was realized in the wake of the Holocaust. Consequently, Israel has developed a particularly Jewish perspective on Holocaust research and education (Cohen & Vazsonyi, 2013; Levy & Sznaider, 2002).

Holocaust education has value in part because it preserves historical memory. The USHMM is a national cornerstone of Holocaust education and offers important guidance in this process (United States Holocaust Memorial Museum, 2018). First, educators should clearly define the Holocaust as the "systematic, bureaucratic, state-sponsored persecution and murder of approximately six million Jews by the Nazi regime and its collaborators" (United States Holocaust Memorial Museum, 2018). This mass persecution was the German policy from 1933 to 1945, growing with the Nuremburg laws that were passed in the early 1930s and accelerating after the 1942 Wannsee conference, where Nazi leaders amplified persecution by designing and authorizing the death camps (Cesarani, 2016; House of the Wannsee Conference Education Department, 2018).

Mass murderers were secretively hidden and obscured by Orwellian propaganda terminology; Jewish populations were "problems" and required "solutions" (including a "final solution"). Nazi government actions, led by perpetrators of mass crimes, were responsible for systematically carrying out millions of civilian murders, most of which were done through "efficient" uses of gas (a chemical weapon) inside crematories between 1942 and 1945 (Browning, 2000). Many other killings were done using other methods, as well. Please remember this: we are not discussing semantics or politics; the European Jewish population was never a "problem" and mass murder is a criminal behavior, not in any sense a "solution" of any kind.

While the German state carried out the Holocaust, the Holocaust was by no means a national event or an event confined to the historical boundaries of pre- or postwar Germany. The major impact (the majority of the mass murders) took place in Nazi-occupied Poland and other territories to the east of Weimar Germany, which Snyder describes as the "bloodlands" of Eastern Europe (Snyder, 2015a, 2015b). Much of the territory affected by the Holocaust, and the vast majority of its victims (including Jewish victims), were not (initially or subsequently) nationally or culturally German. Many counted themselves as other types of Europeans but were mistreated simply as Jews. Many major sites of mass murder and persecution (including Auschwitz and the other death camps in Poland) remained somewhat obscured for decades after the war because the locations of these crimes fell within the Soviet occupation zones and thus behind what became the cold war "iron curtain."

Also, while many German Jews were patriotic and some veterans of the German military, "racial" classification by Nazi law undermined any national or military status held by German Jewish people. But this hardly mattered at the time since Nazis dictated racialized law and policies, removing Jewish people from occupations, locations, and any privileges of national citizenship (Yahil, 1990). During the Holocaust, Jewish people were denied a wide range of human rights, regardless of their past.

While the force and violence of the Holocaust are clear and powerful, we should not teach that the Holocaust was an *inevitable* historical event. In fact, few historical events are inevitable. Neither should we stoically compare experiences of suffering. Instead, we should contextualize history, showing those involved before, during, and after the Holocaust of 1933–1945 (United States Holocaust Memorial Museum, 2018). In general, as with all forms of historical education, we should make responsible choices in selecting and sharing examples and materials, working from primary sources when possible.

While teaching, we should avoid simple answers to complex questions. Popularized postwar obedience experiments notwithstanding (Milgram, 1963), here is no single universal human nature that explains cruelty, nor can we find behavioral patterns that simply explain why people did what they did during the Holocaust. Perpetrators had many different motivations, as did bystanders and resisters (Hayes & Roth, 2010). Victims were diverse, experienced countless difficulties, and often faced with inconceivable and sometimes tortuous "choiceless choices." Perpetrators were not simply monstrous thugs; some were well-educated military men or white-collar bureaucrats. Bystanders and "bystander nations" had varied motives and global policies that changed over time (Hilberg, 1993). Upstanders and righteous heroes, including people of faith, acted ethically, but many others did not (Rittner & Roth, 1997). We can recognize these diversities and strive for precision of language and for balance in representations of different perspectives. We can also recognize the difficult debates that often ensue when choosing any one or only one representation of the Holocaust (Magilow & Silverman, 2015).

Subsequent to the Holocaust, world nations created a more sustainable global organization (many through the United Nations). We slowly and surely learned a series of important lessons for the world, generating shared global principles (human rights) and our international (UN) convention against genocide (Altman, 2012). The development of education for and about human rights also grew, encouraging social justice (Wronka, 1998, 2017).

Cultivating *respect* for humanity and for human cultures is a second reason for Holocaust and Human Rights Education. We learn about and respect many cultures. We recognize and remember those harmed by violence, including people harmed during the Holocaust, and including victims and survivors of many different cultural and national groups. Holocaust education has developed in part because we respect the survivors, who testify to the catastrophe using the power of human stories, like those of Elie Wiesel (Kolbert, 2001; Wiesel, 1999).

We respect those harmed and also those who resisted (Rohrlich, 1998; Tec, 2003). We respect the righteous among nations (memorialized by Yad Vashem in Israel) and recognize their connections with all people who stand up against injustice, speaking and working for justice everywhere. We apply the lessons of the Holocaust across times and places. Respecting and dignifying humanity is one step in repairing harm caused by genocide, moving beyond perpetrator perspectives, replacing cultural defamation and racist discrimination with historical and respectful cultural representations. As part of teaching tolerance through multicultural education (Martin, 2014; Southern Poverty Law Center, 2017), we teach and learn to respect our fellow humans and human cultures. Respect is essential and ethical, constructive, and instructive.

Holocaust education helps us humanize not only the victims of the Holocaust but also one another, illustrating why human rights require that we grant the status of human and full, legal personhood to all people, questioning terms and concepts that separate human beings into unequal categories, even with casual language, such as "us" and "them." Educational and humanistic inclusion, through better conceptualization and through creative processes like writing, is an important principle that nurtures each and all of us, encouraging us to transform, create, and find expression (Carini, 2001). Writing and other forms of expression can help all of us to appreciate the difficult facts that we encounter during the many challenging episodes of Holocaust history.

In learning about and from war and conflict, we celebrate our military veterans, especially those who sacrificed life or limb for our national and international values. Veterans have, for centuries, joined tribes of warriors and endured unspeakable dangers (Junger, 2016). We also respect many types of rescuers and resisters, Holocaust heroes and "upstanders" who resisted the catastrophic harm that was perpetrated by Nazis and their allies in many nations (Bartrop, 2016; Rohrlich, 1998). We can educate students about both armed resistance and diplomatic efforts, reminding others that both were dangerous and heroic. In 1944, when the world was more fully aware of the Holocaust, diplomatic and international efforts to help Hungarian Jewish people were also notable and sometimes successful. Legal and illegal migrations helped save lives; ships to Palestine ran legal and illegal immigrants from the 1930s until 1942 and also after 1944, though these efforts and thus legal immigration were delayed by Germany and also limited by the terms of the British and the League of Nations as well as by multiple forms of required documentation (Yahil, 1990).

In postwar decades, Yad Vashem and other organizations have fully recognized a variety of both war heroes and Holocaust heroes, celebrating the righteous among nations along with fallen and wounded fighters, glorifying resistors and rescuers along with military veterans (Bartrop, 2016; Block & Drucker, 1992). We have made great progress in memorializing survivors and victims as well, despite the fact that honor was initially more fully focused on those who served in uniform (Stein, 2014). We fully respect those who died and those who were wounded or harmed, those who suffered unjustly and those who were resilient. We respect fellow humans as part of our work to recognize all people who stand up against injustice, speaking and working against "injustice anywhere" and for "justice everywhere" (King, 1963).

Finally, we highlight and participate in *resilience*, showing that surviving individuals and groups went to great lengths to maintain cultures and traditions, even in extremely oppressive conditions. Holocaust and genocide studies are replete with lessons in resilience, including accounts of survival that represent the strengths of our human spirit, our best and bravest behaviors, and our expressions of cultural continuity (Spector, 2007; Wiesel, 1999). For example, Olga Lengyel endures the hardships of Auschwitz, surviving to provide a gripping account of the infamous and brutal death camp (Lengyel, 1995). Tec interviews and works with transcripts from other survivors, especially women, to describe the many forms of resistance to oppression. She concludes that "the more accustomed prospective victims are to performing nurturing and cooperative roles, the more they are able to adapt to changing circumstances" (Tec, 2003).

Scholars and educators, joining with museums and memorial projects, help us hear and learn from the resilience of survivors and witnesses. Those who speak about unspeakable mistreatment help us to endure. People who share resilience show us that we can overcome many difficulties, including disaster and disrespect, dehumanization, and even the threat of death (Frankl, 1992), forging community and peace in our lives and in our futures. Holocaust narratives remain one important and pivotal representation of the need for preservation of human rights. Individual and collective survival of the Holocaust gives hope in the face of cruel and criminal actions, promoting a pedagogy of hope (Carini, 2001). We remain resilient through shared history and memory, even while feeling the pains of such memory can be a "terrible gift" (Simon, 2006).

Resilience narratives help us in preserving and respecting cultural traditions, especially in the wake of ongoing antisemitism, hate crimes, and more recent attempts at cultural destruction or genocide. Scholars and educators, museums, and other memorial projects help us hear and learn from the resilience of survivors and witnesses, who show us that we can overcome both disaster and disrespect, forging community and peace in our lives and in our futures (USC Shoah Foundation, 2018).

Resilience remains a core lesson that we can learn from the Holocaust and genocide survivors and bring to our students. To understand and appreciate the depth of both individual and cultural resilience, we respect and remember those who lived through and died in the Holocaust using a variety of voices and views (Dwork, 2002). Finding resilience in testimonials is engaging and inspiring. Personal histories that involve tragedy or trauma illustrate the strength of the human spirit but also expose us to the cruelty and brutality that were all-too-mundane ("banal evil" in the words of Hannah Arendt) during the War. Maliciousness is manifest in the stunning immorality shown by both Nazi German Fascists and by Stalin's authoritarian Soviet Union (Arendt summarizes both in simple phrases: "Thou shalt Lie" and "Thou shalt kill") (Arendt, 1965).

Surviving war and genocidal crimes requires resilience; just exposure to Holocaust history itself requires a degree of resilience. So take heart; we are in good company. Please continue this process, contributing to a chain of memory, fighting against Holocaust amnesia. The prevention of future genocides and injustices require that we remember and reflect with respect and resilience. As we do, we represent and "carry on" the examples of resilient people and cultural groups. Resilience can help educators and students alike.

Resilience, historical or modern, inspires as it transcends the moment, the individual, and the cultural group. While Holocaust can be considered historically specific and unique, it was not unprecedented. Virulent and historical anti-semitism has parallels in historical and modern racism. We do not revise Holocaust history but we can rethink the Holocaust (Bauer, 2001). Many nations contextualize the Holocaust to illuminate wider and universal social problems (Carrier et al., 2015; Fracapane & Hass, 2014). We can consider a variety of examples of resilience within genocide studies as part of multicultural curricula (Belzberg, 2016). With Holocaust education as part of cultural studies, we can cultivate students and human rights. Teaching about the Holocaust, social justice, and human rights can involve discussing and comparing genocides.

We accept that past racial and cultural injustices are not confined to history; they remain related to profound bases of social problems and thus worthy of our ongoing attention (Patterson, 1998). We share in the duty to remember and honor those harmed and murdered in genocides, to respect those who survived, and to appreciate the resilience of those who have endured great hardships and loss in response to these massive crimes. Catastrophic chapters in world history did not end without resistance as well as resilience (Rohrlich, 1998; Tec, 2003). And not all resistance was military or armed; people were hid and were hidden; people fled, escaped, and were smuggled away. People resisted oppression with actions large and small every day (Friedländer, 2003), and people still do.

Holocaust education includes, but is not confined to, education about anti-semitism. Eugenic discrimination during the Holocaust presents us with a clear case of "both/and," not "either/or." Many individuals and groups were harmed and murdered; Jewish people were scapegoated and harmed most of all. Anti-semitic projects were planned and publicized for decades, including well before the Nazis came to power (Berenbaum & United States Holocaust Memorial, 1993, Luckert et al., 2009). Even so, it can and should be recognized that many different groups, not only Jewish people, were selectively targeted for discriminatory and criminal treatment by genocidal regimes. Cultural groups targeted by the Nazis included two other cultural groups (Roma and Jehovah's Witnesses) and many additional groups (including people with disabilities, political prisoners including communists, and people considered LGBT). Many groups were systematically labeled and degraded, subject to discrimination, systematically targeted, and often murdered through industrialized slaughter of human beings.

We can also link survival and resilience to our wider social responsibilities for inclusion through multicultural education in our pluralistic societies. Using Holocaust and other genocide narratives in our teaching, including narratives of heroic resistance and efforts standing up to Nazi war crimes, we can celebrate both those who served allied armed forces and those who endured the horrors of human rights abuses. We can respect how people endured discrimination, forced labor, eviction, relocation, hunger, violence, and ultimately death of millions.

We can counter harmful and unjust myths that remain, stereotypes and propaganda that diminish any cultural or social group, just as we reject the discriminatory claims of eugenics (Kevles, 2016; Rafter, 1992).

We recognize that Holocaust education continues and that human dignity is enduring. Once we humanize the history of the Holocaust, putting faces on grave statistics, we can begin to see and share a bigger picture with a longer view of history. We can appreciate the catastrophic consequences of genocides. We can see Europe, including Jewish communities and people, included diverse communities both before and after the disastrous Holocaust. We can remember, not forget, creating chains of memory to repair ourselves and our communities from the injuries of oppression. We can continue to "do the right thing" as we did when our nations created the Universal Declaration of Human Rights (United Nations 2017 (Enacted 1948)), along with a convention against genocide (Power, 2002). This is the beauty of inclusive memory that includes respect and resilience: we survived before, and will do so again.

Chapter 3

How We Teach Holocaust Education

Holocaust education is and should be included within many types of curricula. As we provide Holocaust education, we are reminded that effective Holocaust education follows simple principles. We define terms, linking the Holocaust to historical and intentional antisemitism. Teaching the historical context of the Holocaust helps convey the fact that Nazi persecution was intended but not inevitable. Effective use of human experiences, like using survival narratives, effectively promotes empathy, connecting statistics to real lives, countering the vast and horrific dehumanization that was perpetrated through both words and actions. We educate through critical thinking and inquiry-based learning, using primary sources and making the Holocaust relevant to other and modern concerns (ADL, USC Shoah Foundation, & Yad Vashem, 2014).

The Holocaust is an important historical topic on its own and also an aspect of modern history (sometimes conflated with World War II). The Holocaust is also a case study of genocide, an opportunity to learn about human rights, and a context for exploring individual and cultural resilience in the face of persecution. Like other examples of persecution and social injustice, the Holocaust illustrates the need for public and global responses to social inequalities. It prompts us to consider our actions in the face of injustices and to appreciate our civic rights and responsibilities. In the wake of the Holocaust, nations of the world have developed global agreements for human rights and against genocide, and we have developed social responsibilities that prevent simply looking on while fellow humans suffer. Understanding totalitarian societies also helps us to appreciate our civic freedoms (Short & Reed, 2004).

Holocaust education helps improve public knowledge of the Holocaust and of world history (Gray, 2014). Many argue the first place for Holocaust education should be in a history curriculum, though it also belongs in civics and other disciplines (Cowan & Maitles, 2017). Citizenship education involves human rights education, and the Holocaust was one tragic event that helped inspire our world to unite and thereafter codify human rights (United Nations 2017 (Enacted 1948)). Studying the Holocaust can educate students who lack basic information and it can also transform learners (Feinberg & Totten, 2016). Knowledge of the Holocaust can reduce harm that flows from intolerant attitudes (Gray, 2014), including Holocaust denial (Lipstadt, 1993; Shermer & Grobman, 2000).

As educators, we prepare and teach Holocaust education with clear and evolving rationale statements, carefully using terms correctly, limiting comparisons and clichés (Totten & Feinberg, 2016). The Holocaust has become a paradigmatic historical event, helping form a global and educational framework for understanding persecution, mass violence, social injustice, and international law (Bazyler, 2016; Fracapane & Hass, 2014).

Cowan and Maitles carefully and clearly distinguish learning *about* and *from* the Holocaust (Cowan & Maitles, 2007, 2017). This allows us to conceptually differentiate those curricula that offer a *moral* emphasis (moral education involving ethical and legal lessons *from* history) from education that offers primarily a more objective historical review of facts, focused on primary source analyses, regardless of the pedagogical perspectives or protagonists involved. History educators, like historians, help us all to focus on clear and compelling facts about the Holocaust and then allow students to draw reasonable interpretations (ADL et al., 2014). This can involve document analysis and also review of survivor or even perpetrator accounts and narratives.

Five Types of Holocaust and Human Rights Education

For the sake of simplicity, let's first appreciate the axiom that Holocaust educational goals can take two basic forms. As noted, these two basic forms are (respectively) learning *about* and learning *from* the Holocaust (Cowan & Maitles, 2017). These two approaches parallel what have been called "curriculum as fact" (given and uncontested information) and "curriculum as practice," which requires interpretation in educational contexts (Foster & Crawford, 2006). Both focus particularly and specifically on the Holocaust. In addition to these two forms, comparative and global historical education is also possible. If or when we expand our educational goals and choices beyond the Holocaust to include related subjects of genocide and human rights, we then also expand our perspective to include three more types of education, creating five types of Holocaust and human rights education.

First, learning *about* the Holocaust (delivering Holocaust curricula as fact) can be described as an evidence-based, objective, and disciplinary approach, often in the context of historical education (or education in another discipline, as appropriate). Learning about the Holocaust often and also seeks to understand causes and consequences of specific historical events. Second, learning *from* the Holocaust can be described somewhat differently as "curriculum in practice," taking a more sociocultural approach that can make history into a "usable past." Learning from the Holocaust relates historical events to the social and cultural frameworks that are held by those teaching and learning about the topic (Epstein & Peck, 2018). Learning *about* the past involves sharing more primary and historical sources and facts (Cowan & Maitles, 2017). Learning *from* the Holocaust involves *interpretations* of this past and applications of the Holocaust in the contexts of more modern or global concerns, including comparing the Holocaust to other forms of mass violence and subsequent genocides (Fein, 2007; Hinton, 2002).

If or when we open our educational scope to include the problems of genocide and human rights, which became focal after the end of World War II, our educational curricula and goals may need to expand beyond the Holocaust (Altman, 2012; Cooper, 2008). *Genocide education* is a third and more comparative way to provide Holocaust education. Genocide education brings into view other catastrophic and genocidal events, contextualizing the Holocaust within a longer historical arc that includes the Holocaust and which invites more international and comparative studies (Fein, 1990, 2007). This broader perspective is reinforced by the fact that the United Nations has recently expanded recognized *international* holidays to include a genocide remembrance day in addition to a Holocaust remembrance day.

Following a related comparative path, we can see that learning *from* the Holocaust also includes learning to take a more universal (some would now say "cosmopolitan") perspective that is well described as "Holocaust and Human Rights Education" (HHRE). HHRE is accomplished through education that is *about* the history, nature, and importance of human rights, which form a basis for international law (Bazyler, 2016). HHRE sometimes also applies education to social justice and collective action, creating a fifth mode for Holocaust education that we will call education *for* human rights. Applying education as an instrument of democratic and civic social policies suggests that education can, or perhaps must, be a force for positive or progressive social justice and change.

Therefore, this chapter will address and elaborate five related and also distinct types of educational perspectives and goals that focus on or significantly involve Holocaust education. The first two of these modes are "particularistic" and focus primarily on the Holocaust. The last three modes are more "universalistic" in that they describe a broader topic in which the Holocaust can and usually should play a major or central role. While this list is not exhaustive or exclusive, these five types or educational modes and perspectives will frame this chapter. All five have educational value and can help us frame curricula and pedagogy:

(1) Learning about the Holocaust
(2) Learning from the Holocaust
(3) Education about genocide
(4) Education about human rights
(5) Education for human rights

As we can see, these five perspectives involve three different but related subjects. First, all five are ways to educate about the Holocaust. Second, the last three perspectives focus on the related topics of genocide and human rights. A particular and focused study of only the Holocaust is still possible when we study genocide and/or human rights, but we also expand curricula into more "universal" or global issues when we name genocide or human rights among our subjects. When we suggest that we need to learn from the Holocaust or educate for human rights, we also apply our knowledge of human rights to social action and to social justice, although this may be more controversial in some contexts, especially if the pressure of current events distracts from our ability to help our students learn about the Holocaust as a series of historical facts.

We may not have the power in our educational systems to choose whether to educate about the Holocaust in particular or genocide and human rights more universally. Whatever our situations, we may unfortunately encounter long-standing controversies that unnecessarily encourage us to "take sides." There have been many different debates over the best goals and methods for Holocaust education (Gray, 2014). Even so, differences in educational perspectives or goals (whether particularistic or universalistic) do not *necessarily* reflect *conflicting* goals or perspectives (Levy & Sznaider, 2006).

We can teach different subjects and topics while still agreeing that these distinct but related topics are important. For example, learning *both* about *and* from the Holocaust are both central and important goals for many Holocaust education providers, driving curricula in school systems and expanding the impact of museums and memorials. Newer and comparative "universalistic" curricula need not displace a particular focus on the Holocaust. Cosmopolitan perspectives involve a wide range of historical and modern concerns related to genocide and/or human rights; Holocaust education is itself increasingly cosmopolitan and global (Levy & Sznaider, 2002). The bottom line is that human rights and genocide education need not conflict with Holocaust education; in fact, both require Holocaust education as a basis from which we can understand the international genocide convention and the development of human rights law (Bazyler, 2016; Lemkin & Jacobs, 2012).

Nonetheless, given modern forms of intolerance, our curricula may not simply ignore or minimize the Holocaust or antisemitism in the name of comparative concerns (UNESCO: United Nations Educational Scientific and Cultural Organization, OSCE: Organization for Security and Co-operation in Europe, 2018). Rather, we simply have made and will continue to make informed choices to fit our educational contexts and goals.

Some European nations have struggled to learn about and from postwar histories and memories while also retaining or adapting national identities. European nations, along with others, have made a series of increasingly progressive decisions to learn particular, but not always all, aspects of the Holocaust. Germany was an early adopter which boldly and intentionally rejected evasion of historical facts and developed locally specific curricula and directives to deliver Holocaust education. German Holocaust education evolved quickly to focus particularly on Jewish persecution, correcting Nazi-era distortions, while updating curricula to stress problems with Nazi dictatorship (Pingel, 2006). Other European nations, including those which were in the former Soviet bloc, initially developed a more nationalist and less complete perspective on the Holocaust but have more recently been updating curricula to show the full extent of both Jewish and national persecution (Fracapane & Hass, 2014). The United States, Canada, Israel, and other nations have developed curricula and memorial cultures, as we will elaborate in future chapters. Some nations that were more distant from the Holocaust have been less active in expanding Holocaust education (Carrier, Fuchs, & Messinger, 2015), although we find some notable exceptions (Freedman,

2014). All nations and regions now have extensive access to resources for Holocaust and human rights education, as we will elaborate.

Our five types of Holocaust education can help educators like us to create educational rationale statements, specifying our learning goals and curricula (Feinberg & Totten, 2016; Totten, 2002). Clarifying and distinguishing our educational goals can help us achieve specific outcomes. We can better understand why some curricula and texts are focused carefully and narrowly on the specific events within the Holocaust, others use or apply the Holocaust as an important and pivotal example for wider efforts to educate about the wider impact of the Holocaust, genocides, and human rights (Carrier et al., 2015). It seems both logical and inevitable that local and national curricula can, do, and perhaps should use Holocaust education and genocide studies for different reasons and in different ways. While single nations may, at times, establish unified or core educational goals, international variations remain possible and in many cases educational.

How we teach Holocaust history, including which type(s) of Holocaust education we embrace, depends upon our curricular goals and our educational contexts, including our disciplines. Focused and *historical* Holocaust education will usually mean learning about the Holocaust, as we elaborate major aspects of events in German-occupied territories from 1933 to 1945. This is the nature of the path within the USHMM (United States Holocaust Memorial Museum, 2018). Broader Holocaust (and/or genocide) studies may expand beyond these 12 Holocaust years (Power, 2002). There is great value in addressing broader issues of genocide (Fein, 1979a; Fracapane & Hass, 2014; Stevick & Gross, 2014), concentration camps (Stone, 2017), antisemitism (UNESCO: United Nations Educational Scientific and Cultural Organization, OSCE: Organization for Security and Co-operation in Europe, 2018), and human rights law (Bazyler, 2016; Bazyler & Tuerkheimer, 2014). Broader approaches can provide analysis of more diverse social groups and more current situations, taking a global or cosmopolitan view of persecution beyond continental and European nations.

Making and recognizing careful distinctions in educational goals can help us make informed and purposeful choices. We may develop ideas and perspectives (or engage in debates over) which purposes are most appropriate in which contexts. Our goals can include delivery of high-quality Holocaust education; we may not wish to establish the prominence or superiority of one curriculum over all others. Unfortunately, too much curricular variety is not always educationally effective, and sometimes results in ambiguity and confusion, as experts have documented in English curricula, after 25 years of diverse developments within a national curricula (Pearce & Chapman, 2017).

Different nations will continue to make complex choices about which topics and rationales to share and support (Fracapane & Hass, 2014). While we need not select *only* one pedagogical goal, it helps to identify, appreciate, and sometimes compare the important variations in Holocaust education. Just as we find *conceptual* distinctions between the Holocaust, genocide, and other atrocities (Bauer, 2001), we can also find and make subsequent distinctions in educational goals. When time and resources allow, we can explore many different local, national, and international examples. We can compare the Holocaust or genocide to other "human wrongs" that may be considered as related topics, such as slavery, mass violence, or terrorism, which may exemplify different focal concepts, but which have not always been grouped in the same curricula with the Holocaust (Fein, 2007). Whether or not educators can or do discuss or accept the horrors of problems like slavery or terrorism as forms of genocide, we can accept and describe these injustices as important historical facts, bringing all manners of injustice and persecution from behind the fog of war and history, reducing the harm that has come from ignorance and denial.

Curricular Variety

With help from research, we can clearly observe that global variations in Holocaust education now include a variety of curricular forms, only some of which focus directly on the Holocaust or particularly on antisemitic persecution. While student and teacher interest in the Holocaust is strong and curricular options are many, teachers can exercise agency and autonomy in Holocaust education. This is supported by analysis of Israeli education (Cohen, 2016). But in many other national contexts, analysis shows that, while students can learn from nationally recognized texts and curricula, many of these resources may fail to deliver important information (Foster & Karayianni, 2017). Even worse, some nations provide only partial coverage, or no coverage at all, of the Holocaust in textbooks and national curricula (Carrier et al., 2015). Newer "versions" of Holocaust histories appear only as examples within the context of "genocide education" and/or education which is about or for human rights. Thus we can simplify curricula as those with any (or many) of these goals. Findings from recent UNESCO research show that while many nations make direct reference to the Holocaust (or Shoah), other nations use alternative terms, which remove a very first principle of effective Holocaust education, which is simply to define the term "Holocaust" (ADL et al., 2014).

Some nations make "partial" reference to the Holocaust, indirectly stipulating teaching about the Holocaust as an example (rather than a focal topic) within a broader historical topic or as a basis of the need for human rights education. Some nations present it only in the context of other topics, like stages of genocide, human rights violations, and antisemitism, but without specifically addressing the Holocaust as an event (Carrier et al., 2015). Many national curricula are in a state of transition, often toward *more* state support for direct Holocaust education.

In contrast, we find early adopters of *state-supported* curricula include Israel in 1981 (Stevick & Gross, 2014) and the United Kingdom in 1990 (Pearce & Chapman, 2017), followed by more recent changes to national curricula in Brazil and (in 2010) in Finland (Carrier et al., 2015). In recent decades, while national and curricular variations in educational forms have evolved, both Holocaust memory and Holocaust education have also become more "universalized" or "cosmopolitan" (Levy & Sznaider, 2006). Sometimes this has meant that schools adopt a goal of (comparative) genocide education, and sometimes this involves becoming more inclusive. Inclusive education can be taken to mean not being so "particularistic" and studying only antisemitism or Jewish experiences, but instead studying diverse groups of people who were harmed by the Holocaust, including Roma and people with disabilities. Such universal or cosmopolitan perspectives, which have become controversial in some contexts and popular in others, can help bring wider audiences into Holocaust education, and need not necessarily distort, diminish, or deny the Holocaust. We can continue to "globalize" Holocaust education and culture and at the same time recognize and prioritize historical and modern problems of antisemitism (UNESCO: United Nations Educational Scientific and Cultural Organization, OSCE: Organization for Security and Co-operation in Europe, 2018).

Holocaust education can recognize that the Holocaust is a unique and uniquely important event, affecting *both* Jewish people *and* other (sometimes intersecting) groups as well. Therefore, Holocaust studies within genocide education should give careful, not just cursory attention to the Holocaust itself (Totten, 2002). In addition, not all comparisons need to focus on postwar or modern examples of genocide or mass violence. For example, the "concentration camp" is a concept and historical form that has had many historical incarnations, including colonial examples prior to the Holocaust and the notorious "gulags" in Soviet territories (Stone, 2017).

Educators, policy-makers, and human rights advocates apply lessons from the Holocaust in order to prevent and prosecute genocide, to reduce antisemitism, and to continue to develop law that generally preserves and protects human rights (Bazyler, 2016). Some expressly "political" interpretations of the Holocaust may lead educators or learners to go beyond an appreciation for civic participation or human rights to criticize modern authoritarians or unchecked sovereignty in militarized-industrial states. While such comparisons can become powerful and while we are free to consider parallels between history and modern society, this has led some critics to point out the dangers of misusing the Holocaust as a metaphor for other problems in public life (Novick, 1999). Public misuses of the term "holocaust," like public misrepresentations of Holocaust perpetrators, continue to stir up plenty of problems and misunderstandings.

Learning about the Holocaust, some curricular approaches carefully limit considerations of comparative contexts (outside of the Holocaust), other atrocities (including other genocide), or even human rights. Taking a "particularistic" (rather than "universal") perspective on the Holocaust may also be supported by concerns about antisemitic and anti-Judaic hatred. UNESCO recently encouraged members and curricula to include antisemitism education and prevention (UNESCO: United Nations Educational Scientific and Cultural Organization, OSCE: Organization for Security and Co-operation in Europe, 2018). "Particularistic" Holocaust education, though it is considered narrow by some, does take Jewish people and groups as focal or primary educational subjects and victims. But this is a perspective, not a resolution of the need for inclusion. How do we address the intended "genocide of Jews" in Europe while not ignoring other cultures and groups subject to Nazi perpetrator persecution and violence? How do we focus on the Holocaust when prior and more recent genocides are increasingly documented and some are ongoing? Jewish populations were clearly targeted, scapegoated, and harmed to a unique extent during the Holocaust, but that does not mean that there is only one problem or genocide that students should consider. Universalistic inclusion and cosmopolitanism may be desirable for many, but this should not lead to the diminishment or exclusion of a careful focus on the history of the Holocaust itself.

Forced choices presented to us during curricular development or delivery need not dissuade us. Narrow views of Holocaust education may be an indicator of frustration rather than reality. Given academic freedom and some degree of teacher autonomy (Cohen, 2016), many educators can and do purposely and confidently choose any or many from among these five approaches when implementing, adapting, or even designing our curricula. It seems only reasonable that we recognize that there are *many* good options in Holocaust education (along with many problematic issues to address in our classrooms). There are many complex answers to most important explanatory questions about the Holocaust (Hayes, 2017). Certainly, many different ways to teach the Holocaust are now and will be in use around the world (Carrier et al., 2015; Pingel, 2014). While each nation and educational group has rights to make choices about education, it seems reasonable that many diverse nations and groups will continue to make somewhat different choices (Fracapane & Hass, 2014), even with international guidance.

Some national curricula and texts can unfairly compare the Holocaust to dissimilar or simply national tragedies in order to create a context of shared or heroic victimhood (Fracapane & Hass, 2014; Pingel, 2014). While we will live without a standard international curriculum in most subjects, we should not let the Holocaust be replaced as a historical topic. We also can acknowledge that Holocaust is profoundly important to our history and our societies, but Holocaust education also has been and will be used for broader goals and universal concerns, such as education about genocide, the history of world wars, and human rights. In summary, the Holocaust in history stands as an unprecedented (though not unique) and pivotal example of racialized genocide (Bauer, 2001).

While we see gaps in knowledge and in curricula as well, Holocaust education is still an effective way to engage students. Critical evaluations of global and other variations in Holocaust education should and need not prevent us from sharing the best forms of Holocaust education, collaborating to make good choices about how we teach and share curricula on this subject.

Learning Both *About* and *From* the Holocaust

Learning *about* the Holocaust begins with a detailed, historically accurate, and accepted definition of Holocaust (ADL et al., 2014). Particular terms in our Holocaust definitions (especially "Nazis," "antisemitism," "genocidal," and "Jews") often need definition or clarification as well (Cowan & Maitles, 2017). Once educators define key concepts and terms, specific educational goals can direct exploration of multiple topics and subjects from many viewpoints, while still helping students learn about the event objectively and often from primary sources (Arad, Gutman, & Margaliot, 1999). Learning *about* history should be considered a first curricular step; learning *from* history may be considered a subsequent, albeit important second step. We should critically evaluate historical events in order to learn moral and legal lessons from Holocaust history, especially because the Holocaust has become both a global and a historical standard for ethical transgression, evil, and mass crime, a reason to compose and approve international rules against genocide (Alexander, 2009; Belzberg, 2016; Power, 2002).

Many curricula, like history texts and museums, take a chronological approach to presenting the Holocaust, starting with antisemitic laws and "actions" that grew from the Nazi policies that started in 1933 (United States Holocaust Memorial Museum, 2018; Yahil, 1990). Sometimes chronology is mixed with major themes, creating a narrative that includes perpetrators, victims, bystanders, and major themes (ADL et al., 2014). For young learners, Cowan has simplified Hilberg's work (Cowan & Maitles, 2017; Hilberg, 1978) to suggest five thematic stages in Holocaust histories, from alienation and segregation into deportation, then extermination (annihilation or genocide), and finally liberation. Offering histories the Holocaust without discussing liberation and diasporic migrations, like teaching about "the war" without discussing the Holocaust, seems incomplete.

Learning about and from history, for visual learners and for us all, is more "real" when we see or visit Holocaust settings like a concentration or death camps (Cowan and Maitles, 2011; Gardner, 1999). Focal settings can also include ghettos and labor sites, both in Germany and in occupied or adjacent ("satellite") nations (Hayes & Roth, 2010). Holocaust education therefore need not be confined to a class or classroom. Teachers and learners alike are often inspired and engaged by resources in or visits to any of many major museums or memorials (Cole, 2004). Reintroducing the Holocaust as a "multicultural past" that involves Jewish heritage sites has also been shown to be helpful in reducing prejudice through this historical variation on intergroup contact (Stefaniak & Bilewicz, 2016).

The design and experience of Holocaust education can provoke different types of responses. One significant factor affecting both design and response to Holocaust education is described as "national consciousness and the relationship between a country and its past" (Gray, 2014). We expect and find differences in Holocaust education by continent and by nation; European nations in particular differ significantly, both from the rest of the world and in relation to one another. Struggling with issues of national responsibilities, educators and students in Germany and Poland may face some of the most complex responses in this regard. Holocaust education has been less fully developed and perhaps less ubiquitous within many nations that were not at "ground zero" during the Holocaust. Variation is expected since each nation and region both experiences and responded somewhat differently to both the Holocaust and subsequently to the challenges of Holocaust education, which can raise difficult issues of national, social, and personal responsibilities among different cohorts and generations (Fracapane & Hass, 2014; Gebert, 2014; Stevick & Gross, 2014).

While Germany has embraced both Holocaust education and Holocaust memorialization (Kaiser, 2014; Stevick & Gross, 2014), the national and educational responses have been somewhat more complex in Poland (Gebert, 2014). Like other areas that Snyder calls "the bloodlands" of eastern Europe (Snyder, 2012, 2015a), many in Poland viewed the Holocaust as part of a more general and very difficult period of national suffering that was related to oppression by Nazi fascists and subsequently to Soviet communists. Thus educators and students in Poland and other post-Soviet nations may respond to Holocaust education by focusing on the point that the victims of the Holocaust and war were not only Jewish communities but also national groups (like Poles). The problem with such nationalist perspectives on both persecution and memory is that they can minimize the real and enduring legacy of antisemitism and antisemitic violence. In fact, many Polish and neighboring Jewish communities were completely or almost completely destroyed (Bauer and Keren, 2001; Gross, 2013).

A focus on national suffering can arise despite clear evidence of antisemitism in particular and eugenics before and during the Holocaust. Issues of responsibility, intolerance, and nationalism can be politically complex, even among enlightened nations and in modern times. US President Reagan upset many in his recognition of military service by perpetrators in his visit to Bergen Belsen (Jensen, 2007). More recent problems of interpretation were noted to President Obama faced after his lamenting of *"Polish* Death Camps" (Gebert, 2014). Even so, can assessments of national responsibilities for genocide be confined to authoritarians or to policy-makers in "perpetrator-nations"?

As noted, educational institutions in many nations did not provide much Holocaust education at all before the 1960s and 1970s. This was the case in the United States (Fallace, 2008; Napolitano et al., 2007), Israel (Stevick & Gross, 2014), and many European nations (Pearce & Chapman, 2017). The extent of Holocaust education changed dramatically in the late twentieth century, led by early adopters of state-supported curricula like Israel in 1981 (Stevick & Gross, 2014) and in the United Kingdom in 1990 (Pearce & Chapman, 2017). But even now, not all nations directly provide Holocaust education, and fewer require it (Carrier et al., 2015; Fracapane & Hass, 2014). We see great progress during the last half-century, nonetheless. As a recent example, despite a somewhat delayed start, Austria is making very positive developments in Holocaust memory, and these changes have led to recent knowledge gains and attitudinal changes among students (Bastel, Matzka, & Miklas, 2010). Initiatives in Brazil, Finland, and other nations are also worthy of attention and support (Carrier et al., 2015).

One big challenge has been to overcome biases associated with national myths of heroism and victimhood, replacing a distorted, biased, and/or apologetic perspective with viewpoints that are more honest and reflective (Fracapane & Hass, 2014). Especially in Germany and its (wartime) allied nations, there is a modern movement and need to not only accept responsibilities but also to recognize that harm resulted from many (perpetrator and bystander) actions, not just the oppressive authoritarianism of Hitler and his close associates (Kaiser, 2014). Authoritarian leaders (Stalin specifically) have caused great and even concurrent harm and oppression, also including millions of deaths. Even so, Nazis *intended* genocide, and thus it is often a serious mistake and a distortion to simply equate massive harm and killing to the narrowly defined crime of genocide, or to draw a false equivalence between the Fascist Nazi goals and actions and the Communist state crimes of Stalin (Bauer, 2010).

Learning *from* Holocaust education can and should freely take many forms and generate many concerns, even as such education is required by the state (Pearce & Chapman, 2017). While pedagogies and learning objectives may vary, there have been many (often moral, not only historical) lessons taken from Holocaust education and studies. These may conform to the educational principles of the school or governmental authority, but they may also develop from the teachers and students involved (Fallace, 2008; Schweber, 2008). Learning from the "echoes" of history is helpful in critical thinking and moral education, as students and teachers find "reflections" on lessons learned in hindsight and sometimes applied to modern contexts (ADL et al., 2014).

Language, especially careful, concise, and inclusive terminology, is important (not trivial) in Holocaust education. Often students can be taught to correctly use terms including "Nazis," "Jews" (or Jewish people), "Roma" (Sinti or "Gypsies"), and the various types of camps and ghettos (Cowan & Maitles, 2017). As variations in language and terms arise, we can structure a longer historical narrative and deconstruct simplistic perspectives. For example, persecuted members of social groups become "victims" or "survivors"; some heroic fighters become "liberators" of camps; some survivors become liberated by liberators and become "displaced persons" (DPs); concentration camps are closed and replaced by DP camps; many displaced people become emigrants and immigrants; some emigrants become refugees and later nationals and citizens; some refugees become leading scientists and teachers. Perhaps some refugees live among us or teach our classes, as well. We all age; thankfully survivors are not stuck in a time of striped pajamas, mandatory yellow stars, and starvation. We are past, but still shocked and awed by unrepresentable skeletal symbols of catastrophe (Buettner, 2009).

Controversial topics often arise in learning about and from the Holocaust (Lindquist, 2010). Educators may be subject to community or policy-related pressures or even to Holocaust denial. The topics may be difficult or emotionally exhausting for teachers, who must carefully set a balanced (though not biased) interpretive tone for classes. While standard curricula are being delivered to students of many age groups, most at least 11 or 12 years old, justifying Holocaust education in primary schools has become popular based on at least three reasons. First, cognitive learning theory is optimistic that young people can be taught most topics as long as material is organized well, building on concepts learned previously. Second, studies show moral education is promoted by appropriate Holocaust topics during the primary level. Third, prejudicial attitudes also infect young minds, so antiprejudice education should start early (Cowan & Maitles, 2007, 2017).

Even with the protective distance of historical hindsight, immersion in oppressive uses of antisemitic racism to scapegoat, harm, and oppress during the Holocaust can become difficult for (especially Jewish) students and teachers

(Tinberg, 2005; Tinberg, Weisberger, & Project, 2013). Jewish students may also have different (often greater) levels of exposure to Holocaust studies, along with understandably strong points of view. Antisemitism and Jewish experiences can be unfairly minimized or overshadowed by discussions or narratives that prioritize other groups perpetrating or even affected by the Holocaust or other genocides (Lindquist, 2010). These concerns, while worthy of discussion and debate, also point to the fact that Holocaust education in schools is not the only form of education about the Holocaust or genocide that students experience; plenty of information "educates" learners outside the formal curricula.

Genocide Education

Holocaust education is a first step toward the broader field of genocide education. Both the Holocaust and genocide can also be included as introductory topics that address modern developments in international law. The Holocaust was and remains the defining case of the crime that international law now defines as genocide (Bazyler, 2016). The concept and definition of genocide exist in large part, thanks to Raphael Lemkin, a linguist-turned-lawyer, who advanced the concept in law and coined the term "genocide" (Lemkin & Jacobs, 2012). In the early twentieth century, despite a need for international legal protections against religious persecution or intolerance, including state-sponsored persecution, internationally reported and recognized vengeance killings and assassinations triggered both public outcry and sometimes mass violence. In the early 1930s, as a young Polish and Jewish scholar, Lemkin suggested the crimes of "barbarism" and "vandalism" (cultural destruction) to the League of Nations, in light of the (soon to be called "genocidal") violence against of large numbers of Armenians and also Ukrainian Jews (Cooper, 2008).

Lemkin presented his research to a 1933 international conference in Spain, describing mass murders of Armenians by Turkish authorities in 1915 (Cooper, 2008; Power, 2002). In 1921, a survivor of this massacre named Tehlirian assassinated a Turkish minister named Talaat. The assassin claimed vengeance for the mass killings of Armenians, which included his entire family. Lemkin saw major problems (violent barbarity) and forged solutions (international laws against persecution of national groups), but his presentation did not have an international impact. Then, tragically confirming the pressing need for international law against genocide, the Holocaust began. Lemkin and millions of others were persecuted on the basis of group affiliation. Lemkin was forced to flee Poland as a refugee in the wake of the German invasion which arrived in September 1939.

Lemkin and many other Jewish refugees escaped Poland to Vilnius, Lithuania, in October 1939. With help from colleagues, he was then able to escape to Sweden and then to receive an invitation to teach law in the United States from Duke University. He arrived in the United States in April 1941, traveled to Duke and was received enthusiastically by the University, including his friend Professor Malcolm McDermott. In 1942, he accepted new work in Washington, D.C., and developed what became his seminal and extensive publication on genocide, completed in November 1943 and published in 1944 (Cooper, 2008; Lemkin & Jacobs, 2012).

Lemkin developed and coined the word "genocide" to describe barbaric violence committed against a "nation," a "geno" (race or tribe), or what we might now call a (human) cultural group. Discriminatory mass violence and killing ("cide") was conceived as a set of destructive threats or techniques that endangered groups and group health on the basis of religious, national, or other group affiliation (Lemkin & Jacobs, 2012). The profound importance of law against "genocide" had been clear to Lemkin for years, even prior to the Holocaust. Lemkin believed that national sovereignty should not preclude an international tribunal from preventing or prosecuting mass murder of civilians (Docker, 2010; Power, 2002).

As early as 1942, a Polish Bund report had informed Lemkin and others that millions of Jewish people were being killed. Most of ~9 million Jews in Europe were, by design, endangered by Nazi eugenic persecution. After the Allied victory and the end of the war in Europe, an international military tribunal (IMT) in Nuremberg, Germany, was created and operationalized. The United States, with Britain, France, and the USSR, leading the IMT, used German documents and testimony to successfully prosecute some of Germany's leadership for a variety of international war crimes. But these crimes did not (at the time) include the soon-to-be-named crime of genocide, and the Nuremberg trial court's jurisdiction was limited to wartime and so did not include the period from 1933 until the outbreak of war in 1939; this limit represented a great injustice in the eyes of Lemkin, among others (Bazyler, 2016; Power, 2002).

After conceiving of and describing the crime of genocide, Lemkin witnessed and pushed for its inclusion. "Genocide" was mentioned in the third count of a first Nuremberg trial indictment of all 24 defendants in October 1945. He lobbied British and other leaders to include the newly coined crime in the Nuremburg judgments. History shows that he was not always successful in the short run (Power, 2002). But success was clear in the long run, where Lemkin's concept transformed international law and human rights. Success began as the newly created United Nations established a universal declaration of human rights and more specifically adopted an international convention against genocide (Power, 2002).

International laws against genocide were debated internationally and within the United States. In the United States, where presidential approval was quick but Senate approval was delayed for decades, this debate brought important attention to the injustices and perceived crimes of racialized slavery (Power, 2002). It is important to help students learn and appreciate that the UN Convention helped spark public and official recognition of racism, and that this has been a long-standing concern in the United States which remains to this day.

Genocide education in the twenty-first century is more often emphasized in the Americas, Africa, and part of Asia, including in the United States (Carrier et al., 2015). We also see a renewed focus on antisemitism as a form of prejudice and discrimination (UNESCO: United Nations Educational Scientific and Cultural Organization, OSCE: Organization for Security and Co-operation in

Europe, 2018). The related and overlapping problems of racism and antisemitism are addressed well in leading and online curricular resources, like Echoes and Reflections (ADL et al., 2014). Thus Holocaust education is ethically and reasonably linked to genocide education. Rather than choosing one over another, Holocaust content can be both particularly problematic for a group (antisemitism harms Jews) and universally problematic for everyone (human rights should not be denied to any person or group). Some bitterly describe curricula that look beyond Holocaust and its limited historical period as "sociological," perhaps because genocide education can be clearly antiracist (Short, 1999), not just "anti-antisemitic" (Gray, 2014). Even so, sociology has not always been a force in the larger world of Holocaust education. Published sociological and other resources have not always been fully informed about the Holocaust; one analysis found professional disinterest in the topics of Holocaust and genocide (Fein, 1979b).

Lessons from the Holocaust can be part of antiracist education, especially when we appreciate the importance of educating against conformist bystander behavior (Short, 1999, 2003). While teaching for tolerance and respect, we nonetheless have limited tolerance for indifference in the face of injustice. Curricula against genocide are well developed in England, France, the United States, and to some extent in Russia (Fracapane & Hass, 2014), those same four nations that judged Holocaust perpetrators during the influential Nuremburg trials (Conot, 1983; Dodd & Bloom, 2007). British and Canadian curricula have also developed rapidly in the last three decades (Short & Reed, 2004). Even so, variations by nations suggest some perspective focus on diverse groups and inclusion in ways that may be interpreted to minimize the Holocaust. As an illustration, a sample of textbooks and curricula in France sometimes omit reference to "the Holocaust" and instead describe "genocide of the Jews," "destructions of Jews," and "extermination of Jews and Gypsies." Some focus on totalitarianism, which is understandable, but provide less emphasis on the French resistance or Jewish experiences, risking bias by minimizing the perspectives of those harmed by and standing up against the Holocaust (Carrier et al., 2015).

While genocide education against racism is appropriate and is found in many nations around the globe, it is certainly well developed in modern Germany, where analysis of five textbooks and curricula shows that significant detail is provided on many topics including genocide, marginalization, incarceration (including a focus on Auschwitz), resistance, and memorial sites of commemoration (Carrier et al., 2015). While bystanders are subject to less scrutiny, and while National Socialism is a primary context for German curricula and textbooks, this UNESCO study shows German curricular resources contain abundant information along with moral and political lessons for new generations.

The situation in developing nations in Latin America and Africa is somewhat different. Nations outside of Europe and the United States may become even more open to understanding Holocaust through education, but curricula in some nations remain somewhat less elaborate. For some of these nations, it has been possible to employ Holocaust history in curricula without the distractions of what it means for historical or contemporary national consciousness. Some students and teachers in less privileged nations in the global south may relate more fully to the topics of human rights in response to experiences of suffering and prejudice, rather than the topics that become complicated by national identities, anti-semitism, or past versions of international conflict (Carrier et al., 2015; Fracapane & Hass, 2014).

Regardless of national variations, even young learners can learn to understand the Holocaust and genocide as these tragedies often follows a series of five stages (Cowan & Maitles, 2017). First, leaders unjustly alienate and marginalize oppressed groups through national law and social policies (Bazyler, 2016). Second, in a stage that resonates with the history of US civil rights, groups are segregated into ghettos. Third, in a more aggressive forced relocation, groups are sent away to prison camps, which include concentration camps for containment, forced labor, and infamously for mass murder at death camps. Especially with death camps, a fifth stage that defines genocides generally and the Holocaust particularly is thus intended mass killing for the purposes of extermination or annihilation, which differentiates genocide from other forms of mass killing or even mass murder. A sixth and final stage is liberation, for survivors who are able to endure genocidal attempts (Cowan & Maitles, 2017).

Genocide is a major global concern; one leading scholar on the subject calculated that it causes more global mortality than natural disaster (Fein, 2007). But she also recognizes that critics may be concerned that charges of "genocide" may be discredited by its hyperbolic and political misuses to describe any alarming social problem. Even so, misuse of a concept does not mean we should minimize its educational uses. Fein also estimates that, among 18 documented cases of genocide in the years from 1915 to 2006, most have not been adjudicated (no group was brought to trial or punished). Notably, the Armenian genocide, the Rwandan Tutsi genocide, and the Nazi genocide "of the Jews" each resulted in killing over 50% of the intended victims. However we define or compare genocide or *genociadaires* (perpetrators of genocide), we can and should link the Holocaust to genocide. We are also global citizens with global rights, and so we can use Holocaust education to advance global citizenship education.

Education *For* and *About* Human Rights

Human rights and responsibilities, established by nations and by faith traditions, form many important bases for social justice (United Nations 2017 (Enacted 1948)). Education *about* and *for* human rights constitute our final (fourth and fifth) types of Holocaust education. Human rights education, especially through service learning and community partnerships, is a growing curricular trend (Kingston, 2014). Like learning *about* the Holocaust, education *about* human rights (both in the abstract and in practice) can be an important rationale for a simpler, less controversial, and more objective sets of educational goals. There are many internationally accepted documents and conventions that guarantee and specify human rights. Which primary sources should we use? Can we distinguish among and prioritize among these (Fein, 2007)? Crucially, how can we apply human rights to specific examples, including the Holocaust (Bazyler, 2016)? These are difficult questions that open up important curricular opportunities and directions. Holocaust and human rights education become part of civics and citizenship education (Cowan & Maitles, 2017).

Educators also should consider whether and how Holocaust and human rights education itself can or should advance social justice, thus creating education *for* human rights (Wronka, 2017). Education for human rights may, like interpretations made in learning *from* the Holocaust, create a wider, less restrictive, more engaging, but potentially less objective basis for curricula and thus for educational processes. Even so, for many of us, education should respond to ongoing needs to improve our world. Educators share many ethical and social responsibilities; we work as teachers, professionals, and often as scholars, to seek and do acts of social justice—not only to discuss justice—*especially* for groups who are subject to great injustices. For example, my own set of professional ethics include a principle to contribute to (and serve) "the public good" (ASA Committee on Professional Ethics, 1999 (2008)).

After the United Nations was founded at the San Francisco Conference on 25 October 1945, a committee chaired by Eleanor Roosevelt drafted (and in 1948 the General Assembly endorsed without dissent) 30 different types of human rights (Wronka, 2017) in its Declaration of Human Rights (UNDHR) (United Nations 2017 (Enacted 1948)). Since then, organizations and educators have elaborated and promoted human rights and a "human rights culture" that is increasingly consistent with this declaration. Consequently, education *for* human rights can build on education *about* human rights, helping societies put ideals and agreements into practice.

Not all forms of human rights education begin with international human rights documents. Political science and civic education (often called "government" class in the United States) often use our national constitution and other national historical documents to elaborate the scope of human rights and civic responsibilities. As noted, civic education in any nation should work to include the example of the Holocaust (Stevick, 2018). Many different rights were taken away from Jewish and other groups during the Holocaust. This was no accident; denial of rights was the first of the four stages in the Nazi war against Jewish Europeans. Once identified (on documents and on clothing), Jews were banned from government service and professional life. A racialized definition of Jewish identity, based on genealogy and not religious faith or practice, was legally established to ensure administrative distinctions were possible (Bazyler, 2016). Intermarriages were forbidden in Germany in 1935. As in other nations (like the United States) during other periods, blood quantum became a federally defining criterion for ethnic or racial classification (Snipp, 2003, 2010). As German power and jurisdiction expanded, so too did the scale of human right abuses (Yahil, 1990).

Violations of human rights, individual and social, depend in part on the way that rights and responsibilities are iterated, classified, assigned, organized, legislated, and adjudicated. Major challenges for learners and educators include finding acceptable systems by which different rights can be ranked or prioritized; sometimes specific rights conflict. This is not a new challenge; both civic and faith-based values, which also may often come into conflict, are at the root of human rights in the UNDHR (United Nations 2017 (Enacted 1948)).

Educational initiatives can be designed to teach both (descriptively) *about* human rights and (progressively) for human rights. Core notions that are found in global human rights documents (like conventions against racial and gender-based discriminations) include human dignity and respect (the core of UNDHR article 1) and nondiscrimination (Wronka, 2017). Additional core notions include civil and political rights (fundamental to the US Bill of Rights); economic, social, and cultural rights; and solidarity rights. While the classification and operationalization of these rights can vary, these are important bases by which major "human wrongs" (like the Holocaust) can be fairly evaluated (Fein, 2007). Thus, education *about* and *for* human rights can both spur and reinforce lessons learned about and from the Holocaust.

Texts and textbooks from many nations emphasize human rights in teaching about the Holocaust (Pingel, 2014). A human rights–based teaching approach to the Holocaust helps students appreciate global notions of human rights as central to international society (Bromley and Russell, 2010). National "master narratives" that summarize historical trends are complicated by a focus on the Holocaust as definitive violations of human rights through genocide, but this creates an opportunity to discuss global concerns and inequalities among multicultural students from multinational backgrounds (Pingel, 2014).

Holocaust education is one way to address important topics of prejudice and discrimination (Cowan & Maitles, 2007). As we will see in future chapters, discriminatory regimes and laws have some commonalities. For example, Jewish exclusions and ghettos during the Holocaust have similarities to decades of discrimination that found enforcement through Jim Crow laws in the southern United States. Educators can explore how antisemitic ethnocentrism, like racism, attempts but ultimately fails to create and sustain its own harmful logics (Bonilla-Silva, 2018, 2015; Zuberi & Bonilla-Silva, 2008).

Human rights–based Holocaust education is consistent with many different forms of citizenship education as well (Cowan & Maitles, 2017). Human rights and responsibilities of citizenship include the protections of civil and other rights for individuals and groups, along with responsibilities to the state. As citizenship education develops, it provides political literacy, community involvement, and positive values (Gutmann & ebrary, 1999). Even so, some evidence from both Europe and the United States shows declining political literacy and growing disinterest in some aspects of both government and social concern (Maitles, 2014; Mirel, 2002). Connecting human rights education to citizenship education can help address this problem and link local, regional, and national responsibilities for citizenship with global responsibilities (Stevick, 2018).

Representing, Reading, and Writing the Holocaust

Accepting the benefits of using text in Holocaust education opens up a world of textual Holocaust representations. These include "documents, testimonies, photographs, memoirs, novels, interviews, dramas, artworks, films, monuments, and other symbolic depictions created at the time and after the fact, whose subject matter is the Holocaust" (Magilow & Silverman, 2015). The Holocaust has become a symbol representing many types of evil and injustice, the foundation for the construction of universal and global moral standards (Alexander, 2009; Levy & Sznaider, 2006). But we also see that the Holocaust has been used as an allegory for other national and global narratives, like Zionism, socialism, and American heroism (Jay, 2009).

We remember and represent the Holocaust as both a particularly antisemitic and Jewish tragedy and a universal concern with genocide and all persecution. While "particularism" focused post-Holocaust efforts on the founding of modern Israel, universalism was at the same time enshrined by the newly created United Nations in our global declaration of human rights and a convention against genocide. These two developments were each and both historically important and consequential. While Zionist interest in Israel and universalist interests in human rights did not remain complementary in the latter twentieth century, the early postwar period included international acceptance of the importance of *both* perspectives and thus forged what we now see as a "transnational memory cultures" in our cosmopolitan age of globalization (Levy & Sznaider, 2006). Modern conflicts in the Middle East do cloud some political versions of memory (Olick & Levy, 1997), but political and other conflicts need not impede our abilities to understand both the history of the Holocaust and other histories of genocide. All history can contribute to the growth of human rights.

Holocaust education uses and creates forms of cultural and historical representation. These representations include survivor and witness testimonies, in an extensive tradition of shared memory that goes back to the early postwar period (Waxman, 2006). Testimonials inform and persuade; accounts are used for both education and social justice. Historical trials in Germany and in Jerusalem created some degree of justice, precedent, and also education, prompting Germany to prosecute perpetrators and later to issue reparations (Bazyler, 2016).

Anne Frank was perhaps among the first faces visually representing the tragedy and injustices of the Holocaust (Prose, 2009). Her biography was rescued by her father, translated, and became popular. Anne's short life was then dramatized for English-speaking and other audiences. She is also now a subject of authorized graphic novels (Jacobson, Colón, & Anne Frank, 2010), suggesting a new genre of Holocaust education, which was first popularized by the darker and respected representations of survivor memory in the publication *Maus* (Spiegelman, 1997).

When educators and content creators bring attention to criminals like Eichmann or survivors like Wiesel or Levi, we make choices about which and which types of protagonists to introduce to our classes. Do we start with or privilege the perspectives of genocidal perpetrators, who were criminals, after all? How do we describe those persecuted, disproportionately Jewish people, of many nationalities? Who do we present first and how are they presented? What about the Germans or other "public Europeans," who were not always empowered by roles in government or military, or whose inactions lead many of us to apply more judgmental descriptions like "bystanders" or "onlookers" (Hayes & Roth, 2010)?

How are these people, groups, and populations cast and performed in our "educational dramas?" Which Holocaust representations could be considered culturally appropriate and which might be unfair cultural appropriations (Magilow & Silverman, 2015)? These questions require discussions of culture and transformations, attributions and misattributions of objects that represent memory and cultural heritage. The Holocaust involved many crimes, including grand larceny and mass murder. Theft from individuals was systemic, for example, from prisoners entering Auschwitz (Lengyel, 1995). Cultural appropriation thus went beyond misrepresentation; it included stolen property and distortion through propaganda (Luckert, Bachrach, & United States Holocaust Memorial Museum, 2009), it also involved the destruction and transfiguration of cultural wealth.

How do we show the harsh realities of persecution, respecting victims of mass violence without upsetting some audiences? Should we even describe those harmed as *victims*, contributing to potentially negative stereotypes, when there was also resistance and rebellion? Especially if students are unfamiliar with Judaism, should we first introduce Jewish people primarily as victims of anti-semitism or the Holocaust, without first introducing us as subjects of a longer and respected historical tradition and trajectory (Lindemann & Levy, 2010)? Such questions lead to complex situations; how can we proceed beyond "Holocaust hesitation" to share curricula? Do we need to start from a more distant beginning and/or tell a longer historical narrative to avoid all possible misunderstandings?

Interpreting Holocaust representations, we quickly find that there are many different ways to represent the types of protagonists in the catastrophe. One image or example is too simple to represent historical events. No single perpetrator or survivor can represent all who were in these categories. Many different diaries show many types of children in different nations and circumstances endured all kinds of Holocaust experiences (Zapruder, 2002). Those who escaped or were hidden had different experiences from those in ghettos and those in camps; many experienced more than one of these oppressive conditions (Hayes & Roth, 2010).

In postmodern times, the same individual can of course be represented in multiple ways. Anne Frank's famous quotation portrays her as an optimist, despite concurrent and grave concerns that are also within her diary (Frank et al., 2003). We less often visually represent the nightmares she must have known, minimizing the clearly adverse conditions that led to her murder (along with most of her family) within the vast system of death camps (Jacobson et al., 2010). Critics of early forms of "Americanized" Holocaust culture have been reasonably concerned that glorifying the subjects of Frank's diary risks minimizing the darker reality and the broader, genocidal, and criminal realities (Flanzbaum, 1999). Perpetrators are also subject to complex and conflicting representations (Foster & Karayianni, 2017; Lewy, 2017). As noted, Eichmann on trial publically represented himself as a blameless bureaucrat, while showing himself in private to be a hateful mass murder (Bazyler, 2016).

Our modern appreciation of history through Holocaust memorials and museums are one venue for "judgment" of the past, even as memorial representations are reshaped by modern concerns (Tumolo, 2015). We can learn from the challenges of Holocaust representation within the context of more difficult historical or modern cultural conflicts, like modern Poland, where collective memories of communities compete to define a shared vision of a traumatic past (Kapralski, 2018). We endeavor to respectfully represent Holocaust-impacted cultures, as we also use care when facing inappropriate or derogatory cultural representations (Magilow & Silverman, 2015). As educators representing the Holocaust, we carefully and clearly share our sources, making sure to note if or how any stereotypic misrepresentations were designed as hateful propaganda (Luckert et al., 2009). Even so, we cannot avoid the fact that people are free to, and often do, express freely, creating sometimes argumentative and even distracting debate over our choices and forms of Holocaust representation.

In choosing what to share, assign, and read about the Holocaust, we both exercise freedom and work within existing curricular frameworks (ADL et al., 2014, ADL, USC Shoah Foundation, & Vashem, 2017). We select student-level appropriate writings and images from both primary and secondary sources (Cowan & Maitles, 2017). With historical focus, we can prioritize primary sources, like diaries salvaged from the ashes of history (Zapruder, 2002). We respect primary source documents that illustrate those chilling legal directives which created oppression throughout Nazi-occupied territories (Arad et al., 1999). As time and resources allow, we can explore a range of perspectives; many educational choices can be good choices.

Misrepresentations and stereotypes about both the subjects of the Holocaust and about the Holocaust as a subject can cloud cultural currents of Holocaust representation and education. Antisemitism was a central, powerful, and pervasive force before and during the Holocaust (Gerber, 1986; Lindemann & Levy, 2010; Julius, 2010). In the context of Nazi oppression, antisemitic and other propaganda were frequently used and still sharp weapons of aggression, strategically effective in scapegoating Jews to justify German aggression, national expansion, and war (Luckert et al., 2009). Both cultural and political groups, including Jews and communists, were targeted and stereotyped through misrepresentation, Jews as greedy criminals, at once capitalists and communists, scheming world domination. Racialized antisemitism was introduced into a sequence of German laws. Jews were legally and racially defined by heritage and not by faith (Bazyler, 2016). Jewish and other communities were subsequently terrorized and systematically sent out to various diasporic locations; those who remained were subject to greater harm. Misrepresentation was only part of cultural dislocation and destruction.

Representations were intentionally and systemically distorted by Nazi leadership, and they built on propaganda techniques that first empowered Hitler and Nazis to succeed in German elections. Once the Nazis outlawed opposition parties, propaganda would help dictatorial leaders to rule as the sole political party (Luckert et al., 2009). From the very first year of Nazi authority (1933), vilified groups were grouped with and portrayed as criminals in national newspapers, described and soon treated as "others," classified as subhuman or nonhuman animals, stereotyped as pests or vermin. Once dehumanized, Jewish and targeted groups were forcibly removed from homes and home cultures, segregated, and eventually slated for "extermination," a process "sanitized" with doublespeak as a "solution" to a "problem" (Dwork, 2002).

To survive persecution, many fled or hid to prevent being subject to increasingly discriminatory and unjust laws and consequent mistreatment (Dwork & Pelt, 2009). Once deported from homes and imprisoned in ghettos or "camps," incarcerated civilians were subject to mistreatment and had to learn very difficult new attitudes and survival skills (Levi, 1989a). To represent these experiences is to lead the learner, reader, or viewer into a difficult and sometimes traumatic world that belies belief, even for those who experienced it first hand (Waxman, 2006). Even so, forcible dehumanization is not without the potential for retrospective resilience or resistance (Tec, 2003). Even so, oppressive agents can be subverted in many ways, including creative representation; Nazis were the cruelest in a different animal farm: pigs made use of cats and dogs, as we see in the graphic narratives of Maus (Spiegelman, 2011).

Bearing Witness

In choosing how to interpret testimonials and testimonial writing from the Holocaust (including survivor and victim autobiographies), we are assisted by the insights of many guides, including feminist scholar Zoe Waxman (Waxman, 2006). Waxman recognizes that bearing witness to the Holocaust is related to contemporary concerns with identity, memory, and representation. Students and educators are among audiences that can "relate to" testimonies by children, women, parents, and working people. Witnesses to the Shoah are found in diverse linguistic and national groups. Witnesses were and have since become aware of and some experts in their roles as people documenting a mass crime of global importance. Witnesses to the Holocaust can bring to students heterogeneous cultures and experiences, along with unusual locations and historical ways of life. Testimonies are also available in English and in other languages. We are indeed privileged to have a large variety of both primary and diverse perspectives on the Holocaust and increasingly to other examples of genocide (USC Shoah Foundation, 2018).

Waxman finds that fewer testimonials were written during the Holocaust while more were written afterward. Some were written in ghettos but fewer were possible in the cruel and oppressive conditions of the camps (Lengyel, 1995). Writing and representing Holocaust experiences was more possible in the contexts inhabited by "liberated prisoners" who, while often DPs, also became known as "survivors" (a term we continue to use to this day). We cannot reconstruct or even imagine a single, homogenous experience of the Holocaust, but we must start somewhere; Waxman herself has focused on the experiences of women (Waxman, 2017).

Concentration and (especially) death camps can transfix us, representing the worst of human conditions (Stone, 2017). These sites of oppression produce a rupture and a disjuncture in testimonial writings that portray Holocaust experiences from a "victim" perspective (Levi, 1959, 1989a). Other forms of testimony come from one of the many ghettos or "labor camps." Memories of the Holocaust are often softened by retrospective reflection of survival after the "miracle" of liberation (Waxman, 2006). The audience of survivors may be better able to endure the camps once a narrative arrives at liberation; 1945 can be a victory and liberation for us too. Learning from the Holocaust in this respect can be transformative, allowing us to find a greater meaning in the Holocaust and in life, which can be a profound result and even an educational outcome (Frankl, 1992).

Written witness testimonials follow themes that will receive detailed elaboration in subsequent chapters. Some recounting begin with life prior to the conflicts, proceed through deportation, and continue (for those who survive) through liberation (Waxman, 2006). Deportation takes people from suffering in homes or ghettos to face unimaginable new challenges; initial and deluded forms of hope and excitement (what could be worse than confinement in ghettos) are crushed by brutal treatment, cattle cars, and severing of human relationships (Frankl, 1992; Lengyel, 1995). Holocaust-related violence and cruelty is extended by arrival at concentration and death camps; this horror is dramatically represented in "Sophie's Choice (Styron, 1999)" and the filming of an arrival platform scene where a fictional mother (portrayed by Meryl Streep) is asked to choose between saving one or the other of her two young children (Pakula and Styron, 1982).

New arrivals at camps were both horrified and incredulous (Waxman, 2006). Humans in the camps were routinely and severely mistreated, some to the point of torture. Those who were spared an expedited murder, perhaps selected as "able," struggled to survive and to avoid further degradation (Levi, 1989a). Initial selections, some immediate on arrival and others at regular camp "roll calls," were daily, uncertain, traumatic, and dangerous matters of life and death (Lengyel, 1995; Levi, 1989a). Many public hints of dignity and self-respect in the camps led to abuse and were potentially lethal. Initiation to degraded living was followed by terrifying lessons in learning to survive.

Educators and students may not wish to delve deeply into these concerns, but we can still teach and learn about the resilience and resistance of Nazi prisoners by recognizing the ways that oppressed prisoners sometimes cling to remnants of culture (including religion). Jewish prisoners could (at times) reflect on religious topics, keep time, mark the Sabbath, barter food for candles, or improvise ritual items (Waxman, 2006; Wiesel, 1999). Retaining some connection with the past, individuals helped cultures continue, under duress, even without openly rebelling, resisting the endless forms of mistreatment. While many flatly presume Jews and others did not resist, the truth of diverse forms of resistance and resilience is important to share (Rohrlich, 1998).

Many corrosive forms of disbelief and denial, both during and since the Holocaust, represent difficult barriers to developing Holocaust history and education (Lipstadt, 1993). Disbelief was a major concern during the Holocaust (Alexander, 2009), even as the press covered the war and even when American Jewish rabbis marched on Washington in 1944 to alert the government to the ongoing crises (Sarna, 2004). Prisoners and resisters of all kinds tried to subvert or rebel against oppression (Bartrop, 2016; Rohrlich, 1998), but only a courageous and privileged few would live to witness the full extent of the Shoah (Tec, 2003). Prisoners in camp administrative roles made reports to underground operatives, and these were shared by the BBC in June 1944. Some forced to work as *sonderkommando* (Venezia & Prasquier, 2009) were able to record the dark details of the mass murder in the crematoria. Even so, most of Holocaust witnesses who wrote while in imprisoned in camps were killed; some of this evidence was destroyed by Nazis during the final days of camp operations, but a limited body of evidence survives (Waxman, 2006).

In many currents of writing, representation, and narration, most after liberation and displacement, we can see evolution in the nature of memory and the selection of memorial narratives (Levi, 1989a; Waxman, 2006). In the wake of the war, the vast scope of destruction, famine, and posttraumatic stress complicate both memory and history. People were traumatized by degradation and choiceless choices; "the drowned and the saved" were revealed to the world as victims of mass violence and abuse. The primary historical narrative clearly identifies moral lessons (Alexander, 2009), identifying Nazi criminal perpetrators in the press as nothing less than evil (Arendt, 1965), but moral and reflective clarity was more difficult for those who faced what Levi calls "gray zones" during Holocaust incarceration (Levi, 1989a). Many survivors and others remained silent rather than revisit the hellish past that they had experienced (Stein, 2009, 2014).

Providing one witness testimony to students is an important first step but not a final destination for Holocaust education; Wiesel, Frank, Levi, Lengyel, and Frankel are only a few of many who have provided this service to modern readers. Uses of survivor and witness narratives will be addressed in later chapters. Some historians note that survivor accounts are necessarily singular and not fully representative and thus illuminate only a corner of the sprawling tragedy we call the Holocaust (Cesarani, 2016).

As no single account can capture the full sweep of history, diversity in educational content and perspective remains of value, even within the limited context of one twelve-year narrative. While there is no singular or representative Holocaust experience, and while there are no universal Holocaust experiences, respecting and representing the Holocaust through witness testimony both enshrines the memories of those harmed and provides broad and universal lessons regarding morality and the human condition (Waxman, 2017). Still, we can learn even more from a more elaborate historical perspective. And we may also choose to educate about the Holocaust as an example of genocide that fits into a human rights culture of concern for current social problems. Many forms of Holocaust education can therefore contribute to our appreciation of history and social justice.

Chapter 4

Realizing Our Responsibilities

How should we clarify and discuss our responsibilities for Holocaust education? As educators using guidance from leaders in Holocaust education, we should provide students with information that is well defined, contextualized, individualized, age appropriate, and culturally appropriate (ADL, USC Shoah Foundation, & Yad Vashem, 2014). We should create supportive and safe learning environments that allow complex answers and which foster empathy. In addition, we should regularly reflect upon our perspectives and our objectives. In this chapter, I suggest that we carefully emphasize humanity and dignity in our treatments of the people and groups who were persecuted and harmed during the Holocaust.

As educators, we dignify those affected by giving voice to individual survivors and other victims of persecution. As noted, we can both focus *particularly* on Jewish people and populations *and* we can inclusively educate about all additional people and populations who were harmed by catastrophic mass violence perpetrated during the Holocaust. We should consider those human rights abuses that were perpetrated during the Holocaust, *and* we may consider comparable and other forms of human rights abuses, including other genocides. We can also consider the growth of national and international human rights laws that tie together and attempt to redress these successive concerns (Bazyler, 2016). Developing more global, universal, and cosmopolitan perspectives on the Holocaust and human rights does *not* necessarily preclude understanding, developing, or appreciating particular perspectives or differences in national or cultural perspectives (Levy & Sznaider, 2006).

In humanizing the Holocaust, we help the survivors and other victims to "speak up" in the face of horrific criminal perpetration. We put faces on statistics, bringing back to life elements of Jewish and European cultures that existed before the Holocaust, endured during the Holocaust, and continue, sometimes transformed, after the Holocaust. As we share educational responsibilities, we do justice to the memories of these and all victims of violence: we create chains of memory, support cultural survival, and respect cultural resilience. We can also recognize and appreciate those who uncovered and adjudicated the crimes of the Holocaust to establish and expand international law, realizing the fundamental goal of genocide prevention by working to define, establish, and enforce a fuller array of human rights (Bazyler, 2016; Bazyler & Tuerkheimer, 2014; Lemkin, 1944).

Humanity and Dignity

Our responsibilities to Holocaust and Human Rights Education (HHRE) include dignifying the lives and memories those harmed by the Holocaust and by other genocides. In addition to national and international commemorations designed specifically for Holocaust remembrance, in 2015 the United Nations established December 9th as a universal commemoration to dignify *all* crimes of genocide, helping to prevent genocide. HHRE can recognize particular *and* universal cultures and memories; prevention and care for harmed individuals and groups is best when we emphasize humanity, dignity, and respect. Teachers and others are called to educate; some of the best education involves including and embracing the humanity and dignity of people, groups, and cultures (Carini, 2001). The Holocaust has become a symbolically "sacred" topic, a first *named* genocide and the one that has first been subject to universal condemnation (Levy & Sznaider, 2006).

Dignity and respect for humanity are particularly important when groups or cultures have been systematically or intentionally dehumanized through oppression. Responding to intersecting forms of oppression, we find common cause in social justice (Collins, 2016; Collins & Bilge, 2016). We find gaps in cultural inclusion and recognition (Lamont, 2018). Dehumanized and oppressed groups remain fully human, but oppression and persecution can rob individuals or groups and individuals of respect and recognition. Leading historian Yehuda Bauer reminds us:

> By dehumanization I do not mean that perpetrators or victims ceased to be human. I do mean to describe acts of humiliation and oppression so extreme that the victims were deprived of... any kind of individuation in their surroundings, of their names, personalities, and family connections... (Bauer, 2001)

Dignifying humans is a humane, respectful, and corrective response to many types of efforts to dehumanize many groups of people. Dehumanizing distinctions and stereotypes of Jews and other groups were part of prejudiced and antisemitic public discrimination during the Third Reich. These actions were intentional and state-sponsored aspects of Nazi and fascist misinformation campaigns (Luckert, Bachrach, & United States Holocaust Memorial Museum, 2009). Nazi dehumanization was built upon tragic and long-standing histories of both antisemitism (Lindemann & Levy, 2010) and eugenics (Kevles, 1985). Whether an animus or an ambiance, antisemitism has been a global problem (Marcus, 2015, UNESCO: United Nations Educational Scientific and Cultural Organization, and OSCE: Organization for Security and Co-operation in Europe, 2018), evolving in many cultures, including in the Anglo and English-speaking world (Julius, 2010).

Holocaust perpetrators threatened, conspired, and intended to commit this mass crime (Dwork, 2002). Primary documents, including the 1961 testimony of Adolph Eichmann, show that there were clear decisions and directions to force out, force to work, and mass murder the Jewish population. These decisions were communicated throughout the German government (House of the Wannsee Conference Education Department, 2018). Consequently, six million Jewish Europeans were murdered and 11 million prisoners of war and displaced persons were liberated from Nazi confinement and forced labor at the end of the war (Bauer & Keren, 2001). Nations and organizations around the world had to work to remediate additional Holocaust losses, after economic, cultural, and human capital were systematically stolen and destroyed by Nazi German state policies and consequent actions. A variety of national and cultural memorials stand to mourn the losses and represent justice through public recognition of the Holocaust (Tumolo, 2015).

Over time, as Holocaust consciousness grew, public attentions have expanded from particular concerns about those harmed by the Holocaust to more general concerns about *all* genocides. All social and cultural groups, *especially* those who faced genocide or were systematically denied human rights, deserve dignity and respect. We can universally and globally dignify humanity; universal rejection of all genocide need not negate the foundational example of the Holocaust (Levy & Sznaider, 2006).

We can take care not to perpetuate past injustices or inequalities while we share educational information about the Holocaust or genocide. Blaming crime victims for crime, and blaming victims more generally, is both unjust and aggravates harm done (Ryan, 1971). Scapegoating people in stigmatized or disempowered groups is another way in which victims of oppression can be harmed. Any genocide is a mass crime that, by definition, creates many crime victims. Victims of crimes may and should report and bear witness to these injustices. This raises an important question: who is responsible for explaining the *motives* of criminal perpetrators? Is explaining perpetrator behaviors a fair task to assign to any victim of any crime? This aspect shows only one of many sometimes naïve or challenging questions that confront and may upset survivor-educators who speak to public audiences (Levi, 1989a).

We should recognize the dignity and humanity to victims of violence in general and Holocaust victims in particular. While propaganda and some scholarship has focused on the perpetrators and often their propaganda (Luckert et al., 2009), a perpetrator perspective or viewpoint should not be our first or only perspective. Why do we gravitate toward *The Boy in Striped Pajamas* story when it misrepresents camp guards and life in concentration camps (Cowan & Maitles, 2017)? Why not use "a Boy in Terezin," based on a real child's diary (Weiner, Weiner, & Dwork, 2012)?

While there are broader and universal problems of human rights and genocide that should be taught, the Holocaust is not simply a secondary story or example that can be subsumed by a larger moral or cultural narrative. The Shoah was first and foremost a catastrophe, a mass murder, and a crime that targeted Jewish people. Most of the mass murders were committed on the basis of that people simply belonged to a racialized group that was classified as Jewish in order to make Germany, Europe, and the world "free of Jews" (Bergen, 2016; Cesarani, 2016). There were many heroes who resisted these injustices, but there were many more who stood by or did not question antisemitic policies and procedures. Why do critics question the actions of Jewish and other victims and not question the non-Jewish beneficiaries of Jewish and other persecutions (Rosenberg & Rozwaski, 1999)?

We diversify our conceptions of Holocaust victims when we accept that genocides, including the Holocaust, have been perpetrated against many different groups. The ("cosmopolitan") memory of the Shoah is not minimized or desecrated if we compare it to other forms of genocide (Levy & Sznaider, 2002, 2006). Education should, within reason, promote inclusive understanding and description. Holocaust "victims" and all those harmed by genocide also can easily be considered members of oppressed status groups who were harmed disproportionately on the basis of unequal treatment. In the Holocaust, we recognize that the first discriminatory Nazi laws targeted and harmed not Jewish people but people with disabilities. We also recognize Nazi policies against Roma people and cultures, people identified as LGBT, and political dissidents, among others. Members of these status groups were also sent to ghettoes, prison camps, and death camps (Dwork & Pelt, 2009).

Perhaps we demand too much of our educational materials; we imagine our curricula as half-empty. Our texts, even when they contain only minimal information about the Holocaust, are necessarily limited sources (Fein, 1979b; Pingel, 2014). Our course books should be points of departure, not simply incomplete or end points. Curricula and outcomes are only part of the educational process. Education and schools should also support and empower learners with dignity and respect by caring and working cooperatively. In education, we value each other, regardless of our reading lists. Students, educators, and the subjects of our lessons are all human and thus interdependent. Even when our work is incomplete, we can respect one another and create collective work.

Humanizing the Holocaust

While the scale of the Holocaust emphasizes its importance, educators should also provide individual and testimonial accounts to help humanize the many and varied people and groups involved, especially people who were harmed by the Holocaust. Historical timeliness, geographic images, and mortality statistics become even more compelling educational materials when illustrated by "human subjects" who endured the Holocaust (ADL et al., 2014, USC Shoah Foundation, 2018). Living "arrangements" and housing changed dramatically for millions of people. While some were privileged and able to flee persecution (Dwork & Pelt, 2009), most could not, and not all who fled could get far enough away to escape persecution (including the family of Anne Frank). Millions of people living in rural and urban areas were forcibly relocated, often more than once, and robbed of their livelihoods. A major but not final step in this "process" was the establishment of Jewish ghettos in cities and some large towns (Dean, 2010;

Dean & Hecker, 2012). These ghettos, like some modern urban neighborhoods, can serve as iconic representations of racialized social inequalities and discrimination (Anderson, 2012). During the Holocaust, ghettos served as segregated but temporary locations for Jewish people (Cole, 2011).

Jewish people and communities were subject to discrimination and dehumanization in many familiar respects: segregation in ghettos, forced relocations, and ultimately by confinement and incarceration in prison "camps." A system of punishment and substandard housing, systems of camps ("Lagers," in German) were established across central Europe. Concentration camps (using the term generally) included hundreds of slave labor camps, thousands of concentration camps, and the six infamous death camps (Wachsmann, 2015). All types of confinement imprisoned and punished innocent civilians in ways that were barbaric and grossly inhumane. Historians remind us that concentration camps were not a new creation of the Nazi era (Stone, 2017). In concentration camps, modern military industry was combined with discrimination, slave labor, and mass murder, a combination of forces which enabled Nazis to commit large-scale genocide using modern technologies while still fighting on multiple fronts (Wachsmann, 2015). This is one reason that some scholars have treated the Holocaust as a critique of industrial development or even an end to modernity or social progress (Adorno & Tiedemann, 2003; Bauman, 1989).

Catastrophic mortality and disease rates, among other Holocaust statistics, attest to the horrific scale, scope, and transnational distributions of the Shoah (Bauer & Keren, 2001; Bergen, 2016). But in order to see real people and not only the geopolitical or international perspective on the Holocaust, we "zoom in" on survivors and other persecuted individuals who struggled within the seas of suffering. We tread lightly in this respect; the Holocaust can be sacred ground where we remember many lost lives (Levy & Sznaider, 2006). For those involved, we do justice in offering dignity and social agency to the memories of people who were both harmed and dehumanized. Metaphor is insufficient; mortality statistics do not refer to livestock of any kind; these were all people. We face the catastrophe through direct contact with the complicated lives and narratives of real people who were involved, witnessing survivors and their testimonies when we can (Des Pres, 1976).

Survivor narratives and testimonies both humanize and individualize the tragedy, providing personal examples that add meaning to potentially overwhelming or incomprehensible statistics. Survivors and others involved, including rescuers (Block & Drucker, 1992), allow us to see and understand human experiences of historical events. Educators and learners can stand with those harmed. We can find humanity within primary sources; we can stand up to and against the impersonal, violent, and demeaning Nazi policies and actions that, even with historical distance, can be painful (ADL et al., 2014). We become solemn witnesses to history, we carefully hear and view testimonies, and we help others to respect and dignify people who were subject to the sweeping destruction of genocide. We need not arrange guest speakers for this to occur; plenty of well-organized and respected online sources are free to us all (USC Shoah Foundation, 2018).

It can be simple to hear but complicated to relate to people who were subject to grave harm. As we listen to survivor and witness presentations, we understand that, like all victims of crimes and violence, most people (past and present) are worthy of respect simply as human beings. While we may share the pain of any victims of violence, we may and can also learn to see survivors as people, not *only* as people who have been forced to endure suffering, not only defining people by their worst moments.

Once we introduce real people and sometimes fuller biographies into our lessons and plans, we become links in a chain of memory, we are no longer bystanders, and we have taken a stand for justice (Roth, 2016; Roth & Roth, 2004). We help learners to push against many forms of dehumanization, we help respect cultures and individuals past and present, and we can also learn to see that there is no one or single story that can represent this or any major chapter in history (Adichie, 2009). No single person, however charismatic, can simply represent all victims or all heroes; there exists no typical perpetrator or bystander, no standard victim or survivor. One personal encounter with a survivor can lead us to teach and learn about all sorts of different Holocaust and related human experiences. We can even compare ourselves to people who experienced genocide. All humans need to be resilient. How should we respond to complexities or difficulties related to persecution? What do prejudice and discrimination mean for us now?

There is little reason to ask teachers or students to suffer through what has become an ongoing debate over which historical group was most harmed, during the Holocaust or during a historical period (Rosenbaum, 2009). Students and teachers can quickly and easily become distressed by confronting or reflecting upon the Holocaust or any genocide. We need not require that "Never again" become "Again and again." "Why the need by each new set of victims to reach the apex of genocide that was reached in the Holocaust? Prevention is our goal, not comparison." "The Holocaust can be a precedent or it can become a warning…we ought to… make sure it is a warning, not a precedent" (Bauer, 2001).

Antisemitism has been a deep root of the dehumanization that characterized the Holocaust (ADL, USC Shoah Foundation, & Vashem, 2017; Lindemann, 2000; UNESCO: United Nations Educational Scientific and Cultural Organization, and OSCE: Organization for Security and Co-operation in Europe, 2018). As many scholars and materials show, antisemitism was neither new to the Holocaust period nor unique to Europe. Antisemitism has also had a long history in the English speaking world (Gerber, 1986; Julius, 2010). Antisemitism (or perhaps anti-Judaism) evolved based on a long (but not continuous) history. Antisemitic prejudice can be divided into two main forms (as identified by Gavin Langmuir). First, *xenophobic antisemitism* is a discomfort with Jewish people, who are portrayed as visibly different (with horns, racialized by facial features or other ethnic typologies). Second, *chimeral antisemitism* sees Jewish people as dangerous to others in some imagined ways, suggesting a defensive response, which has been all too frequently used to justify offenses against Jewish cultural groups (Hayes, 2017). It is also important that, like racism and sexism, antisemitism is not confined to human attitudes or prejudice, it is also a structural problem; systemic discrimination of any kind is a basis for patterns of social inequality (Desmond & Emirbayer, 2016).

Historian Peter Hayes reminds us that "antisemitism" is a relatively new term (arising in 1879 in Germany) that has in its root a misunderstanding (Hayes, 2017). There is no singular "Semitic" culture or ideology called "Semitism." Since the Holocaust, Western antisemitism has not disappeared but instead (like modern anti-black "colorblind" racism) become covert, tacit, and coded (Bonilla-Silva, 2015, 2018). Modern antisemitism includes *anti-Zionism*, a set of prejudices or biases against the state of Israel. Some use the term "anti-Judaism," as noted. In addition, there is renewed global interest in preventing contemporary antisemitism (UNESCO: United Nations Educational Scientific and Cultural Organization, OSCE: Organization for Security and Co-operation in Europe, 2018).

Holocaust persecution, while based on a particular series of events, can be carefully compared with modern forms of persecution, xenophobia, and eugenics. During the Holocaust, disabled people were first from among multiple status groups to be targeted and cruelly treated, facing sterilization laws as early as 1933 (Bergen, 2016). Roma (the other targeted cultural group) were treated as "asocials" and systematically removed to prison camps. Discriminatory Nazi laws were the basis of ongoing injustices for many different and intersecting groups and one set among many injustices that have spurred global antidiscrimination efforts (Bazyler, 2016; Wronka, 2017).

Nazis also ruled by force, eliminating all political opposition. They scapegoated, arrested, imprisoned, enslaved, and often killed people and groups who were considered political opponents, sensationalizing singular events and occasional political crimes as a justification for brutal laws and violent police actions, including Kristallnacht (Bergen, 2016). Even Christian leaders were harmed when they simply questioned or did not support those in power (Bauer & Keren, 2001; Lewy, 1965). These leaders included the well-known pastor Martin Niemoller, who lamented the lack of upstanders ("first they came for the Jews..."), Dietrich Bonhoeffer (who was murdered), and Provost Bernhard Lichtenberg of Berlin (one exemplary leader of the 30 million Catholics residing in Germany in 1937).

We can offer many lessons along with our work to humanize and diversify Holocaust narratives. For example, while there are many important patterns among those harmed, there are no single stories that are typical of Holocaust victims or survivors (Adichie, 2008, 2009). Questioning oversimplified or single stories can help limit the force of singular, generalized stereotypes (e.g., Jews went like sheep, non-Jews were bystanders). This can help us move beyond the popular but overly optimistic representations of Anne Frank (Prose, 2009). Sharing and appreciating multiple experiential perspectives can provide opportunities for discussion and more nuanced appreciation for the people and events in this and other historical chapters. While there are well-known tropes in Holocaust studies, it helps to broaden our perspectives beyond "Americanized" and popular narratives, and thus appeal to diverse and new audiences (Magid, 2012). A global and cosmopolitan culture of Holocaust memory has grown in recent decades (Levy & Sznaider, 2006).

Regardless of our approach, we can remain respectful and on topic. The Holocaust and genocide are topics that suffer from some degree of ignorance, what one historian called a "yawning gulf between popular understanding of history and current scholarship on the topic" (Cesarani, 2016). Effective Holocaust education can narrow this gap, but we should not ignore the history lessons that are required. Students and teachers alike should know the timeline and the geographic scope of both the Holocaust and the war. We can then learn and share compelling accounts of people who experienced unusually difficult and often traumatic events. It is important to recognize genocidal scope of the disaster. At the same time, the Holocaust should not be just a term adapted to describe every injustice or atrocity. Again, *the* (not *any* kind of) Holocaust should not be lightly compared to other forms of persecution or used carelessly as a metaphor (Novick, 1999).

There are other reasons to use care in presenting the specific crimes of the Holocaust. While many materials and some curricula begin with the Nazi policies that led to catastrophic persecution, it is not sufficient to only present the perpetrator perspectives, regardless of our interpretations or how much we condemn them. When we explore the details of crime, do we ask the perpetrators to explain the conditions of those they harmed? Do we only see violence from the viewpoint of people who are violent? So why privilege a Nazi perspective, which has been shown to be intentionally deceptive and propagandistic? Why prioritize the study of power, continuing to focus on authoritarians or fascism, when a primary concern remains the human consequences of such crime? Holocaust victims, along with the upstanding and righteous allies, should never have been ignored. They can now, in historical memory, stand first and foremost among the many groups of "Holocaust protagonists" who narrate the historical record (Hayes & Roth, 2010).

Some Holocaust witnesses wrote about their ordeals and some witness have been interviewed, providing a rich variety of oral history, recorded video material, and first-person testimony, suitable for all kinds of learners (Gardner, 1999). We can access recorded (including video) testimony by streaming or showing recorded testimonies from reputable online sources (ADL et al., 2014). Many resources now include survivors of other and more modern genocides, not only Holocaust survivors. While we might not want to limit ourselves or our students to a single story, we can *start* with just one person, perhaps one remarkably resilient or heroic person, perhaps a person like us, or at least a person who we would like to admire or like to emulate. We are encouraged to build topics, units, or modules around themes that include individual and testimonial experiences, such as Kristallnacht (ADL et al., 2014; USC Shoah Foundation, 2018).

In the United States, many learners and teachers have started with the iconic diary of Anne Frank, a popular symbol of resilience and hope, whose hiding, writing, and diary have come to testify to the human spirit. The subject of both the 1955 Broadway show and multiple films, Frank's diary is seen as a symbol of optimism, at once universally appealing and uniquely important to Jewish youth (Magid, 2012). Frank is brave and resilient, despite being a child and thus a noncombatant in an otherwise conflicted situation. "Frankification" of the Holocaust is humanistic; it remains perhaps the most important popularized educational material in the world, perhaps as a form of collective redemption, optimistically recognizing human potential even in the most distressing situations a child can experience or imagine.

Anne Frank's diary represents one of the millions of tragic stories. Finding optimism in her diary is one way to remember and take to heart the resilience of people and actions that stand in contrast to wartime and eugenic violence that has harmed our world. Still, cultural development can be affected by leading cultural representations. Anne becomes heroic and almost saintly as a universal symbol of innocent suffering in American (and English) dramatizations; her experience and example become a symbol for all humanity, not only or primarily a Jewish cultural symbol (Magid, 2012). Anne is optimistically portrayed as a hopeful, resilient, and resourceful girl who shows "grit" in the face of nightmarish Nazi persecution.

Our methods for humanizing the Holocaust depend on our goals and rationale (Totten, 2002). For example, we may pair narratives with historical events, using narratives as primary sources to support historical elaboration (ADL et al., 2014). Survivor stories can even lead us into postwar periods, when some scarred immigrants became "silent survivors," perhaps seeking home in the United States (Stein, 2014).

While we appreciate humanized Holocaust experiences, we must also share wider perspectives. What can happen if we teach or learn only one Holocaust narrative? What ensues if there is ambiguity about or even denial of that story? What if the story is fictional, perhaps created as a film for sensational appeal? Does the learner give up on understanding the complex histories of the Holocaust? What happens when one story becomes two, or hundreds, or more? We can hope that, with more stories and perspectives, the stories and the statistics convey both the breadth and depth of humanity affected by the Holocaust.

Where can we start? Which narratives can we choose? More importantly, which stories *should* we choose, and why? Answers to these questions do and must vary; there is not one perfect example for any discipline or any one singular learning objective. We must define terms, of course, and we can present a simplified historical narrative. Curricula like Echoes and Reflections (ADL et al., 2014) build in excellent examples for many types of curricular uses. Open resources like iWitness (USC Shoah Foundation, 2018) have both premade curricular examples and open choice options. People harmed in the Holocaust can be represented by the living, speaking directly to the learners, people who can still provide accounts of the Holocaust in active voice and with human agency. Even if Holocaust consciousness or memory reduces us to silence, speechless accounts are possible, as shown by mime and survivor Marcel Marceau (Marceau, 2002).

People are not statistics, so we are able see, hear, and read accounts from each Holocaust narrator as a person and as a unique individual. We find Holocaust and other genocide survivors are far from monolithic. Old and young, men and women, girls and boys, Poles and Germans, tradespeople and elites, Jews and gentiles, all types of human beings are present as subjects and objects in the narratives of the Holocaust (Bergen, 2016). Nonetheless, people harmed were most often stigmatized and persecuted, being forced by Nazi laws and actions into degraded social categories (Dwork, 2002).

Before, During, and After the Catastrophe

Our responsibilities to provide Holocaust education include taking a longer view of Jewish and European cultural histories. While the US Holocaust Memorial and Museum is fairly focused on and limited to 12 years (1933–1945), some histories extend coverage beyond 1945 and liberation (Cesarani, 2016), while others start a second postwar narrative with liberation (Celinscak, 2015). Important modern scholarship focuses entirely on consequential and postwar topics, including survivors (Stein, 2014), the development of international human rights law (Bazyler, 2016), and constructions of memory (Alexander, 2009).

Many authors divide post-Holocaust history into several periods or decades. Initially our interpretations of Holocaust history were shocked but muted, with some forms of sacred silence and an emphasis on allied heroism (Stein, 2014). Terms for genocide and "Holocaust" were developed; Holocaust awareness focused particularly on Jewish experiences, generating limited memorial cultural and minimal Holocaust education (Fallace, 2006, 2008; Levy & Sznaider, 2006). Even in the United States, and in Germany, where the topic was most important, Holocaust consciousness was not well developed. There was little public awareness of the Holocaust in the United Kingdom or in Canada, and so the topic was not often taught in schools (Short & Reed, 2004). Jewish memory books and testimonials were an exception to this global pattern; Jewish audiences were not silent or disinterested in the 1950s, with many wanting to record and hear about the Shoah (Magilow & Silverman, 2015; Waxman, 2006).

Holocaust memorials, supporting new forms and styles of Holocaust education, have grown rapidly. Holocaust education has been diversifying in many ways, sometimes incorporating universal lessons about genocide, or global "cosmopolitanized" form of memory that the whole world can appreciate (Levy & Sznaider, 2006). In addition, most of human history, including most of Jewish and European history, remains prior to the Holocaust. Many historical and important topics and patterns, notably including Jewish culture and religion, require cultural or other forms of representation of life before the catastrophic events of the Holocaust. As was suggested by one expert in Holocaust education, the Shoah could affect young Jewish people who are seeking to embrace cultural identity; it was not the most glorious moment in the longer sweep Jewish history (Short & Reed, 2004). Pre-Holocaust education is also crucial for explaining the rise to power of Nazi government in Germany (Hayes, 2017), a process documented in film and supported by effective propaganda (Luckert et al., 2009).

We can also understand post-Holocaust histories, including those of displaced persons known as "DPs" (Wyman, 1989). Humane representations of Holocaust refugees have important modern parallels; we continue to struggle to assist major global flows of migrants and refugees (Türk, Edwards, & Wouters, 2017). We can see that conflict and war create increases in migrant flows, bringing attention to the current debates about immigrants and children of immigrants around the world. We know that immigrants have helped build the United States, replenishing and reinvigorating urban communities (Alba, 1999; Kasinitz, 2008). US postwar immigrants included a hundred thousand survivors of the Holocaust and their offspring (Stein, 2014). "Reanimating" people and groups affected by conflict and genocide, showing the transition from huddled or skeletal masses into working communities, can benefit from a longer time frame and perhaps a wider geographic window on historical processes. Some scholars and educators are doing this in other ways by extending the narrative both in time and beyond the boundaries of postwar Germany into the formerly occupied (Soviet and post-Soviet) nations that were less open to Western historians when they fell under Soviet control after the war (Snyder, 2012).

By including representations of cultures before the Holocaust, we further humanize people harmed during the Holocaust, and we more fully appreciate all that was destroyed and lost. By continuing to show historical representations of Jewish and other communities (in Europe and emigrating elsewhere) after the Holocaust, we help us all to recover from the violence of historical crimes and develop ways of creating new narratives. Zionism and modern American Jewish communities can be seen, in part, as major Jewish initiatives to continue culture after the Holocaust (Alexander, 2009; Sarna & ebrary, 2004). Describing Jewish survival and continuity through longer time frames affirms both humanity and religious traditions. It shows resilience both to the challenges of antisemitism and to changes related to modernity. Jewish life and cultures do change over time, for some groups more than for others, but many streams of faith and culture continue to flow into the future. Judaism itself remains resilient, having celebrated a transformative postwar period that featured religious renewal and new growth in the United States and in Israel. Jewish populations, while damaged in Europe, found new communities and nationalities, assembling mid-century migrants who shared and still share in renewed American and new Israeli forms of modern Jewish life (Sarna & ebrary, 2004).

Yad Vashem was founded in Israel as a memorial staffed entirely by Holocaust survivors and dedicated to the collection of testimonies (Waxman, 2006). It stands as both an educational center and the Israeli memorial to the Holocaust, recognizing heroes who supported survival for migrant refugees. Yad Vashem started as a way to collect the many disparate and difficult stories of many Holocaust survivors. Our heroes and our communities are proud of our efforts against injustice; our postwar responses have also been impressive and often heroic (Stein, 2014). But we are not limited to one theme, one person, one story, or one hero that should or must personify any complex story of resilience and survival. Respect and remember many different stories. Six million creates a lot of possible combinations.

When catastrophes happen, we are obliged to respond and help. In time, we can retrospectively piece together the sequences of events and experiences that subject people to harm and subsequent stress. When the World Trade Center towers were destroyed on 9/11/2001, and when natural disasters subsided, we spent months and years picking up the pieces, rebuilding our communities. We even found silver linings to our difficult situations, while also involving the very best mental health systems and professionals (Holder, Holliday, &North, 2017; North & Pfefferbaum, 2013). After the Holocaust, while survivors and their families worked to build new lives (Stein, 2014), reconstruction was required and recovery took place in many nations. Some camps remained open while refugees sought surviving relations. Many organizations and people struggled with relocating displaced people (DP), "surviving remnants" of Jewish populations and cultures (Dwork, 2002; Wyman, 1989). Coming home was not always easy or successful for those displaced; many relocated to Israel and started new lives in new nations (Rice, 2017). But these migrations were not new; safe passage to a new home or homeland had been sought by European Jews throughout the war, as well (Yahil, 1990).

Remembering Together: Forming Chains of Survival and Memory

We share solemn and collective responsibilities to preserve and protect Holocaust memory (Jacobs, 2010; Magid, 2012). Holocaust educators, among others, form a "chain of memory" that helps to ensure both cultural continuity and broader understanding of historical facts (Cohen et al., 2013; Roth, 2016). Holocaust education is a shared global effort and a state-supported endeavor that promotes collective memory, just as the text and rhetoric of public memorials inspires reflection and respect for major historical events (Carrier, Fuchs, & Messinger, 2015; Fracapane & Hass, 2014; Stevick & Gross, 2014).

Remembering together, we join international efforts to collaborate in making good choices while sharing Holocaust education. These efforts involve work to improve our understanding of both the Holocaust itself and the process of Holocaust education. We continue to develop our skills in providing and updating curricula in disciplines through topics that include the Holocaust. We aspire to share inclusive and respectful pedagogies, helping us all to learn both about and from the Holocaust (Cowan & Maitles, 2017). We encourage educators to offer integrative curricula that connect Holocaust studies with education about and for human rights (Eckmann, 2010); both types of education advance our collective goals. We can, we should, and in some nations and locations we *must* (by law or policy) choose to responsibly provide and thus extend the scope of Holocaust education. We have too many available resources and few excuses not to do so.

In 1945, British attention to the Holocaust was, for a time, eclipsed by the bombing of Japan. There were decades after the war when the Holocaust was not a subject of major public concern or historical education (Short & Reed, 2004). Many people wanted to put the war and it's injuries behind them. It's hard to imagine now, but many Holocaust survivors, including many in the United States and in Britain, did have real difficulties being heard, respected, and recognized. Levi's groundbreaking book on survival in Auschwitz was a best seller, but only after being rejected by multiple publishers and lying dormant (in Italian, not in translation) for a decade (Levi, 1986; Thomson, 2002). In the United States, public glory and attention was earned by military heroes, while some survivors were reticent about speaking up (Stein, 2014). Some survivors did not like to revisit catastrophic events or topics and others were simply and tragically ignored (Greenspan, 2010a). The very meaning of life had been complicated by living inside prison camp; time and supportive care were required to help many survivors to regain a positive outlook, health, and human functions (Frankl, 1992). In recent decades, and among more privileged generations, it is difficult to imagine the silent suffering that was endured. Now, we have many respected survivors who serve as public speakers and many fewer obstacles to sharing Holocaust narratives and memories.

The Holocaust and other forms of multicultural education have evolved and flourished, offering diverse and inclusive ways to recognize and interpret social problems. We have learned that we need not reinvent Holocaust education (Fallace, 2006, 2008; Gray, 2014). There are many good ways to provide Holocaust education (ADL et al., 2014; United States Holocaust Memorial Museum, 2018).

We carefully, fairly, and truthfully represent the major milestones in history, noting the vast harm done, selectively tailoring disclosures of violence to our audiences. We may question any oversimplified progress narratives that excuse or rationalize the intentions of the perpetrators. We may choose not to ignore the problems raised when we realize the many bystanders or other onlookers, within or outside of central Europe. In providing Holocaust education, we see clear evidence of mass murder and persecution; in this context, we must reestablish our human and moral nature, seeking redemption and working for genocide prevention, hopefully finding common ground and universal values (Alexander, 2009). We should not minimize the importance of these horrific 12 years of oppression; we must deliberately include information about the Holocaust as we "tell the war" to new and sometimes curious generations of learners (Fallace, 2008).

We teach about and with sources from the people and groups involved, most often but not always through history curricula. We reflect on antisemitic persecutions authorized in Nazi-authorized public law and policies, aggressively enforced through a series of horrific events that expanded with Nazi Germany during the years from 1933 to 1945 (ADL et al., 2014; Bergen, 2016; Cesarani, 2016). Thereafter, we can and should also educate about both national and international human rights, promoting a human rights culture that includes both negative rights (e.g., freedom from ethnic or racial persecution) and positive rights (e.g., to education) (Wronka, 2017).

Our curricula can also help us learn lessons from the Holocaust, even as there is debate about whether and which particular lessons should be learned. We aspire to reach higher in our taxonomy of learning when we apply historical information to related historical or modern concerns, particularly those related to prevention of and justice in response to genocide (Bazyler, 2016; Power, 2002). Even so, we must use care when using (at times misconstruing or Americanizing) the Holocaust as a metaphor (Novick, 1999). The Holocaust itself creates a "traumatic drama" that requires the construction of postwar moral universals and thus a metric for progress through redemptive responses (Alexander, 2016). Universal human rights principles, applied through human rights law, then become (even with their limitations) global standards that apply beyond the scope of the Holocaust and genocide.

Teaching and learning about the Holocaust is a particular and often historical objective that often comes with a set of specific objectives (Cowan & Maitles, 2017; Totten, 2002). As noted, learning *from* the Holocaust is more interpretive, raising more universal topics and thus taking us outside of historical and geographical boundaries. We can apply the lessons learned to other and modern contexts. We can see that international law responded to Holocaust crimes, including and specifying the definition of genocide. We appreciate that the global response to the Holocaust includes a Universal Declaration of Human Rights. After the Holocaust, and with more open societies and more pervasive media, we have been better able to see and more cooperatively respond to other mass injustices. To borrow and adapt phrasing from Dr. Martin Luther King, we can learn and teach about *injustice anywhere* (particularly in Nazi Europe during the Holocaust) and also *injustice everywhere* (across the globe and throughout the history of our world) (King, 1963).

Since there are many of us involved in attending to educational projects, our work need not explore only one path; in fact, it may be our shared responsibility and obligation to explore both.

In the age of the Internet, we are privileged to learn, incorporate, and share new forms of Holocaust education, taking advantage of digital media to both distribute and preserve memory (ADL et al., 2017, USC Shoah Foundation, 2018). We proceed with respect and must consider the pervasive violence in our subject. We can approach, with care, even taboo topics. Hate crime remains (United States Federal Bureau of Investigation (FBI), 2017); we may be asked to contextualize even the ugliest and degrading legacy of Nazi antisemitic propaganda and policies (Luckert et al., 2009). Blending primary sources with comprehensive narratives helps us all to realize the scope of human harm and to overcome the stereotypes and culturally misrepresentative single stories that perpetuate misinformation and injustice.

As we are empowered by taking a longer historical view, we see the resilience of European and Jewish cultures before the Holocaust and also after liberation (Cesarani, 2016; Sarna & ebrary, 2004). We can share stories of rescue, resistance, and survival (Tec, 2003), elaborating the good deeds of rescuers from many nations and backgrounds (Dwork, 2010). We can discuss continuity and change, including assistance for immigrant in- or outflows, helping construct diverse chains of memory. Emigrants pushed by Holocaust persecution left Europe to create new communities in new nations, especially in the United States and Israel (Dwork & Pelt, 2009; Stein, 2014). We can recognize the promise of renewed Jewish cultures is maintained by the cooperative growth of these two national communities in the wake of the Shoah (Sarna & ebrary, 2004).

Millions of people were harmed by, often killed in, the Holocaust. As a result, the topic is certainly dark, often violent, and sometimes horrifying, forming a cloud over modernity and history which dissuades too many educators and learners from delving into or even approaching the subject. Entire nations, not only those which bore some responsibility, skirted the subject for decades (Levy & Sznaider, 2006; Short & Reed, 2004); some still do (Fracapane & Hass, 2014; Pingel, 2014). With a few exceptions, we are often unsure if the topic of the Holocaust is appropriate for younger children (Cowan & Maitles, 2017). We have and can respond to this "cloud" by imagining and representing more optimistic or progressive narratives, stressing Anne Frank's humanism or something equally hopeful to find a silver lining. Even so, we deliver our content and respect our subjects with care, sharing with audiences in mind, improving our curricular materials through careful use of well-defined terms, fair comparisons, and not classroom simulations (Lindquist, 2010; United States Holocaust Memorial Museum, 2018). We cannot do otherwise; we remain links in a chain of memory and responsible stewards of Holocaust education.

The Holocaust and International Human Rights Law

The Holocaust, a catastrophe that shook modernity, has become a precedent for any gross injustice and a model of genocide (Bazyler, 2016; Bazyler & Alford, 2006). While interpretations do change, we largely agree that the Holocaust is also a universal example of evil, a moral failure that has required repair (Alexander, 2016; Arendt, 1965).

We did not always have comprehensive international law. Nations were not always responsive to the limited reach of international law, even after the Holocaust. Many oppressive nations and leaders were and are not always willing or able to conform to the difficult demands of human rights law. After the Holocaust, international legal bodies advanced the process of legal reckoning with human rights abuses. The full force of international law developed with a set of trials prosecuting Nazi war criminals, most famously in Nuremberg, Germany (Bazyler, 2016).

After the Holocaust, only a few leading Nazis were brought to justice; some 8 million Germans were Nazi party members at the end of the war (one motto became "let the last lie"). Still, ~6,000 Nazis stood trial and another ~100,000 were investigated but never tried. A famous few were tried early on in Nuremburg under international military tribunal authority, but most accused Nazi war criminals were tried simply as common criminals for derivative crimes under German penal law. Sadly, the nation of West Germany did not generally accept the precedent set by tribunal uses of *ex post facto* laws against international war crimes (including crimes against humanity) in the Nuremburg trials. In addition, many major crimes were not even under the jurisdiction of the postwar international military tribunal because they took place prior to a declaration of war (Bazyler, 2016). Still, an international military tribunal brought leading war criminals to trial in Nuremburg (Conot, 1983; Dodd & Bloom, 2007), exposing the extent of the catastrophic Holocaust and starting a long process that involved improvements to international law and global human rights.

Two significant prosecutions included the 1958 trial of Nazi Einsatzgruppen (in Ulm, Germany) and the 1963 Frankfurt-Auschwitz trial (Bazyler, 2016). The Nazi Einsatzgruppen murdered over 137,000 people, mostly Jewish. The "EK3" group, led by Karl Jager, during five months in 1941 killed thousands along the Lithuanian border. Ten leaders of these "killing (commando) squads" were tried for 5,502 civilian executions (many arranged for efficiency at the edges of mass graves). This trial in Ulm may not have even taken place but for one defendant (Brigadier General Bernhard Fisher-Schweder) who revealed himself in 1955 when he went to court to protest being denied civil service status and benefits. In trials for the EK killings, evidence from the defense and even from some of the accused clearly supported the shootings. Defendants used the (previously unsuccessful) argument that they were only order-followers, "an order is an order"; all 10 were found guilty only as accessories to murder, perpetrators but not "excess" (hatefully motivated) perpetrators, receiving sentences of 3–15 years in prison. One legacy of these Ulm trails was the creation of more organized criminal investigations (through a German agency called the "ZS").

From 1963 to 1965, 20 Auschwitz personnel stood trial in Frankfurt Germany. After 183 court sessions and over 200 witnesses, cruel crimes were exposed. Seven of the accused were convicted of "excessive" murder (motivated by hate) and sentenced to life in prison. Ten were convicted of being accessories (for reasons noted above), sentenced to between three and nine years. Few served their entire term and three were acquitted (Bazyler, 2016). One important legacy of this trial was that the important legal principle of universal jurisdiction was affirmed. In addition, these trials led to German media (including TV) reporting somewhat retroactively on the true crimes of the Holocaust; prior to 1958 the film and television companies largely ignored the subject, leaving the public somewhat uninformed, and off-loading postwar responsibility only to the judiciary.

Adolph Eichman, Nazi and former Lt. Colonel, was tried in 1961 in Jerusalem. One of the greatest criminal trials in modern history, it helped Eichman become a metonym for Nazi murder and persecution of Jews (Cesarani, 2006, 2010). His appearance in a glass box on television helped increase public awareness of the Holocaust. His testimony and biography clarified his leading role in the logistics of the "final solution." Arendt called his actions and directives "the banality of evil," and "terrifyingly normal" (Arendt, 1965) in comparison to the monstrously sadistic personalities being attributed to other Nazi leaders and criminals. But Arendt's perception of a "banal evildoer" is likely misplaced; Eichman on the stand was pretending to be a befuddled bureaucrat. Less public statements show that he would remain forever proud of the mass murder that he and others had perpetrated (Bazyler & Tuerkheimer, 2014). Eichmann on trial was an actor; in real life he was willfully evil, not a clerk (Browning, 2000).

Ethics often require doing justice and standing against injustices. We are not doing good work if we stand by while injustices harm people. Working and living justly, promoting human rights, is required in many professions and professional organizations, particularly in applied areas like education, public health, and social work (Wronka, 2017). While social justice for human rights is sometimes represented as an optional or activist enterprise, some form of social responsibility is fundamentally an ethical undertaking that shapes workplace and professional practices. As such, teaching about human rights (and this can mean including Holocaust education) is part of helping learners prepare for doing justice as members of occupations and professions. Holocaust and genocide education also challenges us to expand our knowledge of histories, cultures, and ethics. We can and should bring human rights to life in our professional and cultural work, moving us away from a world that tolerates oppression and genocide and toward a world that shares a vision of beloved community (Smith, King, & Zepp, 1986).

In the postwar founding the United Nations (25 October 1945), nations ("member states") immediately formed a committee (chaired by Eleanor Roosevelt) to create document that would teach the world about human rights (Wronka, 2017). This document became unanimously accepted and endorsed (on December 10, 1948) as the universal declaration of human rights. It served as an example and a basis for subsequent international human rights agreements, including conventions against discrimination and for the rights of status groups with fewer rights (like women and children). Professional organizations affirm the importance of these agreements in both statements of professional ethics and collective resolutions; human rights have become a corollary of human dignity for entire occupational groups (Wronka, 2017). Consequently, both within and beyond the scope of Holocaust studies, we have seen the creation of a "human rights culture" (Wronka, 2017).

Chapter 5

Teaching Strong Cultures

As educators, we continue to collaborate and improve our goals and methods with new materials and newly redesigned curricula. We affirm the importance of our objectives by reflecting upon why and how we teach our subjects. When we are teaching about the Holocaust, we are privileged to share new and improving resources, including materials easily available online. We discover and use online materials including vast archives of survivor testimonials that were previously limited to archival uses (Langer, 1991), new and often professionally produced videos that offer excellent summaries (ADL, USC Shoah Foundation, & Vashem, 2017, USC Shoah Foundation, 2018).

If we need to design our own materials and courses, we help humanize the Holocaust through accessible and individual accounts. We need not become distracted from our goal of providing Holocaust education by angry critics, cynics, or public debates; we will not be dissuaded from our goals by hateful materials or a narrow, singular focus only perpetrator perspectives. We can and should listen carefully to the voices of those oppressed by both the Holocaust (Frankl, 1992; Tec, 2003) and by all forms of social inequalities (Collins, 2012, 2016).

Thanks to public resources and educator training (The Olga Lengyel Institute (TOLI), 2018; United States Holocaust Memorial Museum, 2018), we are able to see and share cultural strengths through humane perspectives. We can describe the resilience of human groups in the face of the Holocaust and genocide as "strong cultures." Strong cultural representations of people who were subject to harm in the Holocaust show the dignity, resilience, and courage of people and cultures (Tec, 2003). Strong cultural representations, even in the context of oppression, honor Holocaust and genocide memory. We can look for human strengths as we share and discuss images and examples of individual and cultural resilience and resistance. For example, the examples and memories of many diverse children and youth, including but not only Anne Frank, provide educational testimonies to all of us (Zapruder, 2002). Examples of resilience, even with unhappy endings, support the strength of the human spirit during and after the Holocaust (Fogelman, Cohen, & Ofer, 2017). Righteous upstanders also included all sorts of heroic people who "said no" to the crimes perpetrated by Nazis (Bartrop, 2016).

Now, with the benefits of hindsight and multidisciplinary research and development, we each can also teach about the Holocaust from a position of strength. In hindsight, educators and others can be strengthened by the knowledge that many Holocaust-era injustices were ultimately recognized as criminal actions and that preventative international legal systems were developed thereafter (Bazyler, 2016). Another way to both develop and strengthen our work is to advance the integration of Holocaust education into multicultural education, as noted earlier, so we are not alone in teaching about persecution (Grever, 2018). We can explore more global and cosmopolitan perspectives on the Shoah without forgetting the particularly Jewish experiences involved in this history; we need not be forced to choose either particular focus on antisemitism or universal inclusion of many types of oppressive injustices (Levy & Sznaider, 2002, 2006). Finding common purposes by teaching about "strong cultures" that are resilient in the face of persecution promotes more humane forms of Holocaust education for wider audiences. Strengths-based education builds common understanding that symbolic, structural, and individual dimensions of oppression can be effectively addressed through empathy and coalitions around common causes (Collins, 2016).

We discovered that our cultural roots strengthened of our national histories. We are proud that both African American heritage education and Holocaust education expanded and flourished during the 1970s (Fallace, 2008). We have seen remarkable growth in many forms of multicultural and inclusive education ever since, extending cultural studies and critiques of inequality from anthropology and sociology into history, literature, and political sciences, among other disciplines. In the United States, as in many nations, strong multicultural educational and scholarly traditions now support expansive educational curricula which strengthen cultural heritage education. "Standard" national and increasingly global historical and other curricula have grown to include Native Americans (Garroutte, 2001), Asian Americans (Chang, 2001; Ngai, 2004), and Latin-Americans (Portes & Rumbaut, 2014; Rumbaut & Portes, 2001), among other culturally defined ethnic groups. High rates of migration have diversified student populations and cultural dynamics in many nations and in most social institutions. This continues a trend that literally "took flight" as global transportation options increased after World War II.

We also need strength because we live in strained times. Racially identified (racialized) immigrant groups, including some Asian and some Latino groups, are once again been treated xenophobically as culturally or nationally "different." This was a concern in previous generations, when some groups were treated as perpetually foreign or suspect (Chang, 2001). First-generation "immigrants" may still identify with (and be identified by) languages and nations-of-origin, but Ngai suggests those who retain identification with nations-of-origins are better described as migrants or *emigrants* (Ngai, 2004, 2010; Ngai & Gjerde, 2013). "Old country" cultural knowledge and even social standing can be lost among subsequent generations (children and others descended from first-generation immigrants). Subgroups of migrants fare differently in most nations. In the United States, most work hard to succeed while many face new social problems. Sociologists have advanced the idea that some migrant subgroups structurally assimilate and become successful, while others experience "downward assimilation" (Portes, Fernández-Kelly, & Haller, 2009).

While blending the Holocaust, genocide, and human rights education into multicultural curricula, modern generations of students and teachers need not choose only the study of only one cultural group over others. As in other areas of education and study, insight and higher order understanding can be developed through multiple examples of core concepts. Heritage-related cultural histories help all students feel a part of learning communities. Learning through intrinsic motivation can more easily take place when students feel a sense of belonging, adopting a growth mindset with a cooperative spirit (McGuire & McGuire, 2018). So when we support this process through Holocaust and genocide education, reinforcing human rights, we improve our curricula through fairer and fuller perspectives, more inclusive curricula, and more complete, and sometimes universal, frames of reference.

Holocaust educators best describe people and groups subject to persecution as resilient, using and sometimes discussing terms like "survivors," "resisters," or "victims" of persecution. New possibilities and strengths in Holocaust education arise as we focus on the lives of people who were subject to harm, bringing forward the survivor's resilient perspective, even when there are also tragic and traumatic aspects of exploring deep memories (Langer, 1986, 1991). In exploring human resilience, especially among people in liminal situations, we can find people under stress can retain a desire to cope with even the most traumatic circumstances (Frankl, 1992; Levi, 1989a). In the Holocaust, it is no exaggeration to state that millions were not only stressed but also harmed, robbed, and murdered. Despite stereotypes, these people were not simply walking skeletons or sheep, they were (and many still are) people who wrote and spoke up, people whose testimonies have been recorded and archived (Rice, 2017). In survivor writings and other recordings, educators should find many whose voices we respect, sharing insights from witnesses to catastrophes who still retain human agency. Their experiences and voices remind us that we, like military allies and all righteous people, stood and can again stand up against the injustices of the Holocaust and for human rights. Our resilient strengths need not be overwhelmed by the criminal actions of Nazis past or hateful perpetrators present and future.

Educators can respond with strength to Holocaust injustices even while examining the worst aspects of the catastrophe. As the next chapter will elaborate, testimonials contain competing experiences of both suffering and resilience. Suffering was not new or unique, of course. The worst of the Holocaust was done in concentration camps, and such camps were derived from and have similarities to other conflicted periods in history and to prisoner of war camps (Stone, 2016, 2017). Jewish people also had many social circumstances in Europe; some served honorably in allied, German, and many other military forces (Moore & ebrary, 2004; Penslar, 2013). People who endured the Holocaust or any genocidal persecution were obliged to remain resilient and many also were heroic, saving lives even while imprisoned (Lengyel, 1995). We need not mute the strength and power of personal and cultural resilience during the Holocaust when we can instead raise the level of respect for all groups of humans who suffer violence and harm on the basis of group affiliation. In learning about crimes large or small, we *do not* benefit from blaming victims; we *do* benefit from respecting resilience, even when resilience is ultimately not enough for survival.

Teaching both Holocaust and multicultural education from a position of strength is forging new alliances and new perspectives. In 2018, the Olga Lengyel Institute conducted a seminar on the similarities of exclusion during the Holocaust and in the American South during the Jim Crow era (The Olga Lengyel Institute (TOLI), 2018). Discriminatory laws and policies oppress many cultural groups and require educated responses. As we "reclaim our humanity" in the wake of persecution, we are better able to present these injustices as resilient people and groups, educating from a position of strength, not simply as victims in recovery. As Condoleezza Rice powerfully states in her childhood autobiography, describing her youth in segregated and terrorized Birmingham Alabama, people who are subject to unequal treatment do not often appreciate the label of "victims," even in hateful environments where people are subject to criminal violence (Rice, 2010).

How can we learn from multicultural studies of national and migrant histories, building on increasingly diverse and student perspectives on history in American schools (Epstein, 2018; van Boxtel, Grever, & Klein, 2016)? This chapter answers this question by promoting strong cultures of "multicultural Holocaust education." In using shared concepts that are common to many histories of cultural persecution, we identify areas of common understanding and thus allow both educators and learners to expand cognitive and social understanding of cultural history and cultural resilience. We will discuss racialization, discrimination, stereotypes and cultural misrepresentation, genocide, and human rights. We will conclude that education both about and for human rights, like learning both about and from the Holocaust, help prevent future problems and improve our society.

Teaching the Holocaust from a position of strength starts with focusing on the human and cultural perspectives of groups harmed by Nazi and antisemitic aggression. It was and is necessary to also recognize and critique perpetrator and bystander perspectives, but as educators we need to let skeptics or deniers, perpetrators or bystanders, and "haters" or "waiters," dominate our discussions and limited curricular opportunities. This chapter explores ways to include multicultural Holocaust education in fostering respect for individual and cultural resilience. Cultural inclusion is an important way to respond to histories of persecution and inequalities. Finding strength in resilience among those harmed by Holocaust and genocide helps us to engage and inspire present and future generations.

Cultural Studies and Cultural Resilience

As educators, we teach different groups of students at many different educational levels. We educate and learn both histories and cultures through a variety of texts, images, arts, and resources. We may teach about the Holocaust and other genocides as part of a more general task of teaching cultural and multicultural studies (Mitchell & Salsbury, 1999; Southern Poverty Law Center, 2017). We also provide Holocaust and human rights education as one of the many ways to include currently and historically oppressed groups in our curricula, our communities, and in our societies. While the Holocaust is an important educational and historical subject in its own right, and while teaching the Holocaust is a way to redeem or repair past and prevent future injustices, the Holocaust is also a way to introduce or elaborate important topics such as human rights, social inequalities, discrimination, oppression, and persecution of cultural, ethnic, and racial groups.

We educate both about and for human rights. College-aged students in the United States have a lot to learn about global topics, but still have a greater understanding of human rights than any other global topic (Council on Foreign Relations (CFR) and National Geographic, 2016). We have seen Holocaust and human rights education is part of work towards social justice, as championed by Eleanor Roosevelt and the pioneers of the United Nations (United Nations 2017 (Enacted 1948); Wronka, 1998).

We can draw inspiration and strength from a broad-based but sometimes neglected "war on prejudice" in the United States, which followed World War II and paralleled part of the civil rights movement (Svonkin, 1997). The war on prejudice was a broad-based antiprejudice campaign that preceded to the more well-known war on poverty and the mature civil rights movement of the 1960s. This war on prejudice, arising with the postwar social psychology of the 1950s, brought together Jewish and Christian organizations, academics and popular public figures (like Frank Sinatra), all to condemn intolerance based on culture, ethnicity, religion, or race. People in the United States more actively shared the common goals of intergroup (including interfaith) discussion and cooperation. This effort involved not only new initiatives in popular culture but also federal and private funding for social-psychological research (some by German-Jewish refugee scholars) that focused on the newly recognized problems of prejudice, bigotry, and bias (Svonkin, 1997). As the field of social psychology grew to explore problems of prejudice, so did public concern about and support for policies to limit prejudice and discrimination.

Even so, early Holocaust education in the United States was complicated by limited understanding. First, Nazi nightmares were "Americanized" and popularized into metaphors for other problems, including slavery and the oppression of women (Fermaglich & Koret, 2006). Second, few outside of historians knew or could fathom the true extent of the catastrophe. Even among Jewish Americans, there was limited desire to "be ethnic," since Jews and other immigrants had been actively assimilating or assimilated for decades, especially in the 1950s, prior to more recent "identity" movements in culture and politics (Sarna & ebrary, 2004). "Traditional" and conservative Jewish Americans has a history of affiliating with an idealistic view of our American dream and some were not eager to embrace Holocaust studies that suggested a more general critique of authoritarianism, since this could challenge a dominant narrative that centered on American and allied war heroism (Stein, 2014). This began to change in the late 1950s and early 1960s, when social transformations raised criticisms of conformist and authoritarian social forces, promoting greater autonomy and new expressions of freedom (Fermaglich & Koret, 2006).

Prior to the more recent growth of modern identity politics and expressively cultural conflicts, representations of Nazi and related forms of destruction multiplied in the early 1960s. Some popular Jewish authors of this time, including Betty Friedan, Staley Elkins, and Irving Goffman, used Holocaust *analogies* (though without any actual studies of or many specific details of the Holocaust) to critique restrictive social conditions and norms. These authors often did this while also eliding their own cultural locations as Jewish Americans; some assimilated Jews were still uncomfortable addressing "Jewish issues" while looking back at the fading forces of antisemitism; some were also ambivalent about being identified with uniquely or specifically Jewish projects (Fermaglich & Koret, 2006). A number of other popular and influential authors and filmmakers created Holocaust-linked projects to great acclaim. Milgram studied authoritarian situations and Kubrick invented strange new dystopias with characters whose behaviors parodied recent totalitarians. But still, the details and dark realities of the Holocaust remained outside the consciousness of many.

Even families of Holocaust survivors were "desperately seeking normality" during the 1950s and early 1960s (Stein, 2014). Prior to the fast growth of Holocaust consciousness in the late 1970s, the goals of assimilation and normalization (according to middle-class goals) limited the appeal of retrospection and inspection of the Holocaust. Some followed the Eichmann trial and Hannah Arendt's critique of mundane bureaucratic complicity (Arendt, 1965), and others could view Anne Frank's life in dramatic detail, but the Holocaust remained a dark well for many.

We appreciate historical growth in both legal and social acceptance of civil and human rights for many groups, in the United States and globally. Social studies have been one arena in which a rising tide of social inclusion has brought people back to historical reflection as a way of affirming ethnic and cultural identities (Totten & Pedersen, 1997). Jewish subjects became "mainstream" and represented in film on Broadway (Most & Project, 2013), and soon African American authors and playwrights were also shaping cultures and histories in the United States (Gates & West, 2000). Before the rise of angry debates over Affirmative Action policies, representatives of many groups were able to realize social advancement and inclusion; human rights remained a shared goal of both national and international movements.

Many aspects of multicultural education have grown to affirm our cultures and to accept our differences through what may be called a "human relations approach" to education (Appelbaum, 2002). In sociology and in our wider world, we have a pressing, ongoing, and current need to reaffirm and strengthen *all* cultures *and* to support cross-cultural coalitions (Collins, 2016). Multicultural education, institutions, and public spaces can create opportunity, hope, and cosmopolitan canopies in our schools and our communities (Anderson, 2011). But our best work can be challenged by sometimes hostile social and political environments. We can live "at risk" of social degradation or even exclusion, despite antidiscrimination laws. As educational curricula evolve and grow, so too does criticism of diversity, inclusion, and curricular innovation. Can we expand our curricula without sparking less constructive arguments, especially over migration and national inclusion, which irritate many pundits and aggravate mean-spirited public debates?

There are many questions to consider. How does Holocaust education fit into our larger projects of multicultural education, teaching respect, and social inclusion? We have made arguments for including the Holocaust and human rights education for both preventive and ethical reasons. But then which topics do we include? Do explore or prioritize antisemitism, and thus first focus on Jewish persecution? Which "other" groups do we include in our descriptions of the Holocaust? If we start with studies of people with disabilities or Roma, or if we raise persecution on the basis of political party or sexuality, will we have time to discuss antisemitism and Jewish persecution?

What about Holocaust-based xenophobia, which is an increasing contemporary concern in the context of immigration issues? What materials do we use and interpret? Like any content providers, film directors, or memorial designers, our educational choices may always be debated. Will our artifacts, whether primary sources or material cultural examples, become a focus of debates over representation or free speech? Is Holocaust education saddled with bearing a "terrible gift" so that learners receive just to experience the sad truth that our nations were, for a time, blind to a crime that murdered millions (Simon, 2006)?

We can respond with strength to any and all criticisms of our work. We need to increase justice; there is no gain to ranking comparative genocides (Bazyler, 2016). Holocaust education is and will remain essential and important, especially as it is mandated in many nations (Fracapane & Hass, 2014; Levy & Sznaider, 2006; Short & Reed, 2004). The question of how to offer Holocaust education can and should have many answers. Holocaust education as a part of multicultural education is an important and modern, even cosmopolitan variation. Our audiences and our histories require educators to identify and explore key concepts in multicultural Holocaust education. We welcome choices and push past divertive debates between *either* in-depth and particularistic studies of the Holocaust *or* universal and cosmopolitan topics relating genocide and human rights; both are welcome and important (Levy & Sznaider, 2002, 2006). Once we identify concepts that are key to both Holocaust history and human rights protection, we can proceed on both fronts.

Topics in Multicultural Holocaust Education

Responding to any social problems requires delivering and improving education. In designing and improving our educational responses, we recognize that Holocaust education and the concurrent study of antisemitism can be part of but not necessarily central to multicultural education (Mitchell & Salsbury, 1999). We have precedent for discussion of antisemitism in our public education against prejudice. In the decades after the Holocaust, the United States created an underappreciated "war on prejudice." This effort supported public relations and also social sciences to advance postwar human rights (Svonkin, 1997). Multicultural education has been evolving ever since, though it is not without its critics.

We also appreciate that public attention to social problems follows patterns, rising and falling over time, developing new concerns and multiple (sometimes competing) frames of reference. Patterns in attention to social problems are affected by events, the media, and sometimes dramatic representations. One consequence is that social problems are constructed according to new paradigms for new generations and in new ways (Best, 2013; Hilgartner & Bosk, 1988). Holocaust education, which has been "particularistic" and centered on Jewish experiences, has also developed versions that are more "universalistic," "cosmopolitan" and often blended with global concerns, other genocides, and human rights (Levy & Sznaider, 2006).

The Holocaust in social sciences often arises because it illustrates genocide, and genocide is the most contentious form of intergroup relations. It is also true, though rarely emphasized, that the Holocaust includes important and distinct forms of racism and ethnocentrism, discrimination and persecution based on culture, nationality, ethnicity, race, and other social classifications. As such, multicultural education can and should include examples of inequalities from the Holocaust and its context in European history. Holocaust *narratives*, which will be explored in subsequent chapters, are full of examples of prejudice and discrimination, including moments of acute disrespect, "everyday racism," and incivility, further illustrating that historically racialized and oppressed groups are subject to differential treatment (Anderson, 2011; Bonilla-Silva, 2014; Desmond & Emirbayer, 2016). Inclusive education, including Holocaust education, can move us toward a more enlightened and more cosmopolitan public and public sphere.

Once we define the Holocaust and genocide, how can we proceed? There are many possible directions for teaching many different subjects. Which concepts and terms do we select to drive our educational goals and lesson plans? Which topics in multicultural education help students learn about the Holocaust, and which aspects of the Holocaust help learners learn and appreciate multicultural values, like inclusion, diversity, respect, and resilience? In the following section, we explore six specific concepts: antisemitism, racialization, discrimination, xenophobia, stereotypes, and denial as key concepts that can be used in multicultural Holocaust education. These concepts improve our understanding of genocide and link the Holocaust more fully with multicultural and human rights education.

During the Holocaust, Nazi officials developed intentionally antisemitic propaganda that systematically targeted Jewish people and cultures in a series of intentional, discriminatory, often deceitful and hateful "actions." Germany's occupation of European nations extended antisemitic policies and practices across the continent (Hayes, 2017; Yahil, 1990). Nazis in Germany developed propaganda first for electoral purposes, helping Hitler and the Nazi party usurp political power. Once Nazis dictated their own rules, propaganda was used along with discriminatory laws and actions to deceive and scapegoat Jewish and other populations during the extended period of persecution that we now call the Holocaust (Luckert, Bachrach, & United States Holocaust Memorial Museum, 2009).

Nazi propaganda, albeit distasteful cultural misrepresentation, helps us to discuss the Holocaust as an egregious example of antisemitism. The Holocaust was also the event that awakened the world to the universal problem of genocide and to harmful aspect of eugenics. The Holocaust remains, like all genocides, an affront to everyone and to our ethical systems, a betrayal of all religious and secular principles of justice, and thus a universal concern for educators and learners alike, especially after the UN Convention against Genocide (Lemkin, 1948). As a consequence of the Holocaust, our nations have agreed to a historical and universal condemnation of genocide, a universal declaration and affirmation of human rights, and universal applications of law to a number of global injustices (Bazyler, 2016).

Many forms of persecution and conflict involve antagonistic ideologies that posit cultural or racial forms of inequality. Antisemitism is one such ideology which can be considered an "antitype," an irrational phenomenon that, for some, is not amenable to explication or moral critique (Yahil, 1990). Antisemitism, describing anti-Judaic behavior, concepts, and culture, is a long-standing form of irrational hatred. This helped the Nazis use antisemitism to scapegoat Jewish populations, both through their media and through German law. The legal basis of antisemitism *racialized* (made into a racial group) the definition of Jewish people and Jewish heritage in Germany, creating their own distinctions and false categories based on genealogy and designed for exclusion and persecution (Bazyler, 2016).

Categorical exclusion, in the name of a false science of eugenics (elevating "Aryans"), was an engine that drove Jewish and other populations into exile, creating homelessness and ending in mass murder (Bergen, 2016). Jews and many other groups were displaced. Some initially became what we'd now describe as "transit migrants" leading liminal lives in diasporas that stretched across many continents (Paynter, 2018). For those who were unable to leave Nazi-occupied lands, racialized Jews were mistreated systematically as a "race" according to German national law, which was extended by force to cover many areas of Europe. Livelihoods were stolen; it was not possible for most Jewish people to hide or to assimilate; it was also impossible for racialized groups (Jews and Sinti/Roma) to live as or "become white folks" in the context of Nazi Germany, as it was in other and more recent contexts (Brodkin, 1998). Antisemitism had deep roots and the power of German law.

German Nazi leaders implemented a form of legalized barbarism during the Holocaust, beginning with the Nuremburg laws of September 1935, but apparent in 1933 when Nazis expelled all Jewish people from civil service and later issued a decree that outlawed listing Jewish holidays on office calendars. Law was used to transform Jewish people from citizens to noncitizens and then to "subhumans." Nazi laws removed both legal and professional protections previously present in Weimar Germany and later in occupied nations. Nazi power was centralized under essentially martial law, Hitler ruled as "supreme leader" and by decree, and law was used to persecute Jewish and many other groups (Bazyler, 2016). The legal measures against Jews took place in successive historical stages of identification, expropriation and emigration, "concentration," and "extermination" (Hilberg, 1978).

The Nuremberg and other German laws defined and classified Jews by *genealogy*, not religion, using a concept of a Jewish "race" that was based on blood quantum. By this law, not by faith or religious practices, three or more Jewish parents (or two grandparents and a Jewish spouse) established a person as "Jewish." Only one Jewish grandparent made a person a mixed race *Mischlinge*. Civil rights for people so defined as Jewish in Nazi Germany, including voting rights, were abolished on November 14, 1935. Marriage rights and certain types of sexual relations were also constrained by decree soon thereafter. Jews, along with additional groups, described by Nazis as "Gypsies and Negroes" were grouped as of "alien blood" and deprived of rights. Jews, among others, were compelled to wear identifying symbols (stars of David, for example). Jews were obligated to take on a biblical middle name and passports were marked for simpler identification purposes. Jewish property was looted as Jews were excluded and forced to relocate; "Jewish-free living" was legislated and aided by police and citizen persecutions, called "actions," most famously in Kristallnacht (Bazyler, 2016).

Jews were racialized by the Nazi government, however irrational this may seem, clearly defining groups of people who were literally marked (with stars and otherwise) for extensive antisemitic persecution. Many nations, including the United States, use evolving and complex categories to racialize human populations (Iceland, 2017); many national racial and ethnic categories are diverse and change over time (Snipp, 2003, 2010). Native American tribes have independent and highly variable criteria for inclusion (Garroutte, 2001). Unequal and disparate classification systems create many challenges and problems for demographic analysis (Zuberi, 2001; Zuberi & Bonilla-Silva, 2008). Antisemitism in Nazi law can thus be compared with histories of legalized racism in many nations. Jews were also ghettoized during the Nazi era, and during other periods in European history, creating additional parallels with the histories of African American and other black populations. Jews were forced to relocate, as were Native and Latin-Americans during recent centuries. While each of these historical chapters is unique and deserves careful study and attention, it is important to identify patterns of structural inequality persecution across groups, above and beyond individual or single-group experiences of mistreatment (Desmond & Emirbayer, 2016).

Racism in Nazi Germany rested on three problematic propositions: race is a biological force of nature that determines behavior, race has a genetic basis, and race is a basis for hierarchy (including political power). "Racialist" Nazi practices built a racist government on Social Darwinism, ranking certain appearances that reflected "ideals" of Aryan race and culture above the "antitype" of "Jew," along with people grouped as disabled, criminal, inferior, or potentially political enemies (Yahil, 1990). Political antisemitism as a form of racism became a "revolutionary instrument," used to both seize property and expand state power.

Using antisemitic racism as a basis in Nazi law allowed large-scale persecution and discrimination. As students learn about histories of discrimination and prejudice in modern texts (Desmond & Emirbayer, 2016), historical examples are often included. Nazi discrimination was not limited to Germany, of course. Unequal treatment was expanded to occupied territories, creating ghettoization in Europe (Yahil, 1990) and eventually the mass violence and murder that took place in the first half of the 1940s.

The analysis of inequality through discrimination is another important parallel that helps justify multicultural Holocaust education. As Nazi Germany expanded into Central and Eastern Europe in 1939, their "Justice Ministry" was aware of international laws on occupation that remain applicable to this day (Bazyler, 2016). As German military units rolled into Austria, Poland, France, and other nations, discriminatory German laws would immediately apply, forcing large numbers of Jews to give up civil rights and subjecting many Jewish populations to stigmatization, terror, abuse, and violence. New laws that were context-specific would also be developed and applied in occupied territories. These included laws to suppress underground resistance and laws that would "solve" the "problems" associated with large Jewish populations in occupied nations, such as Poland and neighboring regions. One decree ("night and fog" in December 1941) allowed detained political suspects to be "disappeared" and be jailed or murdered. Analysis of these unjust laws was started even before the war and Holocaust were over (Bazyler, 2016; Lemkin, 1944).

As the Nazi German state expanded, systematically spreading fear, historians document consequent problems associated with Jewish migration (Dwork & Pelt, 2009). Then as now, transitory refugees were not easily accepted as immigrants to other nations, even while persecution was clearly evident. Xenophobia is an applicable concept related to this process; many national publics and policies were (and some are now) fearful and even intolerant of "foreigners" and associated global or international cultures. This is a topic with growing importance for multicultural Holocaust education. In the Holocaust, xenophobia is clearly found in the terminologies that Nazis used to describe (and the policies used to persecute) Jewish and other oppressed groups (Dwork, 2002; Hayes & Roth, 2010). In a variety of laws, decrees, and judgments, "non-Germans" were pronounced by the conquering state as aliens or (literally) "foreign people" (*fremvolkische*). German Nazi powers established "special laws" and rules for "non-Germans" in occupied territories based on the concept of "racial inequality" for "foreign" groups (Majer & United States Holocaust Memorial, 2003).

Xenophobic "special laws" for "foreign" groups were not limited to Jewish people. Poles who were Christian, for example, could also be subject to extensive persecution and discriminatory laws and policies. Poles and Jews could even receive a death penalty when evidence showed they had "particularly objectionable motives," giving occupying police freedom to terrorize any act considered criminal. The uses of unjust law were designed to be both terrifying and extortive; some people were systematically robbed and it was known that some officials could sometimes be bribed (Bazyler, 2016; Majer & United States Holocaust Memorial, 2003).

The Holocaust thus provides examples of dramatic and racialized injustices that echo the experiences of many different oppressed ethnic, racial, and cultural groups. For example, several successive injustices can be clearly identified in (Chief of Security Police) Heydrich's instructions and policy outlining "The Problem of the Jews in Occupied Areas" (Arad, Gutman, & Margaliot, 1999). After a Berlin Conference on September 21, 1939, Reinhard Heydrich outlined secret and evolving measures to evict, concentrate, organize, extort, and work Jewish populations throughout the occupied territories. Eviction was to start with clearing small cities and setting up isolated "concentration centers" along rail lines. These populations, some forced into ghettos, would be organized under "Jewish councils" who would be responsible for feeding these deportees. Administrators were to conduct a census and coordinate with the army and police. Measures for appropriating Jewish industries and labor were also expected to be planned. Thus there was planning (and some legal basis) for segregation, ghettoization, discrimination, and even enslavement (Arad, Gutman, & Margaliot, 1999; Bazyler 2016; Yahil, 1990).

There are also abundant and sensationalist examples of stereotypical cultural misrepresentation of Jewish and other groups in Nazi propaganda and law (Luckert et al., 2009). These stereotypical cultural misrepresentations were designed to scapegoat Jewish and other "antitypes" as the causes of problems and the reasons for expanding control over (eastern and other) European territories (Yahil, 1990). Couching policies within a false but scientifically appealing distinctions of "biological" race, stereotypes promoted the rejection of both political opposition and cultural diversity. People and groups conforming to Aryan ideal needed to have families and expand with the nation. Other groups, including people with disabilities, were not encouraged to have families, mate, or reproduce. Harmful stereotypes shocked the public by associating Jews and others with vermin and conspiracy, greed and harm, drawing on long-standing myths and misrepresentations of Jewish and Hebrew cultures. Much like Asian immigrants in America, populations that included citizens and veterans were "xenotypically" misrepresented as a peril, "forever foreign," and thus enemies of the state (Chang, 2001).

Historical and modern Holocaust representations both raise the question of how to fairly represent or misrepresent this important, if not sacred, historical event. Memorials and museums must work to make the "terrible gift" of Holocaust memory and culture something more than "just remembering" (Berenbaum & United States Holocaust Memorial, 1993; Tumolo, 2015). The historical process of representation has many facets associated with many kinds of media and certain iconic moments and representations (Magilow & Silverman, 2015).

The Holocaust was first represented on film in the 1940s. "Atrocity films" were, early in post-Holocaust history, some of the most important visual representations of the Holocaust. These short films show the world horrific murder scenes as they were just after the (usually US military) liberation of concentration camps. One of these films was used to support the Nuremburg trial indictment of Nazi war criminals in November 1945. Some of these short films, often shot by

US military men, were narrated with a scripted statement, to ensure credibility. These films were not simply random footage or systemic representations, they were designed to arouse shock and horror. But even these films were "spun" to support certain interests. Images of atrocities were incorporated into later films that had more nationalistic purposes (making heroes of the French resistance), raising early criticism that some films were ignoring the antisemitic aspects of the Holocaust, or the particularly systematic genocide that was targeted at the Jews (Magilow & Silverman, 2015).

The 1961 Eichmann trial in Jerusalem was the first time a Holocaust-perpetrator trial was held for the purpose of doing justice and improving collective memory (Magilow & Silverman, 2015). It represents an important historical representation, both engaging general audiences through television (and print) and representing survivor voices to the mass media for the first time. Leaving aside many complex questions and concerns surrounding Hannah Arendt's analyses of the trial and the antisemitic actions of its infamous protagonist (Arendt, 1965), we note that the "art of trials" presents the Holocaust as a drama (Magilow & Silverman, 2015). This drama continues to evolve in literature, on stage, and as a medium for addressing moral, psychological, and cultural concerns, even when more accurate chapters of history dissolve into historical fiction.

Educational representations even go so far as to show that school-aged children can help teach about the Holocaust. In the small US town of Whitwell Tennessee, a middle school has hosted a children's Holocaust memorial, where the scale of six million is represented by six million paper clips. A paper clip collection is but one of several different ways that school children have developed to represent and display "six million" (displays also including buttons, butterflies, and diversity statements). So we see that the sheer scale of the catastrophe inspires social action for the sake of memory (Magilow & Silverman, 2015).

A final parallel between Holocaust education and modern multicultural education relates to the subject of intolerance through bullying and hate crimes. Some Holocaust scholars have incorporated the concept of "bystanders" and shown how this term applies to those individuals and groups who have been called onlookers, gainers, or other "helpers" during the Holocaust (Hayes & Roth, 2010). While different nations and national groups have considered many different perspectives on the Holocaust at different points in time (Levy & Sznaider, 2006; Pingel, 2014), a growing concern with bystanders shows that more could have been done to help address the mass crimes of the Holocaust, even if it was dangerous to do so (Cesarani & Levine, 2002; Tinberg & Weisberger, 2014). Standing up to injustices is not easy or always safe. An iconic call to stand up against injustices, anywhere and everywhere, was written eloquently by Dr. Martin Luther King from a city jail cell in Birmingham, Alabama, during a time when African Americans were being terrorized in the name of unjust laws (King, 1963). "Justice everywhere" suggests we should not ignore these parallels; find common cause between histories of the Holocaust and other civil and human rights violations through multicultural education.

Cultural Misrepresentation Through Holocaust Denial

Historians have immortalized the words and actions surrounding General (later US President) Dwight D. Eisenhower's arrival at Buchenwald concentration camp on April 13, 1945. He and others in service witnessed "indisputable evidence of Nazi brutality and ruthless disregard of... decency." Consequently, he anticipated denial by future generations, advocating that we testify and witness against this brutal crime (Shermer & Grobman, 2000). His words included the famous "never again" slogan that remains written in stone on the US Holocaust Memorial Museum (USHMM). Some degree of cynical doubt had tinged some public conceptions of the Holocaust prior to the arrival of allied armies (and photographers) at the Nazi concentration camps. Not everyone had known or believed the Holocaust was such a catastrophic event, despite growing evidence to the contrary. While Americans and others may have had reason to be uncertain or even skeptical about some global information during these times, as propaganda and deceit were common during wartime, the public became much less willing to ignore the tragic disaster after the war's end and the liberation of survivors (Shermer & Grobman, 2000). Still, the uncertainties of doubt and distrust were not attempting to rewrite history through Holocaust denial.

Denial is one of the most disturbing and cruel forms of cultural misrepresentation applied to the Holocaust. Modern Holocaust denial (not to be confused with intentional secrecy or Nazi perpetrator double-speak during the Holocaust) is part of a more diffused subject called "revisionist history" (Lipstadt, 1993). Denial can be elaborated as an expression or manifestation of "denialism." Any modern false claims about the Holocaust suggest, at minimum, an educational response. Education seems to be a reasonably moderate contemporary response to Holocaust denial, in contrast to more "aggressive" tactics like legislating against denial claims. Even so, in some nations that include the United States, general or public antipathies can work against any mandated form of multicultural education, where curricular obligations may be considered challenges to some of our freedoms of expression. Holocaust denial is just one more reason that we should help our curricula and our students to stand up against intolerance (Chelsea & Greg, 2009; Southern Poverty Law Center, 2017).

As noted, a popular reason for advancing and delivering Holocaust education has been to remember (or not to forget) those harmed by the Holocaust and the broader crime (and moral transgression) of Nazi-perpetrated genocide. Another reason for promoting, delivering, and institutionalizing Holocaust and Human Rights Education (HHRE) is to speak up against denial. "Denialism" can be loosely defined in this case as an antisemitic ideology or systematic practice that promotes Holocaust denial. Denialism is more than simply a historical position in a "debate" about the "truth" of the Holocaust; it can be a corrosive force, perpetuating antisemitism and intolerance using the guise of alternative histories (Lipstadt, 1993). While evidence and recent British legal proceedings discredit denial (Evans, 2001), it continues to fester in segments of the public imagination.

Lang posits three major (false) "denialist" claims before addressing larger issues in the study of (and responses to) Holocaust denial (Lang, 2010). Shermer and Grobman add a fourth false claim (Shermer & Grobman, 2000). The most common types of false claims regarding the Holocaust include the following:

Denial of established statistics: The (six million) number of Jewish people murdered during the Holocaust is falsely suggested to have been exaggerated. Reasons for this include the following:

Denial of the purposes of the gas chambers. Deniers suggest that the Nazi-designed crematoria were not (sufficient) infrastructure to generate established mortality statistics.

Denial of intent: Some claim that Nazis did not intend to commit genocide.

Denial of the Holocaust: It is a myth invented by propagandists in allied nations during the war and sustained by Jews who wished to gain political and financial strength (in and through the state of Israel).

Each and all of these claims have been successfully disputed and refuted by evidence and respected scholars (Evans, 2001; Lipstadt, 1993; Shermer & Grobman, 2000), though this refutation of denial does not by itself prevent or eliminate "denialism" generally or the perpetuation of false claims. As with the "antitype" of antisemitism, progress though rational debate is not a goal of most Holocaust denial.

The most popular recent controversy over denial, which has become a popular film (Lipstadt & Hare, 2016), finds historian Deborah Lipstadt defending against a libel accusation made in Britain by Holocaust denier David Irving. Irving brought suit when Lipstadt's historical text indicated he was a falsifier of history (Evans, 2001). Irving was not the first to make strong claims of Holocaust denial. Others before him often sold books, sometimes by mail order, as popular history, profiting from controversial claims circulated by authors on the fringes of public life (Evans, 2001). A series of denier-authors start shortly after the war with a Frenchman named Paul Raissner. Raissner was a prejudiced author who suggested Jewish people started the war, defended the actions of the SS, and disputed the accounts of the uses of gas for murder. Raissner survived an assault by a German communist while in prison during the war, then was transferred to better conditions and well treated by SS officers (Evans, 2001).

Subsequent deniers including Austin J. App, a German-American who defended the murderers, disputed the statistics, and denied the existence of murder-through-gas. Arther Butz, professor at Northwestern, published a more professional book with denial, *The Hoax of the Twentieth Century* (in 1976). Butz and other members of the Institute for Historical Review (in CA, United States) are more recent deniers, gathering and publishing the JHR (Journal of Historical Review).

The last of the four common false claims, emphasizing a "conspiratorial side of Holocaust denial," furthers an anti-Jewish agenda using a culturally misrepresentative stereotype to advance an antiglobalist claim. While much of the content in the IHR oversimplifies and focuses on "the Jews," a global conspiracy myth revolves around the Holocaust as a lie perpetuated by Zionist-Jewry in hope of making Germans and others feel guilty enough to cede Palestine to become (again) the state of Israel (Shermer & Grobman, 2000).

As with antisemitism generally, there is more to denial than irrational thinking. Lang (2010) helps us to understand that, if we expand our perspective, there are many and differently motivated forms of denial (and/or denialism) that can fall between complete "recognition" of or acceptance of the full historical record of the Holocaust and complete rejection or denial of the Holocaust. For example, not all "denialists" are negating the fact of some degree of mass murder, not all are openly antisemitic, and some present as people simply trying to present alternative historical facts.

Clearly, there are many people (especially young learners) who may be simply or blissfully ignorant, unaware of the Holocaust (Jedwab, 2010; Pettigrew, 2017). Research shows that a large majority of people in the United States agree with a need for Holocaust education, but younger cohorts including millennials are more likely to lack awareness or basic knowledge of the Holocaust, underestimating the number of Jewish people killed in the Holocaust (Schoen Consulting, 2018). Those who do not know history may simply need time to learn well-delivered information. Not all who lack knowledge are "condemned to" or intend to repeat past mistakes. We can imagine, following Primo Levi (Levi, 1989b), that the Holocaust remains so enormously horrific that common reactions can include incredulity, denial of historical accounts, or even refusal to accept it ever happened. Six million is a large and sometimes unbelievable number of deaths, the "greatest ever" mass murder (Belzberg, 2016). Skepticism is more suspect, but must we blame people who have not had the privilege of Holocaust education for naïve moments of disbelief?

Many less pernicious groups of people can also occupy a "middle ground" between outright Holocaust denial and complete "acceptance" or recognition of the Holocaust. According to Lang (2010), these viewpoints do include the following:

The relatively indifferent: Many people do not think the Holocaust matters any more than other genocide, and thus may become irritated by or resistant to Holocaust-specific or antisemitism-centered perspectives, including a focus on Jewish victimization during the Holocaust.

The less empathic: Many groups suffered in the past, why choose those harmed by the Holocaust, or even the Jewish victims of the Holocaust (who were, of course, not alone in being persecuted or killed in large numbers).

Once we see that not all forms of skepticism and "denial" are angry, conspiratorial, dangerous, or antisemitic people trying to revise history or to minimize the harm or crimes committed, we see that what we have termed "denialism" (much like racism) can be considered a wider spectrum of problems that develop around the process of sharing accurate Holocaust history. Denial does not just include (and is thus not confined to) a small group of revisionist historians and antisemites who benefit from free expression. That kid in class who wants attention may just be unafraid to be rude.

The consequences of recognizing such middle groups within a spectrum of "denialism" are complex and can be profound. Some groups and people may or are able to move toward either side of this artificial and potentially harmful "debate," either embracing the need for Holocaust consciousness and thus education, or alternatively rejecting such goals as lower priorities or misguided. Lang (2010) points out that some leaders in some Muslim nations can "swing" some of a populace toward skepticism toward the cause of anti-Zionism through Holocaust denial, creating greater interfaith hostility for political ends (Lang, 2010). Absence of Holocaust consciousness need not be a threat or a harm to the goal of historical memory.

Thus Holocaust education of any sort can "fill the gap" left by either ignorance or denial. Educating through Holocaust, genocide, and human right topics can also help address a wider "genre of denial" (Lang, 2010); more than one historical atrocity has been met with immoral (and sometimes official) silences. For example, Japanese aggression in "the Rape of Nanking" during World War II (Shermer & Grobman, 2000) and the Armenian genocide (1915–1917) by Turkey were not recognized by the nations which perpetrated these respective examples of mass murder.

Denial and denialism, while an affront to inclusion and morality, have, perhaps ironically, also contained a silver lining. Lang (2010) reminds us that putting forth false claims forces us to articulate the truth of Holocaust history, bringing a humane and human rights perspective into our educational efforts. We also must face the issue of "criminalizing denial," where policies or statutes can "legislate" and prosecute some expressions of Holocaust denial (Lang, 2010). Along with wider debates over "hate speech," a legislative option risks limiting free expression. Still, laws against denial have been created (targeting either the Holocaust or genocides generally) in 14 nations, from Canada to Australia, a list notably including Germany and Israel. Legislating "undeniable" histories has consequences, including possible deterrent effects, backlash, and costs to the public (such as enforcement costs).

So it seems that simply responding to denial is too limited a response, while legislating and enforcing criminal sanctions may be (for some nations or interests) too strong a response or perhaps too controversial. Even so, we cannot simply dispute denial and denialism, even while we may not be able to forcefully or fully legislate a stronger response. Thus our work in Holocaust education takes on even greater importance.

In a world limited by indifference, standing up against hateful social problems means responding fully and systematically against denialism and associated forms of antisemitism and racism. In this light, HHRE remains both a moral imperative and a temperate response, even in a modern context that includes more abundant Holocaust culture and consciousness. While we may fall short of criminalizing denial, we need not simply accept denialism as simply a hateful form of "free speech" that we must accept or endure. "Giving the devil his due" allows denial of the Holocaust a wider circulation (Shermer & Grobman, 2000).

Beyond Perpetrator Perspectives: Not Just or Unjust Nazis

Perpetrator perspectives, full of images and text that focus on Nazi power or terror, crowd Holocaust sections of libraries and bookstores, not to mention some locations on the Internet. Perpetrators and their actions have subject to extensive analyses. Historians and others work tirelessly to find motive and methods to perpetration of mass violence, including murder (Longerich, 2010; Lower, 2017). The spotlight was and often is brightly focused on a goose-stepping Nazi soldier or Hitler and his henchmen. Should we focus on the perpetrator? Must we review their authoritarian personalities, military might, and evil ways, banal or not?

Who, among the Holocaust trio of perpetrators, bystanders, and victims, should be first and longest in our educational focus (Hilberg, 1993)? Perhaps we could help our students see past the swastikas and the uniform cruelty of the perpetrators and perpetrator perspectives. Perhaps we can review but not become fixed upon images or examples of Nazis. Perhaps our curricula, not only our respect and memories, should intentionally focus on those who were harmed by, and sometimes survived, the Holocaust. Can we help return names and faces to people who were harmed? They were not animals, neither sheep nor cattle, despite being treated as such. Isn't it bad enough that Nazis successfully misled much of the world into believing that the crime was not a crime while it was in progress, disguising the horrors of the Theresienstadt prison camp (Adler, Cooper, Loewenhaar-Blauweiss, & Adler, 2017)? The injustices have been proven by international courts; at what point can we turn away from the criminal perpetrators so we can learn from those resilient survivors and souls who were harmed in the Holocaust?

The Holocaust as a topic can and sometimes does attract defensive or prurient forms of attention, especially when the narrative involves national or collective responsibilities and memories, for example, in Poland (Kapralski, 2018). Global concern and attribution of responsibility has often been specifically and narrowly focused on the Nazi and German perpetrators and less on those complicit in other allied or occupied nations. When we are first or only concerned about the motives of any perpetrators or authoritarians, we may lose track of the injustices and the experiences of those persecuted. Too often the perspectives of an account or story can be considered from a perpetrator or a bystander perspective rather than the perspective of a victim or resister.

Some criticisms of Holocaust education point to this as a problem of viewpoint, privileging the experiences of people who caused harm while not giving similar or any recounting from a subjugated or victim perspective. For example, characters in propaganda, popular accounts, and scholarly representations of wartime cultures often include strong images of Nazis (Hitler and the SS), shown as powerful men in military uniform and marching in lockstep to strict discipline ("jackboots") (Luckert et al., 2009), in contrast to denigrated images and representations of Jewish and other persecuted groups as criminals, paupers, orphans, disabled, or subhuman people (Spinelli, 2003).

The popular use of the text or film *The Boy in the Striped Pajamas* points to another problem. "Blind space" in film or literature, where groups or problems are behind a wall or fence, invite curiosity but may also prevent witnessing or experiencing the perspective of a persecuted group, like Jewish people during the Holocaust (Boyne, 2006; Curry, 2010). What are the ethical and representational consequences of showing or filming as Nazis or bystanders rather than as resisters or "victims?" Does this offer a fair or full view of the true problems created by genocidal cultures?

Perpetrator perspectives survived the destructions of war, given that much of the material cultures, not to mention the lives of Jewish and other victims, were destroyed during the Holocaust. Theories of totalitarian and authoritarian states were and are popular veins of Holocaust interpretation; concern with these perspectives can unintentionally restrict our understanding of the experiences of Holocaust victims and survivors (Novick, 1999). Even the material culture of the Holocaust favored the perpetrator. To illustrate, a leading American lawyer was able to send home to his wife and children some Nazi helmets and other artifacts as "spoils" from his work on the Nuremburg trials (Dodd & Bloom, 2007). In contrast, Jewish ritual objects were stolen and less abundant, when not destroyed or converted to different wartime materials (Berenbaum & United States Holocaust Memorial, 1993; Levin, 1968).

Both popular culture (Styron, 1999) and important primary sources (Lengyel, 1995) may also put the reader, viewer, or other witness to the Holocaust, directly on the spot where life-or-death selections were made, often forcing us to face the cruelty of perpetrators. This tense location of selection procedures often occurs at a railside platform, on the site of one of the six infamous Nazi killing centers (death camps that included Auschwitz-Birkinau and Treblinka). The "workflow" of the six Nazi killing centers started at the point where a transport of human prisoners in cattle cars arrived at a platform (Berenbaum & United States Holocaust Memorial, 1993).

Sorting separated people able to walk from those who were unable to walk or dead. In all six camps, sex segregation followed. Then, if there were forced labor (slave) camps associated with the center, people condemned to work were selected out from those condemned to immediate death. In all cases, people were forced to surrender valuables and clothing and often their hair was removed. Gassing, shooting, or (in some locations) "extermination through work" followed. Gold fillings were removed after people were killed; most mass killing also involved cremation and the deposit of ashes into pits (Berenbaum & United States Holocaust Memorial, 1993).

We can become more hopeful and resilient because some people who lived during the Holocaust did not simply look away when faced with crimes, genocide, and unjust violence. These righteous allies are quite diverse. Righteous people do not simply ask or demand what others must do or do for us. People of good character ally with victims, do for others, for our countries, for other countries, for those in need. Righteous allies were upstanders, not bystanders. It took grit and guts to do the right thing. Many died in hiding Jews, resisting, or simply standing up for humanity during this darkest hour. Janusz Korczak, author and physician, made the ultimate sacrifice, entering the ovens and dying from poisonous gas, in order to keep his commitment to orphaned and isolated children during their darkest hours (Cohen, 1994).

Pushing past the cruelty of perpetrators, let us not forget the heroes, including the fighters, the righteous with weapons, the forces and the troops, the greatest generations of men and women, who are supported by families and by nations. Fighters bravely joined, both militaries against fascism and internal resistance, and together became part of Holocaust resistance (Rohrlich, 1998). People stood up for principles, suited up, fought in difficult situations, and ultimately succeeded, enduring great losses. Rescuers came from all nations and all occupations (Dwork, 2002). Fighters represented great nations in times of great duress. Fighters bore the mantle of the United States and many other nations, heroic soldiers and sailors, airmen and marines, marching across continents and crossing channels, dropping into bulging battles with meager rations and worn weapons. Nazis were shattering our lives, burning our families and cultures; military heroes gave them hell in return.

Finding Heroes: Our Inspirations and Models for Resilience

After the war was won, survivors were nourished by a variety of international allies. Our cultures were resilient, thanks to blue-collar workers and white-collar professionals: generals, diplomats, and lawyers; nurses, physicians, and medics; people who rescued lives and cultures from the rubble of destruction. Health-care workers helped skeletons grow back into bodies. Nations engaged in synagogue salvaging and national rebuilding. Families worked toward reuniting, when possible, all while recognizing those lost in unspeakable years of pain. Fields of graves and gravestones grew like weeds on the shores and in the cities. Remembering the fallen, remembering the slain, we remained vigilant.

After the disaster, healing wounds with time, a new world can allow refugees and veterans, along with all kinds of students and teachers, to go back to visit the sights of violence and injustice, now scarred but sacred places, to preserve and memorialize those harmed by the Holocaust. In educating, we inform but we may not benefit from simulations; there is no need to recreate the catastrophe by subjecting anyone to excess stress or choiceless choices (United States Holocaust Memorial Museum, 2018). Let us respect and remember and then let us appreciate that we did survive the fear and discrimination, and we live now, after the war. Anne Frank was a hero who did not survive, but her family record remains, and her words remain an "afterlife" that gives witness to the injustices that she and her family endured (Prose, 2009).

We are all with and grateful to the survivors, many of whom left us gripping and moving accounts of resilience (Auerbacher, 1993; Roth & Roth, 2004; Weiss, 2013). When we recount survivor stories, we may be transformed; we learn to thank God for the food, the water, the bed, the help, the ticket, the chocolate. Allies help end the war, liberate the camps, and then we, like survivors, can move on. And we see that we also must move on now. Refugees need resettlement. Improved public and social policies need development and enforcement. The world needs healing again. But never again shall we allow such a transgression as the Holocaust. Genocide is illegal now, thanks to our ability to see problems past and cast the Holocaust as the trauma drama of the century (Alexander, 2009; Power, 2002).

Reconstructing and preserving cultural memory becomes a shared project, the work of many. We practice educational pedagogies of hope. We start with community, with "us," with people, giving each person the full and human "status of a person" (Carini, 2001). Humanistic work creatively gives each individual and all groups the power of agency, the decency of capacity. Giving voice to suffering is transformative, generating imagination and creativity. To deny personhood unjustly separates a person or group from humanity. Thus humanity requires vigilant protection. We can share Holocaust education in this spirit. We have allies among us; survivors have provided accounts that will persevere and inspire. In respectfully remembering the Holocaust, they help us to prevent further harm and to repair the injustices that plagued our past.

Chapter 6

Survivors Share Resilience

Humane Holocaust education involves learning about and from Holocaust survivors. As educators, we can select, convey, and help interpret the narratives and accounts of survivors. Whether or not it is part of our given curricula, we can be privileged to listen and, when possible, interact with people who had firsthand experiences with catastrophic historical events. It is estimated that there have been over 100,000 recorded accounts of Holocaust survival, only some of which have been examined and appreciated by scholars or educational audiences (Greenspan, 2010b). Survivor accounts tell and retell Holocaust narratives in many ways and from many perspectives. Survivor narratives extend educational options well beyond the important "cannon" provided by well-known authors. Navigating selections from survivors is a great opportunity for educators and provides "relatable" information to students and for Holocaust studies of all kinds.

Introducing learners to survivors and survivor narratives provides us with both sight and insight. Within survivor narration, we learn to imagine and see the Holocaust from the historical ground, thanks to eyewitnesses in many locations. We are able to envision the details of camp, ghetto, and box cars, as we could do in a well-designed museum. We do not arrive late at the catastrophe, when gruesome mass graves and starved skeletons can horrify all who can dare to look. We walk with people who were part of this history and learn to connect lessons learned from historical genocides with modern concerns for human rights. We appreciate and gain insight from real people who endured this mass crime.

We can then arrive at deeper interpretations of history and human behavior based on our understandings of people who endured the Holocaust (Greenspan, 2010a; Langer, 1991). Survivor narratives testify to the Holocaust and also provide life histories, guiding readers, viewers, and listeners through experiences before, during, and after catastrophic events. We respectfully witness the abilities of human beings to endure what we may be almost unable to imagine: the pains of persecution, anguished memories, and the necessities of resilience (Frankl, 1992).

We need not reduce Holocaust survivor narratives, or their more formal versions called "testimonies," to a simple or singular lesson, although many of us may wish to do so. A *variety* of details and insights are provided by each narrative and by each survivor. When we put any set of narratives together, we find many important themes and gain a fuller understanding of historical events (Greenspan, 2010a). Recounting complex experiences is an iterative and potentially cooperative process that often need not be formalized; "testimonies" is a formal term that could also describe a legal statement in a court of law. We need not be so formal or so focused on the legal aspects of Holocaust history. As noted, recorded testimonies are abundant and online, both on their own (USC Shoah Foundation, 2018) and as illustrations that are integrated into explanatory video presentations (ADL, USC Shoah Foundation, & Vashem, 2017).

As educators, we once again can make many and responsible choices about how to inform our classes. We can serve as guides, introducing, linking, and hyperlinking learners to a variety of informative survivor-witnesses, sharing spoken, performed, and written accounts. We join a tradition of recording memory that goes back millennia and specifically includes the early documentation of the Holocaust and the creation of the Yad Vashem museum and memorial in Israel (Vashem, 1963). Writing about the Holocaust was and is itself a form of survival, *writing to remember* (Waxman, 2006). We humanize and respect survivors by speaking and listening to our historical guides.

While the "ruins of memory" can be complex and difficult to share and compare (Langer, 1991), we need not remain pained by anguished memory. As noted, we can become links in a chain of memory, humanizing the Holocaust in conversation with the past (Greenspan, 2010a), bringing lessons and resilience out of the past and into our present and our future. Especially for women who endured the Holocaust (Tec, 2003; Waxman, 2017), and for all who suffered silently or who were ignored during the early decades after the catastrophe, we are obligated to at least pay attention. We can find all sorts of accounts: those tragic and courageous, profound and mundane, inspiring and upsetting, spoken and unspoken, composed and distressed, practiced and prompted, articulate and otherwise.

When sharing narratives from the Holocaust, educators serve and preserve collective memory, helping cultural resilience and continuity. As we remember, we pay respect to those who have suffered injustices and harm, and we may learn from their experiences. We have abundant opportunities to explore, share, and discuss lessons from the Holocaust, based on voices and writings from survivors who witnessed the catastrophic events. Showing and describing human resilience can help us to appreciate the many skills and communities required for human and cultural survival.

Accounts of survivor experiences can create what Friedlander termed an "integrated history" that uses voices of victims in representing the history of the Holocaust (Friedländer, 2003; Rice, 2017). While we should not ignore the full range of protagonists, including the heroic actions of nations, militaries, and brave people who fought in global wars, we need not remain frozen in awe or anger, only reacting to stereotypes and propaganda or to criminal actions of hateful perpetrators. When we listen and plan ahead, we are able to see and hear those who were targets for genocide on the simple basis of stigmatized identities and thus were forced to flee or live in the criminal conditions of ghettos and concentration camps (Waxman, 2006). We can do this through our curricula and through special (often memorial) observances. Diverse forms of respect for cultural memory, including many different national and international memorial days, do and can have a place in educational schedules around the world (Fracapane & Hass, 2014).

Voices From Survivors

The most immediate and popular way to include Holocaust studies in any curriculum is to see, hear, and read from survivors, opening ourselves to the voices of people who were harmed, the victims of the Holocaust and of all genocides. We prioritize narratives from those who faced persecution along with those who stood up for justice. After the Holocaust, both the victims and the upstanding resisters have become memorialized in Yad Vashem (in Israel). Upstanders who resisted Nazi aggression on principle, even when not directly targeted, are formally described as the righteous among nations (Imber, 2016; Vashem, 1963). Survivor accounts and perspectives, in contrast to perpetrators and onlookers or bystanders, provide both a victim's perspective and a more inclusive narrative to historical injustices. But the surviving accounts are evidence that persecuted people were not "just victims," recording the Holocaust was itself a form of resistance and resilience (Waxman, 2006).

While living Holocaust survivors are a diminishing group and cohort, the words and narratives of "Holocaust generations" are now well preserved in a variety of old and new media, from texts to videos, available through libraries and websites around the globe. Among the most novel of these are video archives, most notably iWitness (USC Shoah Foundation, 2018), which shares testimonies of survival and resilience as easily as YouTube shares a video or Apple Music shares a tune. Video and textual testimonies are also online through approved and flexible curricula like the ADL's "Echoes and Reflections," in addition to the United States Holocaust Memorial Museum (USHMM) and other museums around the world. Plentiful and diverse written accounts continue to describe as well as commemorate the disaster that we call the Holocaust; 75 *memoirs* were written in many languages just during the years 1945–1949 (Waxman, 2006).

There are specific individuals and texts that have become iconic examples extending this chain of memory (Bigsby, 2006). Notably, Primo Levi, Elie Wiesel, and Anne Frank stand out as internationally known "stars" among the many creators of Holocaust memories. Their work is not only well known and profound, each account provides abundant lessons and details that help navigate the sea of information related to and documenting the Holocaust. Authors Levi and Wiesel were among the most widely read "living voices" in this chain of memory, while Frank remains the icon of optimism, despite her fate, an angel of sorts who perennially helps create and preserve Holocaust consciousness for younger and future generations. I was glad to learn that Anne Frank's extended family lives on (Prose, 2009).

Even with our modern appreciation of these prominent writers and voices, it is important to note that earlier generations were not as receptive to the memories and voices of survivors. Italian chemist Primo Levi's first book, *If This Is a Man*, was written to witness and document his 11 months in Auschwitz (Levi, 1979).

After a series of several rejections from publishers, it was published in Italian in 1947, with limited public interest and response. It was then republished to acclaim in 1958, leading to his career as a writer (Bigsby, 2006). A recent biography elaborates Levi's life (Thomson, 2002).

Levi's reflections are profound, culminating in his last work *The Drowned and the Saved* (Levi, 1989a). In *Drowned*, he describes his reflections on the essential elements of self-preservation in the tortured camps. *Drowned* is a bookend to Levi's first testimonial, *Survival in Auschwitz*, first published in 1947 (Levi, 1986). *Survival* offers primarily testimony; *Drowned* includes more reflection and judgment (Druker, 1994). Levi's memory and reflection describe and indict criminal injustices using deep memories of Auschwitz; anguished memory remains. The truth of the Holocaust belies the propaganda (and signage): *Nothing Makes You Free* (Bukiet, 2002).

Primo Levi worked for 11 months in Auschwitz III, a Nazi labor camp adjacent to the infamous death camp. Levi was an Italian chemist who synthesized rubber (Bigsby, 2006). Levi's survival strategies (as a survivor, he was one of "the saved") are interspersed with the fateful horrors of the less fortunate who were "drowned." After his liberation in 1945, he spent almost a year getting home and then wrote his first book. Levi became a writer-witness against perpetrators. In *Drowned*, he reminds us that the Nazi officials tried to cover up their crimes when their loss in war seemed certain (Levi, 1989a). As educators, we remember to share information that many fought and died to preserve, a chain of Holocaust memory, which Nazi perpetrators disguised and intended to remain hidden.

Levi preserves memories to witness the offenses committed by the Nazi totalitarian state through propaganda, terror, and the euphemistically phrased "barriers…against pluralism of information" (Levi, 1989a). The "processing" and treatment of people-turned-prisoners was cruel, unusual, intentional, stigmatizing, and degrading. Violent rituals committed by armed and enraged functionaries were followed by stripping and beatings, shaving, and redressing in rags. Hunger and thirst were familiar enemies. Educators and learners may be put off by horrific details, but these remain the facts of historical record.

Should educators choose to shield learners from this real and revolting violence? Levi himself raises the less violent alternative of Anne Frank, whose diary provides moments of hope for humanity, an early postwar example of empowered resilience, and the basis for transformative popular theatrical productions and Holocaust consciousness (Brenner, 1997; Prose, 2009). Levi's *The Truce* was also theatrically produced, by CBC as a Canadian Radio play (Bigsby, 2006). We remember through many forms of media and varieties of human experiences.

In *Drowned* Levi elaborates moral and experiential "gray zones," ambiguities of interpretation that remain after we simplify history, as well as uncertainties about the meanings of traumatized memories (Levi, 1989a). Levi reflects on feelings that were misunderstood as shame or communication-impaired silence after liberation. He reminds us that some survivors had experiences of or survived by assuming privileges. While Nazis were responsible for inhumane conditions, some prisoners chose or needed to become self-interested to a fault; the tension between survivor-cooperation and self-interest is a point where Levi and Wiesel publically disagreed (Bigsby, 2006).

How should educators describe or represent mistreatment during the Holocaust? Levi writes that "twelve Hitlerian years...were characterized by widespread useless violence" for the purposes of inflicting pain (Levi, 1989a). Persecution was intended and directed. Perpetrators were "rationally" mean, putting unjust law and violence to use for social control, applying military aggression and terror. Life in camps started with a departure: a sealed cattle car becomes a prison-on-wheels, conveying "human material" to distant locations, followed by plunder and cruelty, leading toward sites of mass murder. While we do not need to show all the gory details, we can certainly point out that they exist.

As a trained chemist and scientist, Levi was assigned the "benefit" of wartime work, forced labor rather than "extermination," and a registration number (174517, a permanent tattoo). While dehumanizing, numerical classification protected many workers against death-by-incineration. Still, his culture and education had disadvantages; "intellectuals" were subject to harm and special antisemitic degradations. In Auschwitz and beyond, faith and ritual were difficult and materially challenged during the Holocaust; books and reading were often prohibited (Levi, 1989a).

Who can or should speak for survivors? In *Drowned*, Levi distinguishes people who speak up from those who remain silent. Survivors who speak up about their Holocaust experiences (including Levi during his lifetime) are too often asked why they did not rebel, avoid capture, or escape (Levi, 1989a). Levi writes that this assumes escape is a *moral obligation* and that a prisoner's condition is somehow illegitimate in the context of our presumably free world. But "Holocaust camp" prisoners were dehumanized by systematic mistreatment and abuses. "Camp survivors" were routinely harmed, overworked, starved, cut off, and otherwise degraded. Prisoners were often "foreigners" and thus experienced limited communication capacities, subjected to horrid conditions without clean or sufficient clothing, and under careful surveillance. In the camps, most were forced to speak only their number at roll call, sometimes at penalty of death. In Nazi-controlled conditions, any allies also risked severe punishment. Multiple authors testify that attempts to escape were desperate and doomed (Lengyel, 1995).

Levi's work reminds us that retrospective interpretations can be based on stereotypes (Levi, 1989a). Severe oppression was designed to weaken, demoralize, and prevent the potential for organized resistance or conflict; even pregnant women were brutally harmed in Auschwitz (Lengyel, 1995). To resist or rebel could mean to choose death, creating one of many impossible, "choiceless choices." Subjecting survivors to interrogation or alternative scenarios in hindsight is to blame a victim for the crimes of the Nazis.

This raises an important lesson that we can share with our students and colleagues: innocent victims of *any* crime are not obligated to explain their own motives or behaviors nor the motives driving perpetrators of crime. Crime is immoral. This topic should engage student and other modern audiences; there need be no shame in being subject to racism, sexism, or any form of oppression, especially when it is found to be criminal. Survivors of crime, like Levi and others, may testify in a "court of public education," but testimonial memories need not be subject to hostile cross-examinations that subject victims to false accusations.

Some Holocaust and other survivors have followed this credo: we bear witness and the weight of memory, whether we like it or not (Bigsby, 2006). Levi's writing, posted for a time as a sign at Auschwitz, makes sense in any context of any xenophobic intolerance: "...you are not a foreigner here... our own deaths have not been in vain. For you, and for your children, may the ashes of Auschwitz serve as a warning. And may the dreadful fruit of hatred, whose traces you have seen here, not grow again – not tomorrow, not ever" (Bigsby, 2006).

Accounting and Recounting the Holocaust

Holocaust accounts are abundant, diverse, online, and open to competing interpretations. Not all accounts are formal or complete. "Recounting" by survivors humanizes the catastrophe and helps us realize that the Holocaust created many diverse and profound changes and enduring disruptions for many different individuals, as well as cultural threats and changes for different *types* of people and nations. Holocaust narratives can be optimistic and empowering as they represent resilience and sometimes resistance, but Holocaust narratives can also be very difficult for both survivors and audiences. Accounts punctuated by atrocities and deprivations can be painful, even unimaginable, and become representations of persecution.

Consequently, some narratives may be recounted and interpreted to represent strong examples of resilience, even when the narrator does not survive, as with the diary of Anne Frank (Frank, 1993; Jacobson, Colón, and Anne Frank, 2010; Prose, 2009). Testimonials focus on hopeful insights and profound reflections, standing as symbols of optimistic endurance, and providing us with role models to respect and remember (Auerbacher, 1995; Tec, 2003). Survivors and their narratives can also become symbols of the damages done by ongoing discrimination and persecution, sometimes tortured or humiliating memories, reminding us that life is precious and limited (Des Pres, 1976; Frankl, 1992; Langer, 1991; Levi, 1978, 1986). Survivors and others subject to mass violence can become representations of damaged human communities and lives. In addition, the narrative can grow and be elaborated. The same survivor can even recount multiple experiences to different (and sometimes collaborating) interviewers, creating portraits of survival that can be woven together into stories about both traumatic camp experiences and life after liberation (Matthäus, 2009).

We appreciate the many burdens shared among people who experience the stress of conflict and war, groups which include both fighters and those (like Holocaust survivors) forced into confinement. After the disruptions of traumatic stress, "normal" and less conflicted situations are not always hospitable or even appealing to some of those who endure conflict, such as wounded warriors (Junger, 2016). When we delve into accounts of posttraumatic survival, we are faced with anguished and sometimes humiliating struggles that can involve tainted memories, painful losses of human agency, and the unheroic actions required of people in tragic, sometimes even tortured situations (Langer, 1991).

Wrestling with memory, sometimes being silent, forgetting, or repressing difficult experiences, each Holocaust survivor's search for meaning follows many paths. Some require tragic optimism, a will to find meaning and purpose in life each day, no matter how horrible the situation (Frankl, 1992). Others remain silent or depressed for a time, anguished or shamed by lack of respectful reception, disturbed feelings, or both (Greenspan, 2010b; Stein, 2014). There are many possible lessons that can be learned from difficult experiences. Not all of these "life lessons" are easy to receive or relate to others, but some can be transferred to new generations. Survivor-speakers often echo early postwar public relations, relying on acceptable themes, such as antiprejudice and religious inclusion (Svonkin, 1997).

Still, survivor narratives can be upsetting or disturbing for some and some among school-based audiences. We do not want to force or see our students face the same impossible "choiceless choices" that confronted Holocaust survivors (United States Holocaust Memorial Museum, 2018), though we may want to ask everyone to bravely confront the catastrophic conditions and the fact that most survivors met a myriad of challenges required by these human experiences. Perhaps animal metaphors are limited, but victims and survivors could be compared to lions in cages, not sheep in slaughterhouses. Regardless, Nazi perpetrators were predatory (Spiegelman, 2011) and they stigmatized the victims as vermin, both in propaganda and in practice. This raises many concerns about Holocaust representation (Magilow & Silverman, 2015). Whatever our materials show, we need to appreciate that the extensive and prejudicial misinformation created by Holocaust perpetrators and antisemitic hate criminals makes it more important to receive the voices of the victims and upstanders; truth from witnesses must be presented in any context which is polluted by systemic distortions, propaganda, and outright lies (Luckert, Bachrach, & United States Holocaust Memorial Museum, 2009).

Survivors Show Resilience

We can share messages and examples of resilience by showing or summarizing survivor accounts of the Holocaust. Here, four survivor narratives will be used to illustrate how survivor-resilience creates themes useful in teaching about the Holocaust and Human Rights. These survivors include Inge Aeurbacher (Auerbacher & Gilbride, 2009), Olga Lengyel (Lengyel, 1995), Irving Roth (Roth & Roth, 2004), and Helga Weiss (Weiss, 2013). I was fortunate and privileged to meet both Auerbacher and Roth in person (at an institute named for Lengyel) during a nationally recognized teaching seminar in 2017 (The Olga Lengyel Institute for Holocaust Education and Human Rights (TOLI), 2017). All four of these survivors have provided detailed written accounts of their lives and resilience during the Shoah.

Resilience was required by segregation and stigmatization, which are symbolized by labeling with stars and tattoos. Once the Nuremburg laws were in force, children like Inge Auerbacher and adults as well were denied entry into many public facilities in Germany. For youth like Auerbacher, this meant not going to parks or pools and being forced into segregated schools (Auerbacher, 1993). Inge had to walk two miles and then take a train to attend the only Jewish school in her province of Germany. Jews and others were no longer allowed to intermarry; interfaith working relationships with Jews were also strained and sometimes forbidden, worsening economic hardships. As Germany invaded and laid claim to other nations, such racialized distinctions and laws expanded to include what we now recognize as Austria, Poland, Czechoslovakia, Hungary, and other nations (Bazyler, 2016).

Children in Prague, like Helga Weiss (Weiss, 2013) subsequently faced similar restrictions. Helga was forced out of schooling and thus separated from friends and forced to wear a yellow star, before being deported to concentration or death camps. In other towns in Czechoslovakia, the pattern was similar. Irving Roth was not allowed to play soccer with the non-Jewish kids (Roth & Roth, 2004). Pavel Weiner was discouraged from soccer after being subject to food rations and other forms of scarcity (Weiner, Weiner, & Dwork, 2012). It's easy to forget that discrimination and everyday harm were ubiquitous throughout the Holocaust.

During the Holocaust, segregation into ghettos and deportation to camps required further resilience. Ghettos were suggested as responses to "emergencies" in early as 1938. Thereafter, ghettoization became standard practice for segregating Jewish people and appropriating Jewish assets. Like many forms of extreme persecution, ghettoization accelerated in Poland in 1940 (200 Polish ghettos were listed by August 1942) (Dean, 2010; Yahil, 1990). Ghetto life was recently and popularly represented in text and film by *The Zoo Keeper's Wife* (Ackerman, 2007).

While ghetto life was difficult, and while it was hard to imagine, life would get worse. Survivors, including child survivor-authors, clearly describe painful experiences of deportation and relocation processes. For Helga Weiss and many others, deportations went directly to concentration camps, a more secure form of imprisonment and persecution (Weiss, 2013). For others, deportations offered a motivation to try to escape; Irving Roth escaped to be free for a time, before his latter imprisonment in Auschwitz-Birkenau (Roth & Roth, 2004). As some note, the wider scope and reach of the Holocaust was not always visible to victims "on the ground" or at the time; who knew how far the Nazis would go, or what nations would be safe havens? Perpetrators secretively guarded their wider systems of persecution and genocide, disguising their eugenic operations in deceptive euphemisms and propaganda (Luckert et al., 2009).

Persecution involved concentrating people in prisons, detention in what Germans called "Lagers." Most of these prisons concentrated and detained; six specific locations included death camps (like Auschwitz-Birkenau). Death camps were industrialized murder centers that were covertly developed in 1942 and all located in Poland (Bauer & Keren, 2001; Yahil, 1990). These most lethal machineries of death were formally operationalized at the Wannsee Conference near Berlin (Dwork, 2002). Genocidal methods falsely described as a "final solution" became more "efficient" through the criminal use of poisonous gas; bullets and other supplies were then able to be more fully deployed by Nazi aggressors to battles on the eastern and western fronts.

During the war, thousands of concentration camps or "Lagers" were established in Germany and in German-occupied nations (Wachsmann, 2015). Dachau was one of the first; Auschwitz and the other five killing centers were ultimately the most fatal, the mechanisms for a system of industrialized mass murder that was internationally recognized during the Nuremburg trials and the convention against genocide (Docker, 2010; Power, 2002).

Jews and Roma, among others, classified as less human than a false Aryan stereotype (including people with disabilities, political enemies, and those labeled LGBT), were widely and systematically subject to incarceration. Concentrated camp groups in minimal "barracks" were segregated by sex and confined to inhumane conditions. Sometimes people were selected to participate in forced (slave) labor, taking undesired jobs, including those involving "processing" human corpses in the death camps. In death camps, those confined were regularly subject to selection for incineration or other forms of mass murder (Lengyel, 1995).

> ...Individuals could be incarcerated in concentration camps indefinitely without ever being charged for a specific act... or because the SS and police authorities deemed that individual—often on the basis of alleged racial inferiority or alleged racially driven 'hostility to Germany'—was a danger to German society (United States Holocaust Memorial Museum, 2018).

During the last months of the war, Auschwitz and many other "camps" were damaged by retreating Nazis; Majdanek (near to Lublin, Poland) is one that stands very much as it was, a monument to the memories of millions of victims and survivors. The perpetrators of the "final solution" were unable to disguise the industrial scope of the mass murder. Rail cars remain as containers connoting displacement and death. Museums and tours of the Holocaust have educated millions on these machineries of destruction (United States Holocaust Memorial Museum, 2018). For those outside the carnage, propaganda shared ongoing and harmful lies designed to cover and distract people from the criminal crisis (Adler et al., 2017, Luckert et al., 2009).

Olga Lengyel's gripping and painful account of life in Auschwitz is the subject of her book *Five Chimneys*. Lengyel gives important testimony to the banality of harm and death during the Holocaust (Lengyel, 1995). Lengyel's life and work are commemorated in New York City by the Olga Lengyel Institute, located at her former home in Manhattan (The Olga Lengyel Institute for Holocaust Education and Human Rights (TOLI), 2017). Her descriptions of Auschwitz, which is notable as some of the first published work by women who survived, are clear and complex, reflecting the cruelty of genocidal policies and practices, situating the reader in the daily struggles for life. These struggles include roll call, selections (often for incineration), and choiceless choices, including unethical medical "experiments" that have become an important basis for modern medical ethics. Lengyel's insights and daily actions guide us through the deadliest location of the

Holocaust. Readers and people watching her recorded testimony are fortunate to survive with her, to walk in and out of her shoes (often in cold, bare feet) (Lengyel, 1995).

Incarceration and other harsh Holocaust truths were intentionally and systematically masked by deceit and propagandistic lies in many ways. The conditions in camps were falsely presented to representatives of the International Red Cross (IRC) at Terezin, a "show camp" (Weiss, 2013). Sickness, hunger, death, and brutalization were daily concerns in this and thousands of camps and locations. Slave labor was the basis for most selections of Jews and other incarcerated people. Tattoos, while seemingly stigmatizing, were also signs that a person had value as a worker, and thus were worn proudly by some (Roth & Roth, 2004). Liberation was a great beginning for those who endured and often migrated (or returned to home). Liberation (for the "lucky" survivors) was the start of a new chapter of life after the war. Inge Auerbacher was able to start anew and became a respected scientist in the United States (Auerbacher, 1995). Harm and persecution often had long-lasting and diasporic effects (Dwork & Pelt, 2009). As we know and still can witness, discrimination, persecution, conflicts, and wars are major reasons for migrations and for refugee crises (Türk, Edwards, & Wouters, 2017).

Sight and Insight

Holocaust education, like Holocaust studies, requires at least two complementary perspectives. We can and need to promote both *sight* and *insight* into the Holocaust (Langer, 1991). Just as we learn *about* and *from* the Holocaust, sight and insight help us to envision the past, and thus help us to navigate carefully through historical "echoes" and more interpretive or personal "reflections" (ADL, USC Shoah Foundation, & Yad Vashem, 2014). Primary sources, including documents and images, provide us sight, direct views of the past (ADL et al., 2014). Survivor narratives also speak and write directly to historical events. As we reflect on these sources, we find and discuss many *insights*, both our own and those received from decades of Holocaust and genocide studies.

We need to appreciate that survivors are varied and complex. While we may want them to help in representing human resilience, we must recognize also that humans and human memories can be anguished and damaged (Langer, 1991). Survivors were not all able or willing to relate their experiences to their children, no less to others (Stein, 2014). There were and are many good reasons for this hesitance. As educators and consumer of Holocaust narratives, we may be able to appreciate and represent memories as both examples of resilience and difficult memories of damaging experiences. Survivors can be at once heroic and harmed. With our students, we can see inside the worst of human experiences; we may fall silent out of respect, but we can also discover that there is joy in survival, in contrast to the darkness of mass murder. In comparison to the horrid and oppressive world that was created by Nazi genocide and war crimes, decades of life after liberation and new generations growing up in relative affluence can seem like heaven in almost any nation.

Many survivors come to represent those persecuted as people with strong character who endured great suffering. Some survivors emerged from the fires of the Holocaust as a symbol of hope, resilience, and continuity, even while expressing the dark and melancholy experiences of survival (Kolbert, 2001). Religious interpretations of the Holocaust are difficult but possible (Berenbaum, 2010). Weisel questioned God's role but ultimately kept faith (Wiesel, 1995). Anne Frank wrote in her diary that people are good at heart (Frank, 1993), a sentiment that made it to Broadway and two film adaptations (Langer, 1983; Prose, 2009).

The "gold standard" for "teachable moments" in Holocaust education has been to be able to present a survivor as a charismatic guest speaker. A leading seminar for educators generously offers multiple survivor guest appearances to humanize our histories (The Olga Lengyel Institute for Holocaust Education and Human Rights (TOLI), 2017). A "survivor-in-education," whether speaking in an auditorium or to a class, can directly relate to an audience and recount his or her personal experience, often through practices and polished speaking performance. Respectfully listening to survivors serves our educational participants and also can help the survivor himself or herself (Greenspan, 2010a). This is a wonderful but increasingly rare opportunity that of course relies on an aging cohort of Holocaust survivor-speakers. Fortunately, technologies are coming to our assistance.

In addition to in-person survivor presentations delivered to classes or assemblies in "real time," we can now easily share what used to be confined to a Yale film library collection. We can all now access an amazing variety of recorded survivor and witness film and video narratives, thanks to well-curated online resources. Each resource and its component parts can be used "as is," best following guidance from the host website, and each can also be, to some extent, incorporated into new curricula designed by the educational providers. Along with resources from national and local Holocaust museums, these online resources are quite extensive and currently available to registered public users. Training is available for teachers who wish to use the following:

(1) Echoes and Reflections provides resources, thanks to the ADL, Yad Vashem, and the USC Shoah Foundation (ADL et al., 2017).
(2) iWitness provides an extensive collection of video-recorded interviews with Holocaust and other genocide survivors (USC Shoah Foundation, 2018). This resource is used within Echoes and Reflections curricula.
(3) Facing History and Ourselves is a more general project in multicultural education that offers collections of topical materials on the Holocaust and genocide (Facing History and Ourselves, 2018).

Presentations by and interviews with survivors are powerful ways to humanize an otherwise complex topic. Speakers and texts can help illustrate clearly and immediately a variety of important Holocaust topics, including aspects of daily life in the context of persecution, discrimination, and the extensive array of inequalities and crimes perpetrated by Nazis. Survivors can change our perspectives, as well. For example, we might think a numerical tattoo or a yellow star of David is always and simply a shaming or stigmatizing mark, until we learn about their meanings directly from survivors (Cohen, Boaz, & Vazsonyi, 2013; Roth, 2016). We might find that numerical tattoos are born with pride by people whose capacity to work likely and literally saved their skins.

Research on Holocaust narratives finds that people who describe their survival mix institutionally legitimated information, personal details, and social memory to reinforce their personal accounts of historical events (Beim & Fine, 2007). While there are many reasons to understand and respond to traumatic aspects of survivor memory, this process is difficult enough for those who survive and sometimes for their chosen mental health professionals. Instead of just pitying those affected by traumatic stress, or lamenting how the world "outside" of or after traumatic circumstances can be complicated by the trauma (Junger, 2016), we can also learn from and respond to the resilience of people who endured during and after the Holocaust. Survivors can be models of resilience, a quality which is both necessary to successful education and which can be learned in the face of even the most traumatizing events (Frankl, 1992). In education, we described resilience as one of the "three Rs." Along with resistance, resilience reinforces personal and cultural strengths for all (Hass, 1990; Tec, 2003).

In case students are skeptical or disinterested, direct (in person or recorded) Holocaust witness testimonials, from people who saw the event "with their own eyes," add credibility and trust to the tangled, complex, and often distressing process of describing the Holocaust. While many even simple Holocaust facts may seem incredible or "unbelievable" to some young learners, the voices of real survivors are difficult to deny. Testimonies allow students to relate to victims as people and not just statistics or members of a status group. Even so, delivering and understanding the descriptions of traumatic experiences, sometimes in accented English, is no simple or straightforward task (Greenspan, 1999). Women and girls were only partially represented among survivor accounts, and their stories have sometimes been found less heroic than those of men (Waxman, 2006, 2017). Still, many do relate to the experiences of women and girls, especially Anne Frank and her peers (Jacobson et al., 2010; Prose, 2009).

Holocaust survivor testimonies often provide a compelling form of character education, an "ethics of experience," wherein people who endured suffering (including antisemitic discrimination) describe how adverse experiences can teach important lessons (Beim & Fine, 2007). Survivors credibly recount their real-life experiences and share evidence of these experiences, including and highlighting material cultural objects like their identifying tattoos or stars of David (Auerbacher, 1993, 1995). In providing evidence of their individual experience, they verify and humanize the facts of the Holocaust itself, speaking and writing against the hostilities of denial or the patterns of forgetting.

Human abilities to endure Holocaust experiences, resilience itself, may become the focus of discussion. There are many ways to understand or explain resilience, thanks to important developments in psychology and psychiatry, including an entire (logo) therapy based upon and devoted to what is required for survival (Frankl, 1992). Some explanations, emphasizing resilience through strength and/or intelligence, emphasize human agency, showing the survivor as a powerful social agent able to make important choices than enable survival, even in the worst situations (Frankl, 1992). Another set of explanations, which humbly minimize an individual's social agency, describe survival as "lucky." This more random type of explanation both pays respect to those who were killed and also acknowledges the importance of powerful and contextual social forces like Nazi law, military power, and antisemitic discrimination (Beim & Fine, 2007).

In the United States, personal accounts can be delivered by survivors who may be affiliated with one of the many members of the Association of Holocaust Organizations (AHO). Narratives also reinforce the truth of Holocaust events, working against the problems of ignorance, "forgetting," ("Holocaust amnesia"), and Holocaust denial (Beim & Fine, 2007).

Links in a Chain of Memory

Survivor Irving Roth reminds us that we are links in a chain of Holocaust memory (Roth, 2016; Roth & Roth, 2004). Each one of us can help society recover from "Holocaust amnesia" to extend knowledge about the Holocaust forward and among younger generations. In doing so, we continue expanding human rights through Holocaust education. This simple fact was shared with all of us who were fortunate to participate in the 2017 summer seminar for Holocaust educators at the Olga Lengyel Institute (TOLI), centered in New York City (The Olga Lengyel Institute for Holocaust Education and Human Rights (TOLI), 2017). As each teacher can help hundreds or even thousands of students, so too can Holocaust education spread Holocaust memory and human rights. Through these linkages, memory and cultures will continue and connect us to each other and to our heritages; we can bear the weight of injustice together and recognize that justice does eventually arrive, even if justice delayed is justice denied (King, 1963).

To preserve memory, we need not engage in victim-based suffering competitions, nor bind ourselves or our students to painful past experiences. Historical comparisons, especially with conflicted and violent events, reveal both similarities with and (thankfully) great differences from modern experiences. As noted, the Holocaust generally should not be used as a metaphor for all forms of injustice or violence in modern or American life (Novick, 1999). While it is possible and even helpful to discuss human rights and social justice in educational settings, Holocaust education should first involve learning *about* the Holocaust, through elaboration of historical information. When we then work to learn *from* the Holocaust, we are learning the importance of general principles (including human rights) from *specific* events in history, not simply learning how to describe modern or other events with historically potent language or metaphor. There are many other and even comparable genocides and examples of mass violence (including that caused by atomic weapons), but describing these events or other problems of concern does not accomplish the basic goals involved with learning about the

Holocaust. We attribute eugenic crimes to those who committed them and we remember the documented and many victims as well.

Hindsight views of war and conflict can allow us to learn safely with the benefit of historical distance (Grever, 2018). Like museum curators, educators structure time to be diachronic (spanning long terms) or synchronic (focusing on events). We can use our curricula to "visit" places or people in the near or distant past. We can also encourage students to engage and learn from their curricula without abandoning their feelings, their moral standards, their intellectual interests, or their political perspectives. Even so, aspects of difficult histories can upset any of us, especially when testimonials reveal violence and conflict. We must be sensitive to these concerns and to "triggering connections" to traumatic experiences. But this should not prevent us from exploring the Holocaust.

Memories are carried by individuals and by groups. Collective memories of the past, according to French sociologist Maurice Halbwachs, bind collectives. Each individual can invoke collective memory to reconstruct an image of past community life (Rice, 2017). "Deep" cultural memory of the Holocaust has, for many years, been revealed by oral testimonies (Langer, 1991). But such collective memories should not be taken for granted or as simple consequences of resilience or endurance. Survival was difficult even after the end of the war and liberation. For example, *survival* meant *deprival* for many Polish Jews, who were limited in their abilities to create what we now take for granted: a survivor-based narrative of the catastrophic events that took place during the Holocaust. Local hostility may have slowed the reconstruction of collective memory in Poland; in Israel, the resilient survivor or resister became icon of a newly formed Jewish identity (Rice, 2017).

Greenspan (2010) takes us from survivor testimony to recounting experiences of the Holocaust. From conversing with survivors for more than 30 years, he compares repeated accounts to learn both from and about survivors themselves, learning also about the Holocaust. We learn that survivors live and symbolize both suffering and recovery. Life histories show careful listeners that each survivor is unique, that many lessons can be taken from even one recounting, and that the Holocaust was larger and more catastrophic than any one account can tell or imagine (Greenspan, 2010a).

Accounts of the Holocaust often begin as fragments of memory, shocking and unfinished nightmares in search of larger narratives. When practiced, they often become more structured and insightful (Greenspan, 2010a). Many survivor accounts during the initial postwar decades, and even Levi's first book and Wiesel's first spoken descriptions, were sadly not encouraged and unappreciated. Some survivors learned to suffer in silence or developed partial stories. Some survivors felt at times humiliated or even guilty, or that the heroic memories of military veterans were more acceptable than the unheroic memories of the Holocaust (Langer, 1991; Levi, 1989a).

In addition, we learn that Holocaust education can be both *for* and *about survivors* themselves. When a survivor accounts for his or her experiences in a historical situation, he or she autobiographically helps us to clarify what specific words and experiences can mean (Wiesel, 1999). When an interpreter of accounts, such as an educator or author, describes the experiences of survivors as individuals or as a group, we see the development of theories and evidence about the commonalities (or diversities) among survivors. Survivors may be portrayed as ghostly victims of violence or heroic witnesses resiliently representing enduring life forces, or both.

Just as survivors seek to resolve their own fragmented or anguished memories, so too must we resolve the competing darkness and light that we glean from accounts of survival. Even so, we know our interpretations are incomplete since not all details are "tellable" or "hearable" (Greenspan, 2010a). Many listeners may develop expectations, but few accounts can or do tell a "whole story" about the Holocaust. Ultimately, like many of us, survival accounts represent people attempting to share oral histories, not complete or comprehensive descriptions of historical events. Survival accounts need to be heard, read, and appreciated. The more we learn from survivor accounts, the more we know about the Holocaust, and the better we can share the principles of respect, remembrance, and resilience.

Chapter 7

Global Holocaust Education for the Twenty-first Century

We have bright prospects for global Holocaust and human rights education in the twenty-first century. As educators, we are supported by vast and historically unique technologies that help us share historical hindsight. After a postwar period when Holocaust education was limited, languishing in the context of troubled and sometimes traumatized relationships between history and memory, we are now living with tremendous opportunities for international Holocaust and human rights education. Survivors have spoken and we have heard, formalizing memorial cultures. We have easy access to use amazing educational resources developed by many major organizations, allowing us to facilitate interesting curricular delivery and course development.

In this chapter, we will offer just a few of many ways that new technological and organizational resources enable and encourage both teachers and learners to explore the Holocaust, genocides, and human rights. For students and public audiences in many nations, as for descendants of Holocaust survivors, technologies and museums open up new and often simplified choices in Holocaust and human rights education. Technologies are "airing out" previously cloistered primary sources, including historical documents and survivor narratives, that were distributed in many different and often distant places and collections (Gray, 2014). These resources give voice to history, bringing Holocaust survivors into our view, and connecting us through social media. They also dramatically increase our access to Holocaust curricula by expanding our web-based sources and choices. We need only to select among many high-quality resources and materials that have been developed systematically in recent years, synthesizing important historical and educational work that has been developed by many people and organizations over the decades (Schweber, 2011).

We work carefully so as not to create unnecessary complexity or controversy. The US Holocaust Museum reminds us of at least 14 guidelines for Holocaust education, which reveal common concerns and occasional mistakes. Guidelines start by defining the Holocaust and offering ways to frame its context. We translate statistics into people ("humanize"), striving for precision of language. We avoid simple answers to complex historical events, recognizing that nothing is inevitable. We shun stereotypes and balance perspectives, though most of us recognize that sensationalist perpetrator perspectives should be presented with care. We endeavor to reference sources, and we do not romanticize history, even as we recognize a hope for humanity that fosters human resilience. We use care and sensitivity in selecting appropriate content and assigning learning activities. Our objectives and lesson plans need to be pursued but need not include comparisons of pain or suffering (Napolitano et al., 2007; United States Holocaust Memorial Museum, 2018).

We have shown that we can use a variety of teaching approaches to deliver Holocaust education. As in all educational topics, we can link our curricula to commemoration and remembrance (Cowan & Maitles, 2017). Using survivor testimony, technologies, documentaries, and literature can help give voice to the human consequences of social injustices (Beim & Fine, 2007; Greenspan, 2010a; Waxman, 2006). Educators may also bring our own strengths, styles, and skills into Holocaust education. In comparing teaching orientations, recent research finds that many teachers are passionate about Holocaust history, and some focus on transformative learning for students. Some of us are more pragmatic, teaching Holocaust to reinforce good citizenship, and some of us see the Holocaust linked to contemporary social justice issues. Some educators build on the shock and awe that follows awareness of Holocaust persecution to rivet learners; others humanize the Holocaust, as we suggest in this text, to help students develop skills for empathizing with people (Novis Deutsch, Perkis, & Granot-Bein, 2018). We can practice more than one teaching style, and we can use effective teaching orientations that fit our rationales, our learning objectives, and our lesson plans.

This chapter first provided a brief description of only a few notable and globally available Holocaust educational resources. We only skim the surface of some technologies and museums, providing a few views of the amazing choices available to online learners and course designers, trusting that educators are able and willing to explore many other and new resources as needed. Next, this chapter reviews recent UNESCO reports and summaries that summarize the state of Holocaust education in nations around the world. We also introduce readers to a recent UNESCO report on the topic of antisemitism education.

We briefly explore some Holocaust education variations, including helpful technologies and a small selection from the many amazing and accessible Holocaust-related museums and memorial sites. We elaborate how some of our current educational resources are generated by "directives" that come from nations, jurisdictions, and organizations, including an increasing number of states in our United States. We also explore what kind of future might be anticipated for future global varieties of Holocaust education curricula, given the many current and cosmopolitan variations. Anticipating generational change, we then discuss how descendants of survivors, like survivors themselves, contribute to Holocaust consciousness and Holocaust education. Finally, we will conclude with a call to action that reflects our optimism about Holocaust and human rights education.

Technologies and Museums

As more and eventually all Holocaust survivor-cohorts pass away, and as younger generations face new forms of Holocaust education, Holocaust educational curricula will change and evolve. In fact, the meanings of collective memories are themselves negotiated and thus subject to change over time, though within limits (Olick & Levy, 1997). We appreciate concerns that younger cohorts will have limited exposures to live-survivor accounts; most future narratives from survivors will be in the form of written texts or audiovisual recordings, rather than public speakers. This will limit our abilities to interact and to ask real-time questions. But, thanks to new technologies and growing numbers of museums, most of which provide English language resources, intergenerational changes will not take away our ability to hear accounts and survivor testimonies (Cole, 2004).

Advanced online technologies and museums, run by increasingly sophisticated and global organizations and collaborations, offer a bright future to twenty-first-century educators and learners. A plethora of documentaries and recordings of survivors are available online, most useful when in carefully managed archives, like "iWitness." For educators, it is increasingly possible and simple to "connect kids to museums" without necessarily taking a trip outside of school grounds (McRainey & Russick, 2010). We have and should make use of easy online access to both museums and museum-quality resources. These multilingual and often rich resources remain nothing short of miraculous and inspiring to teachers and students. Museum and memorial sites also help us to commemorate, as possible, and bring remembrance into our courses and classrooms from around the world (Cowan & Maitles, 2017).

We also realize that Holocaust education raises complex issues and difficult choices. People can and do share skeptical and sometimes cynical attitudes on the Holocaust and related subjects, suggesting that Holocaust education and Holocaust-related culture may be overemphasized, that we must also acknowledge other genocides, other perpetrators, and other persecuted groups. If we choose, we can adapt to this more expansive and universal or cosmopolitan perspective, as well. Critics may also and reasonably note that there is not enough time to engage in this subject. Inclusion and time management are always fair concerns, though these concerns apply to most, if not, all educational topics (Foster et al., 2016). It is important to remind one another that, while Holocaust consciousness is now widespread, it is nowhere near universal. Misinformation remains harmful and abundant, along with corrosive attitudes, and is occasionally infused with antisemitism, hatred, or even Holocaust denial (Lang, 2010; Lipstadt, 1993; Shermer & Grobman, 2000).

In our times, the Holocaust has become more established as a historical event which has consequences for our contemporary cultures, some (even well meaning) critics to complain of "Holocaust fatigue" (Schweber, 2004; Stein, 2014). Cynicism and complaints can worsen when Holocaust education is unreasonably commodified, or it is reduced to high-profile public cultural events; a public figure sarcastically remarked in Europe "there is no business like Shoah business"

(Bastel, Matzka, & Miklas, 2010). However, no worthy endeavor is without its social critics. In truth, many Holocaust educational services are free and many curricula are already in open educational and digital formats. We can easily share access, and we can simply pause or stop lessons as we stop playing recordings, providing an impetus to learn but not a sermon on the topic. We should always elaborate realistic learning goals and lessons in advance, and educators must manage our classroom and student contact time, whatever our topics or our educational situations.

It is humbling to remind ourselves that, in the immediate aftermath of the Holocaust, few who were privileged to live in Europe or the United States had *any* personal electronic technologies, such as televisions, that could provide insight by sharing moving or even static images. Wartime and postwar news of the Holocaust arrived with delays and through filmed news reels. Static and often gruesome images of the Holocaust were, early on, seen as incredible and brutal. Nazi-driven and antisemitic injustices were, for a time, even discredited as potentially false or inauthentic, propagandistic atrocity stories, initiating some disbelief for American readers and viewers, especially during wartime (Alexander, 2016). Now, we can immediately access and view a multitude of images and video materials, along with professional and high-quality documentary compilations, making genocide awareness and prevention more of a public concern, facilitating learning for all kinds of learners with our Internet-enabled classroom technologies (ADL, USC Shoah Foundation, & Vashem, 2017).

Introductory units on the Holocaust should make use of multiple and reputable sources of information about and perspectives on the Holocaust. As noted, *Echoes and Reflections,* supported by Yad Vashem and the ADL, is a very fine resource that provides both extensive educator instruction and also curricula complete with student resources (ADL, USC Shoah Foundation, & Yad Vashem, 2014). The most comprehensive survivor and testimonial resource is now the iWitness website that is housed at the University of Southern California (USC) and also supported by the ADL, Yad Vashem, and the Shoah Foundation (USC Shoah Foundation, 2018). Both of these sources can provide ongoing and online education for all people who request free accounts and access using their websites. Professional and curricular development are easier than ever, thanks to technology and the work of our predecessors (Schweber, 2011; Short & Reed, 2004; Totten & Feinberg, 2001, 2016).

In addition, there are a myriad of museums and organizations that offer extensive resources and libraries of online material. Since we cannot describe all of the many technologies and organizations, we will only mention a select few. These websites are designed for public education, but some are also linked to a global effort to boost Holocaust or heritage tourism. The resources described in this text are not representative, only illustrative examples. More can be found through targeted searches in a library, with a search engine, and through building on the work of others through "suggested sites" that are referenced by major Holocaust education sites. Of course, new information is continuously becoming available on the web; so if an interest is not listed or found with your first searches online, do not despair, just take a break, and try again later or in a different search mode.

The United States Holocaust Memorial and Museum (USHMM) provides excellent, diverse, and vast resources for teaching and learning about the Holocaust (United States Holocaust Memorial Museum, 2018). Promoting "the power of truth," it is prominent and one of a variety of organizations and foundations which support teachers and teacher trainings, along with field trips that involve museum visits. The museum's online resources and material artifacts, in both the permanent collection and in special exhibits, provide excellent lessons on the Holocaust, complete with photos, videos, audio recordings, maps, and other materials. Museum resources for educators continue to grow; scholarly research is also conducted at and with support of this Museum. The USHMM is only one of many diverse US museums, however. The Museum of Jewish Heritage in New York (MJH) and the Simon Wiesenthal Center in Los Angeles are also amazing resources. The MJH design is smaller but takes a longer historical view of Jewish life before, during, and after the Shoah. The Wiesenthal Center is a Museum of Tolerance with experiential education and also now includes a film division.

In Europe and elsewhere, we find extensive, diverse, and many new museums that focus on cultural groups, including national or regional museums of Jewish and other formerly persecuted cultural groups. We can also find museums that focus specifically on the Holocaust. We are able to explore in person or online a wide variety of "location museums" which have grown up around concentration camps and other Holocaust sites in Europe, especially in Germany and Poland (Heyl, 2014). For example, we can virtually visit and learn from KL Auschwitz (where Google Arts & Culture has shared a series of online educational modules). We can also explore a new (Ulma Family) museum featuring righteous Poles who saved Jews. Near Berlin, or online, we can visit the Wannsee House to learn about the famous conference that formalized the use of death camps. These European examples are drops in bucket of educational resources; growing numbers of national and international museums and increasingly interconnected monuments are growing up around the world.

If we are seeking speakers, we can search speaker bureaus, and we can find speakers who are linked to organizations that support Holocaust survivors. In the United States, a central resource is the Association of Holocaust Organizations (AHO). When we need advanced teacher training or distributed seminars, both in the United States and international, the Olga Lengyel Institute (TOLI) is an amazing and global resource for educators and organizations (The Olga Lengyel Institute for Holocaust Education and Human Rights (TOLI), 2017). As with the USHMM and other major museums, teacher trainings are offered by TOLI in locations across the nation and around the world.

UNESCO's Global and Comparative Studies

Globally, Holocaust education appears as strong as it has ever been. As a United Nations agency dedicated to international and global educational and cultural collaboration, UNESCO studies Holocaust education around the world. A recent

(2015) UNESCO report provides information about global curricula for Holocaust education, including textbooks. The Georg Eckert Institute, with support from UNESCO and over 100 collaborating researchers, produced important comparative analysis (Carrier, Fuchs, & Messinger, 2015). Findings show how varied historical concepts and narratives both converge and diverge, creating a diverse, somewhat fragmented, but "cosmopolitan culture of memory" through global curricular examples of Holocaust education (Levy & Sznaider, 2002, 2006; Olick & Levy, 1997).

This report can be used to compare nations or to recommend new national or regional policies and directives and to improve any Holocaust curricula. Findings show that Holocaust concepts and perspectives are common in European nations but, particularly in parts of the global south, sometimes absent, muted, or distorted (Carrier et al., 2015). Mutual educational exchange can help improve Holocaust education, particularly for nations and groups that were historically uninvolved in the Holocaust and for nations that have had limited access to global educational resources. Teachers and researchers may learn from UNESCO work that describes national and global educational efforts in Holocaust education (Fracapane & Hass, 2014). Understanding global strategies for antisemitism education is also helpful; UNESCO very recently released a comprehensive report on this subject as well (UNESCO: United Nations Educational Scientific and Cultural Organization and OSCE: Organization for Security and Co-operation in Europe, 2018).

While curricular content on the Holocaust appears absent in only a few nations, and while some major nations provide educational resources on only contextual topics (like world wars or the Nazis), most national curricular materials provide either *direct* reference to the Holocaust (sometimes referred to as the Shoah or the genocide against Jews) or *partial* reference (describing the Holocaust as indirectly an example of genocide prompting the need for human rights law). Holocaust education often recognizes that genocide exemplifies clear and global moral standards of good and evil. This provides educators opportunities to articulate moral and legal standards for human rights and to prevent and sanction injustices (Carrier et al., 2015).

Lessons from the Holocaust may be complicated by nationalistic (and sometimes even biased) narratives and concerns. Some nations tend or tended to present Holocaust information within a more nationalistic (rather than a global) narrative or perspective (Carrier et al., 2015). In addition, an emphasis on national suffering can compete with the topic of Jewish persecution, though any such "Olympics of suffering" is being addressed by new curricula in Poland, among other nations (Gebert, 2014; Gross, 2013; Imhoff et al., 2017). Holocaust education also serves many diverse and often important uses in diverse nations, promoting communications about human rights and civic education that help nations move toward positive national and international transformations, especially since the end of the cold war and the creation of the European Union (Fracapane & Hass, 2014; Stevick & Gross, 2014).

How effective and useful are global curricula, including texts? The UNESCO report by the Eckert Institute examines curricula and textbooks. Across 193 nations, 272 officially recognized curricula for students aged 14–18 years were collected, analyzed, charted, and mapped. Complementary comparisons and assessments summarize 89 textbooks in 26 countries (Carrier et al., 2015). Research explores the educational contexts of Holocaust topics and "metahistorical" questions about if and how the Holocaust has been conceptualized as an antisemitic genocide or/and "universalized" as a model to represent other or all genocides, or even all atrocities. Such "universalization" is a process that can, with potential risk to historical focus and accuracy, generate cosmopolitan, though less culturally focused forms of historic memory (Levy & Sznaider, 2002).

Report authors ask three questions to guide curricular analysis. First, researchers ask about absolute status: Do curricula (in texts and in national curricula) stipulate teaching about Holocaust? In what terms ("semantic status")? How does curriculum contextualize Holocaust in history? Textbook analyses provide national portraits and international perspectives. Global comparisons show that educational portraits in textbooks may not always reflect the status of the Holocaust in the wider media or in family stories. In many ways, the Holocaust becomes many narratives which raise universal questions about civic morality around the globe, as noted by many authors and comparative studies of textbooks (Alexander, 2009; Bromley & Russell, 2010; Pingel, 2014). Comparing texts, we find that the Holocaust is transforming from a European to a global event.

Many nations make *direct* reference to the Holocaust (or Shoah), while other nations or regions use alternative terms (e.g., "the Jewish genocide"). Fewer nations use curricula with *partial* reference to the Holocaust, indirectly stipulating teaching about the Holocaust as an example of another topic (such as genocide) or as a basis of the need for human rights education. Some nations and curricula present the Holocaust only *in context*, noting many problems in terms like the injustices practiced by Nazis, stages of genocide, human rights violations, and antisemitism, but not specifically addressing the Holocaust as an event (Carrier et al., 2015).

In some nations, this UNESCO report finds no or very limited reference to the Holocaust in curricula, even in the context of other topics. Even so, many national curricula are in a state of transition, often toward more state support for direct Holocaust education, as we can see from early adopters of state-supported curricula like Israel in 1981 (Stevick & Gross, 2014) and the United Kingdom in 1990 (Pearce & Chapman, 2017) to more recent changes in Brazil and (in 2010) Finland (Carrier et al., 2015).

As noted, some nations, curricula, and textbooks focus particularly on Jewish victims while others increasingly expand to address Roma cultures, people with disabilities, and other groups subject to Nazi-generated human rights abuses. Within the Eckert report and elsewhere, *terms* for atrocities or genocides which *imply national responsibility* may be muted or limited (with the notable exception of responsibilities forcibly taken by Nazi Germany). As noted, careful use of educational language (Cowan & Maitles, 2017) is essential in this and other contexts, not simply a semantic or political concern (United States Holocaust

Memorial Museum, 2018). Clear concepts and careful word choices help national and other curricula to explore the topic without generating misunderstandings and without overemphasis of events that could suggest "self-incrimination." Holocaust education can address complexities of national exploitation by oppressive authoritarian military regimes, as we find in Poland, where *Nazi* policies (*not* Polish state authorities) assigned and designed death camps to "blood lands" like Auschwitz, forcing east many of the millions of crematoria-based mass murders that took place from 1942–1945 (Gebert, 2014; Snyder, 2015a).

UNESCO authors conclude that a higher proportion of OECD (European) nations prescribe some version of *compulsory* Holocaust education, as do Israel and the United Kingdom (Carrier et al., 2015). In contrast, many nations in Africa and Asia, among others, provided fewer data to the study, and these data show somewhat more limited, partial, or indirect forms of Holocaust education within national educational curricula and textbooks. Evidently, both within nations and across regions, there remains room for growth of Holocaust curricula within multiple educational dimensions, and subsequent research efforts remain necessary. Where nations self-assess and set national goals, the path forward becomes clearer (Foster et al., 2016). There are reasons to remain both optimistic and critical; the field of Holocaust education is experiencing innovation and profound developmental transformations (Stevick & Gross, 2014). In this process, we can help attend to and perhaps help guide the future implementation of these important developments.

Variations and Directives

Different national histories and cultures are related to international and global variations in contemporary Holocaust education (Fracapane & Hass, 2014; Stevick & Michaels, 2013). Each national and local context presents different challenges to design, delivery, and reception of Holocaust education. Nonetheless, Holocaust education has emerged in some form within many if not most national and local educational curricula (Carrier et al., 2015). Curricula are supported in part through national and educational efforts toward Holocaust memorialization. Taking many different and no "standard" forms, Holocaust education also helps address more general social problems including xenophobia, racism, anti-semitism, and human rights, especially when delivered with a "social justice" teaching orientation (Novis Deutsch et al., 2018).

While some nations deferred on Holocaust education for some decades after the Shoah, the subject remains essential and related to other important historical and contemporary topics (Davis & Rubinstein-Avila, 2013). Holocaust history may have been initially understated in parts of Central and Eastern Europe; it was also initially downplayed and often tailored to national goals in the United States and in most nations (Cohen, 2016). In recent times and in contrast, a modern and rather cosmopolitan perspective on Holocaust memory is increasingly accepted by most nations, even with nationalist and other forms of particularistic concerns (Levy & Sznaider, 2006). We also find that Holocaust educational curricula need not be forced to choose between either moral or historical lessons, a topic of much debate in earlier periods of time (Russell, 2006).

In Israel, where the Holocaust has been widely taught and required, a new national curriculum with flexible but defined requirements enables autonomy among educators who actively individualize Holocaust curricula (Cohen, 2016). The Holocaust is a major topic in many educational areas and disciplines; it is seen as a part of the reason for Israeli statehood and nationalism, and it was a particularly Jewish concern that led to the postwar immigration of many Israelis. As Israel embodies a particularly Jewish context for all forms of education, Holocaust education has addressed antisemitic aspects of the Shoah, though not exclusively so. This is evident as effective *multicultural* education (promoting tolerance and providing strategies for dealing with diversities) that involves Holocaust education has been documented in both Israel and Germany (Shamai, Yardeni, & Klages, 2004).

Israeli Holocaust education can be traced to the new national government's institution of a Shoah memorial day (1951) and the creation of Yad Vashem (1953). Even so, curricula and delivery were, like in many nations, limited until the late 1970s. A 1979 Ministry of Education initiative led to more comprehensive teacher training courses and textbook development (Cohen, 2016). Since then, Israeli educational lessons have expanded to include a series of themes, including memory, identity, democracy, and commitment to both national and universal principles. Consequently, mandatory Holocaust education at a secondary level now includes over 130 hours and can involve memorial events, family history projects, and trips to Poland to see memorial sites. Since 2014, Israeli Holocaust education has moved to be included for all age groups and toward carefully developed curricular goals based on commonly accepted principles, which has involved greater standardization (Cohen, 2016).

In Polish schools, perceptions of the Holocaust continue to change, and educational approaches are affected by Poland's social and political contexts. The Holocaust has evolved from a Nazi attack against all Poles to be seen more specifically as a particular attack against Jewish populations (Gross, 2013; Kapralski, 2018). The nature and scope of Polish Holocaust education is actively developing, reconciling narratives which cast both Polish nationals and Jewish populations as targets and victims. Recent developments help in overcoming "suffering competitions" that were occasionally the source of anger and misunderstanding, particularly when Poles were, even unintentionally, unfairly, and wrongly accused of governmental responsibility for "the German death camp enterprise" (Gebert, 2014).

In Germany, where the Holocaust represents perhaps the greatest moral catastrophe in German history, local educational ministries and organizations have been requiring, designing, and overseeing Holocaust education since the late 1940s (Pingel, 2006). Germany has developed an official consensus that the Nazi era and the Holocaust, including Nazi crimes, must be taught and remembered, though this consensus and the subsequent moral pressures on students do not go unchallenged (Kaiser, 2014). In recent decades, this means teaching the subject within local history and geography courses from ages

14 to 16 years and then expanding the scope of Holocaust and national historical education for elder teens. German curricula were initially established during occupation and the foundation of the Federal Republic, but a focus on Jewish persecution actually decreased in the mid-1950s as apologetic narratives increased (Pingel, 2006). Victims of persecution were first allowed to have voice in the history texts of the 1960s, but texts were more focused on the difficult question of how a murderous dictatorship could be allowed to replace the democratic Weimar government. Children's perspectives "broke" with those of their war-era parents, a generation gap that was not limited to Germany. German elders and youth, in postwar generations, struggled with emotion, accusations, justifications, and feelings of guilt; presentation of history was consequently designed to be rational and nonemotional. In the former East Germany (GDR), capitalism was the culprit. In modern days, while a range of well-designed texts are improved and more than abundant, the curriculum has moved outside the text and classroom into the local sites where the Holocaust occurred, through tours and seminars (Pingel, 2006).

The case of German Holocaust education raises two interesting points. First, there is little pedantic debate in Germany as to whether Holocaust education should be a part of curricula; it is taken for granted that it is necessary, even as it can be overwhelming for some students and others. Second, the Holocaust exposed the fact that leaders can radically deny human values, destroying much of civilization in a modern nation (leading some to decry the Holocaust as an end to modernity). This can create, in students and in us all, a sense of distrust in leaders and also the realization that human values are fragile (Pingel, 2006).

Teachers and students in Germany continue to find Holocaust education important but challenging. Why did the Holocaust happen? Why were such harmful policies implemented by so many people? Why was it tolerated? German students are often now encouraged to empathize with victims; textbooks study documents that help them appreciate victim and perpetrator perspectives. The authoritarian context of Nazi rule is fully included in German curricula. Even so, education has many facets and works differently for each student; so, the challenges of humanistic education and harm prevention continue (Kaiser, 2014).

In the United States, seven (soon eight) of our fifty states have passed state laws "mandating" Holocaust education resources be available to and used by school entities. Some other states are in the process of considering such laws. My own home state of Pennsylvania passed such a law in 2014 (Reinherz, 2014, June 19). Subsequent research in Pennsylvania shows that, while *a third* of a random sample of residential households in our state did not include residents with any exposure to Holocaust education in their past (Polgar, 2015), almost *all* school systems are now using some sort of Holocaust education at some point in secondary educational curricula (Snider, Craig, Carol, Glenn, & Wittig, 2017). In US Catholic schools, inspired by Vatican documents and led by a National Catholic Center for Holocaust education, renewed understandings of Judaism and Jewish experiences renounce all forms of hatred and persecution, including antisemitism (Napolitano et al., 2007). Thus, both many public and many private educational systems are actively delivering Holocaust education.

In Britain, we appreciate active and growing traditions of both Holocaust education and scholarship that examine the delivery of Holocaust education (Cowan & Maitles, 2017; Short & Reed, 2004). Holocaust education and curricula have been growing and improving for decades (Pearce, 2008). Recent national studies and reports were published in 2015 (Lawson, 2017; Pearce & Chapman, 2017). British national curricula require some coverage of the Holocaust in preuniversity history classes, but the extent of coverage is unspecified and variable, and there is no standard examination testing this knowledge. Even so, the growth of student commemoration of Holocaust Memorial Day in the United Kingdom has grown, along with calls to broaden the commemoration to include other forms of conflict and genocide (Cowan & Maitles, 2017).

Holocaust education-related innovation and transformation are both possible and illustrated by case studies. An interdisciplinary and multiconcern 12-day "one-world" series of activities in a Scottish school used Holocaust and other citizenship education foci to improve student attitudes along multiple dimensions (Cowan & Maitles, 2017). Helping students explore citizenship, including both individual and collective responsibilities for prejudice, discrimination, or persecution, can apply Holocaust education to more general efforts to promote attitudes of social inclusion and respect, over and above tolerance in multicultural education.

Research with data from over 9,500 British students finds that young people are interested in what they find is an important topic, and that the topic has been a staple in the curriculum, but that some precollege student knowledge was found to be limited or based on inaccuracies, as it has been in many other nations. Some of what was missing among students, according to this 2015 report, were developed understandings of antisemitism, Nazi policies, and Holocaust collaboration by both functionaries and by governments in nations beyond Germany. Research found an underestimation of the scale of the Holocaust and an overestimation of the Jewish population in prewar Germany. A large majority had viewed the film (and some read the book) *The Boy in the Striped Pajamas* (Foster et al., 2016). These findings have been pessimistically interpreted by leading intellectuals like Deborah Dwork and Tony Kushner, but they also provide some optimism as well. Research suggests and reinforces the need for developing and sustaining teacher access to rigorous teacher education and improving student knowledge of the Holocaust through creative and age-appropriate pedagogy (Lawson, 2017; Pearce & Chapman, 2017).

In Austria, truly reflective Holocaust education was dormant into the 1980s (Austrian nationals were portrayed as Nazi victims, also with Jews and other targeted groups), but things have changed in recent decades. Educators now initiate discussions with survivors, and schools can take visits to Holocaust nearby or online memorials. Many Austrian students visit the *Mauthausen* concentration camp while in high school. A central Hero's Square in Vienna has been the site of children's Holocaust memorial activities but also the site of angry right-wing protests since the square includes a Vienna memorial that celebrates Austro-German nationalism, which can serve as a focus for some anti-Slavic, anti-Turkish, and antisemitic attitudes (Bastel et al., 2010).

Authors writing about France, Argentina, South Africa, and other nations explore Holocaust education in a global context (Fracapane & Hass, 2014). In South Africa, obligatory Holocaust education for 9th grade students is now a part of human rights education. The 15 hours allotted to Holocaust education is second only to the hours allocated to the study of Apartheid. Human rights principles are indeed global; the end of Apartheid included a well-received 18-month traveling exhibition about Anne Frank, which had previously respected an international boycott (Reilly, 1997). International examples remind us to learn from teachers in different nations through seminars and conferences (The Olga Lengyel Institute for Holocaust Education and Human Rights (TOLI), 2017). There is no reason to think that innovations and resources for Holocaust education should be nation-specific. In fact, globalized Holocaust memory is growing and succeeding in all corners of the world (Levy & Sznaider, 2002, 2006). Educators and students alike can visit new places, online or through field trips, and help all of us to dig deeper into the lessons we learn from historical topics and subsequent work to repair past persecution (Cowan & Maitles, 2011).

Descendants of Survivors

Holocaust survivors are not alone in finding ongoing purpose and identity in survival. Our first generation of people descended from Holocaust survivors are a cohort also known as "second generation" Holocaust survivors. Like many children of immigrants to the United States, we are partially defined by the dynamic experiences of our parents (Rumbaut & Portes, 2001). Many of us in this surviving second generation grew up during decades when there was more limited Holocaust education in school systems (Fallace, 2008; Napolitano et al., 2007; Schweber, 2010). Even so, some of us sought clarification from our elders about their experiences as survivors, helping us root our cultural and familial backgrounds and our own modern identities, finding common cause with others in our cohort who had survivor-parents (Epstein, 1979). Subsequently, many of us helped recover and share the growing numbers of Holocaust survivor narratives, helping popularize this "genre," writing our own narratives (Bukiet, 2002) and raising Holocaust consciousness to new levels (Stein, 2014).

During our younger years, and sometimes thereafter, our elders who experienced the Holocaust did not always or fully share anguished memories with those of us who were descendants of survivors. We helped others to understand that many Holocaust survivors wanted to preserve optimism about the future, shunning the stigma of needing help or psychological labeling, embracing dreams of recovery and social mobility, and thus avoiding difficult discussions that were seen as challenges to familial progress or well-being (Epstein, 1979). Survivors showed and still exemplify remarkable resilience, which was often unrecognized, especially when the dominant and often necessary focus was on the survivor's consequences of trauma, especially among "clinical cases" (Hass, 1990). Sometimes estranged from their postwar situations, a conspiracy of silence enveloped too many survivors. This silence was sometimes fostered by bitterness, especially when audiences (including some kin) were unwilling or unable to listen supportively.

One asked poignantly, "who would believe us?" (Langer, 1991; Stein, 2014). Who can blame survivors, or blame victims more generally?

We children of survivors number perhaps a quarter of a million people in the United States (most of us born of over 100,000 survivors who came to the United States). As a consequence of our persecuted and complicated lineages, many of us had truncated family networks such as no or few grandparents (Bukiet, 2002). Traces of the past, including taboo subjects, were familiar to us when we found that there were other and indeed many "people like us" who had survivors among our parents. Therefore we contributed actively to the rising Holocaust consciousness of the late twentieth century and the concurrent preservation of cultural memory (Stein, 2009, 2014).

As Holocaust survivors initially recounted displaced lives and reported experiences of persecution, and as audiences listened to and read these narrative accounts, many survivors found little heroism, honor, or distinction in *being* survivors. The "real victims" were those who were murdered, both fighters and other targets of persecution, numbering 6 million or two-thirds of European Jewry who lost lives in the Holocaust. Some survivors did not always feel that they showed the same degree of bravery and selflessness as the fighters or resistance and thus rarely saw themselves as worthy of public attention, no less fame (Stein, 2014). It took new generations, inquiring children, and new contexts to change some of these unfair comparisons and bring survivor narratives from the shadows of suffering or silence.

Many Holocaust survivors experienced assimilative forces prevalent among migrants who arrived during the early postwar period in places like the United States. Lingering and often reasonable concerns about antisemitic exclusion also muted the "Jewishness" of immigrant populations (Sarna & ebrary, 2004). In contrast, we in the second generation experienced cultural freedoms and were exposed to both identity and inclusion movements, fostering multiculturalism and therapeutic cultures. We grew up in cultures and schools which more often encouraged our interests in unique and national heritages. Our generation did not generally have to endure either antisemitic forces separating Jewish people from the mainstream in our "new countries" (especially in Israel) or the memories of personal persecution. We had fewer "bullets to dodge," literally or figuratively, and we did not usually have to adapt our heritage to fit circumstances. We did not perceive or accept stigma associated with our familial cultures; our accounts of our parents were less personally painful and more often accepted on face value (Stein, 2014).

We may note some "tainted heritage" for descendants of survivors; our parents and our peers have been subject to extensive consideration within narrow psychological and psychiatric perspectives (Epstein, 1979). While it helped and still helps to have had mental health support from people who care, we should not ignore or downplay the resilience of our elder kin who learned to survive persecution, often developing an optimistic "faith in life" (Des Pres, 1976). There is an "upside" to comparing modern material cultures with historical deprivation and persecution, as many elders of all backgrounds can probably describe. Even so, surviving generations and audiences of Holocaust survivors should not fool ourselves that the Holocaust is a long story that is characterized an abundance of happy endings. We are skeptical of "the comforts of common memories." We certainly see the variations in Holocaust victim and survivor experiences; we see a vast array of loss and harm, even while we celebrate the gifts of select and redemptive narratives (Langer, 1986; Stein, 2014).

Holocaust Hesitation

I would also like to briefly offer a personal perspective on motivations for Holocaust education. As a sociology teacher for college students in the United States, and also a person whose family members survived the Holocaust, you might think that I have always or often taught about the Holocaust. In fact, I have hesitated to do so for many years. My sociological colleagues and I often use multicultural educational materials and methods to teach about cultures, diversities, and inequalities, but both the Holocaust and topics related to religion are rarely a focus in our curricula. We sociologists are often teaching courses that focus on diversities and inclusion, often teaching about inequalities related to race and ethnicities. I teach such courses at Pennsylvania State University. Sometimes, multicultural education frustrates some educators due to issues related to inequalities, assessment, classroom management, or grouping practices (Appelbaum, 2002). I am happy and privileged to report that I do not often face these or many other problems in teaching multicultural topics to diverse college students. For the most part, my students and I like teaching and learning sociologically about the diversity and inclusion of ethnic and racial groups in our schools and our nations. Instead, I have faced a different and less common concern. I did not usually choose or get assigned to teach about the Holocaust. For my first 20 years as a teacher, I hesitated to introduce the subject into any of my courses; I have only started to do so in the last few years of my 25-year college teaching career. Now, I consider it one of my most interesting topics and foci.

With a few exceptions, I have hesitated to bring my own cultural background or cultural concerns into my courses because I did not think these topics were related to our course topics. As noted in the preface, I am Jewish and also the son and grandson of Holocaust survivors. I do recognize my own gendered, economic, racial, and cultural privileges. I do not often raise "religious topics" in class, though I do describe religion as an important social institution. I believe religion is important to most of us, and I am a regular participant in (mostly Jewish but also other) religious activities. So, why have I (like many other Jewish teachers that I know) *hesitated* to teach about the Holocaust? I have mentioned it on occasion, but I have also hesitated to actively *include* the Holocaust, and even Holocaust-related topics related to inequality and persecution (such as anti-semitism), in our course curricula.

My earlier ambivalence to raise or even include Holocaust topics, which I've called "Holocaust hesitation," likely stems from a combination of factors. One has been modesty; I do not think any course should be "about" the teacher or the teacher's cultural background. Another has been training; I was not fully prepared, despite my family history, to teach about the Holocaust. I addressed this problem by participating in many in-person and online teacher trainings, first with the USHMM, then with Echoes and Reflections, and finally with TOLI (The Olga Lengyel Institute (TOLI), 2018; The Olga Lengyel Institute for Holocaust Education and Human Rights (TOLI), 2017). A third concern may be that people (especially non-Jewish students) could find it unfair; too many other curricular topics and many teachers have diminished certain other cultural histories of persecution for too long. In contrast, some see the Holocaust as a topic that has received the attention that it's due, at least in recent decades, within educational curricula.

A hesitation to include the Holocaust in any curriculum can also be couched in a reasonable and fair concern for teachers of young and/or sensitive learners (Cowan & Maitles, 2017). Young people generally should not be exposed to excessive violence, according to many and to medical experts, and so educators are not often willing to introduce a topic that can lead to the important though horrifying discovery of mass violence, including genocidal slaughter of many innocents and their disposal in mass graves. Reading or learning about a famously optimistic author like Anne Frank, often represented as a happy diarist, despite her tragic fate, is less horrifying when the end is muted. Even so, one narrative, no matter how gently concluded, cannot fully eclipse the true nature of the Holocaust or any genocide. Reading or more vividly seeing the facts of the Holocaust may be truly traumatic for young learners. For older learners, this state of shock may be less problematic and instead motivate social awareness. As a young author, Susan Sontag saw photographs of Dachau in a bookstore in the 1940s. She left the store upset and in a horrified shock; it was a watershed moment in her life (Cowan & Maitles, 2017). Who would do, or better "who *does* such things?" What is represented by these tragic images before us? Herein we find a good reason to learn about the history of Germany and Europe.

Hesitantly, educators may reasonably question the wisdom of raising *any* violent, upsetting, or morbid narratives, especially those that involve genocide and persecution, even into our multicultural studies of interesting and diverse cultural groups. Lynching and other extreme forms of racial violence and brutality are also and similarly terrifying, especially to young people. But can educators actually *avoid* all difficult topics if we fear that a student (or even the teacher) may be "triggered" and have an emotional reaction? How do we soften the impact of our subjects without censoring the reality of real historical violence? I think we do not yet have any simple answers to these questions.

Among Jewish educators and especially those who champion Jewish culture, there are other concerns with a focus on Holocaust education. Jewish studies, including studies of our Bible or Torah, involve a very long historical arc. If or as we may have only limited time to spend on Jewish topics, we might not want to *start* with the Holocaust and thus risk identifying Jewish cultures with such a tragic historical chapter or with events that are sometimes viewed from the outside as evidence of large-scale victimhood. Why substitute a chance to expand interfaith or cultural awareness among non-Jewish students with the tormenting complexities of expanded Holocaust consciousness (Stein, 2014)? Uncertainty about the related roles of Jewish studies and Holocaust studies can lead educators to examine both a longer span of Jewish history and antisemitism as a part of Holocaust education. In fact, as we have noted, Yad Vashem now suggests that Holocaust education involves descriptions of Jewish cultures before and after the Shoah. It seems reasonable and fair to represent our cultures both realistically (in contrast to Nazi propagandistic stereotypes) and as enduring after and since the Holocaust.

We also note that there are systemic forces that can be antagonistic to Holocaust education. Some national and political outlooks, specifically those which emphasize national suffering in the wars, may minimize Holocaust education and focus on broader themes of national victimhood and suffering (Gray, 2014). In Poland, as in other Baltic states, understandable themes of more general national suffering at the hands of Nazi occupiers (and subsequent Soviets) have, at times and in some ways, overshadowed a more particularistic concern of Jewish persecution and also the topic of national responsibilities (Gebert, 2014; Gross, 2013; Imhoff et al., 2017; Kapralski, 2018). In Austria, ambivalence regarding responsibilities is related to a "late start" for Holocaust education (Bastel et al., 2010). Even so, not all nations had delayed developments of Holocaust education. German curricula for Holocaust education was initiated in the late 1940s and, while not always apologetic or fully descriptive, did not evade the subject entirely (Pingel, 2006).

We also appreciate that the Holocaust was not a singular series of events for all who were persecuted. Gender, nationality, ethnicity, and other social distinctions were not only the subject of distinction and persecution during the Holocaust but also representations of different perspectives on the experiences of Holocaust and genocide. Some experiences were specific national cultures, while others diminished (Jewish) cultural identity. Anne Frank had a Dutch girl's experience, while Ellie Wiesel's experience was related to his roles as a male, a Hungarian, a writer, a prisoner, and an immigrant. Understanding multiple experiences and perspectives through Holocaust and Human Rights Education (HHRE) allow us to understand that there were many diverse Holocaust victim experiences and help to repair the damages that are done to cultural continuity.

Educators and students of diverse backgrounds benefit from applying the sociological concept of intersectionality to problems of oppression and inequality (Collins, 2015). We all occupy multiple statuses and groups; we can be subject to mistreatment within more than one of our intersecting statuses (perhaps as a disabled woman). People harmed by violence and genocide are also not all of one group, though they may be treated as such (e.g., by "Holocaust particularism" and by highlighting antisemitism during the Holocaust). Inequalities intersected during the Holocaust too. For example, European and Jewish women were, while quite diverse, also subject to types of persecution that were different from those of men. Women and girls who were and are Holocaust witnesses can now be represented to a wide audience (as we see with Anne Frank), but women as a group have been considered and often portrayed narrowly, usually as selfless caregivers trying to save their families (as in the book-turned-film *Sophie's Choice*). Women and girls are less often represented as heroic resistance fighters, even though there were notable examples like Hannah Senesh (Senesh, 2004). Women were more often in hiding and also subject to sexual violence. All people who suffer violence and genocide live in multiple and intersecting social roles. Singular stories and stereotypes do not serve any historical exploration or analysis.

Holocaust Education in the Twenty-first Century

We all have a great deal to learn and to share through Holocaust education. We can be optimistic that Holocaust education will continue to expand and evolve in our new century, innovating and diversifying throughout our educational and global communities. We hope that Holocaust education will continue to inspire us to appreciate and respect human resilience. Memory and memorial organizations will continue to offer support and solace to help us remember those who were scared or taken by genocidal persecution.

With time, reflection, and preparation, our curricula can help students to appreciate the gifts that we who live after the Holocaust have received. The enduring memories from our histories reinforce our commitments to human rights and civic responsibilities. We can continue to imagine and also witness transformational educational work, where students and teachers learn both about and from the Holocaust, growing to appreciate that this darkest chapter in history helped generate a shared commitment to prevent and prosecute genocide, along with a more universal commitment to help nations and communities articulate and reinforce human rights for all groups and all people.

As professionals and educators, along with students and other learners, we can also develop and update our skills and our specialties. Holocaust and human rights education presents opportunities for growth and enrichment, often finding new interests and colleagues, perhaps reawakening to our calling and improving the efficacy of our professions.

We need also resilience in our educational work; we should not be dissuaded from delivering Holocaust education or discouraged by rancorous public debates. We can consider the Holocaust as *both* a particular antisemitic genocide *and* a universal moral tragedy that harmed many diverse groups. The Holocaust was *both* a unique genocide created by one specific group of perpetrators *and* also one of the many genocides in history. Genocide is a particularly heinous international crime but not the only form of mass violence or persecution that we have or will see in our complex and conflicted world. Antisemitism was both a form of racism in the Holocaust and is now one of the many new problems of human relations, including xenophobia and terrorism.

This book has examined why and how we teach the Holocaust. We can remember both the historical tragedy and the fact that it was not, for many decades, well incorporated in most of our educational systems. We learn about and from the Holocaust, forming chains of memory and teaching from a position of strength. But we are not limited to a narrow perspective on the Holocaust. We appreciate that it has become a cornerstone for the creation of human rights and part of education that helps us all work for human rights. The extreme and inhumane forms of persecution that were central to the Holocaust help us to appreciate the fundamental rights that we share and the responsibilities of democratic leadership and participation.

In closing, I hope that each reader, like each Holocaust survivor and each historical hero, finds our own modicum of respect and resilience as we pursue our ongoing educational enterprises. We join as links in chains of memory that assist the development of successful future generations. Our strength and opportunities allow us to realize a few of the best qualities of those who endured difficult historical injustices. We aspire to create justice everywhere and we can do it. Thanks and keep up the good work for us all.

References

Ackerman, D. (2007). *The zookeeper's wife* (1st ed.). New York, NY: W. W. Norton & Company, Inc.

Adichie, C. N. (2008). *African "authenticity" and the Biafran experience*. 42–53. Bloomington, IN: Indiana University Press.

Adichie, C. N. (2009). *The danger of a single story*. TED. Retrieved from https://www.ted.com/talks/chimamanda_adichie_the_danger_of_a_single_story.

Adler, H. G., Cooper, B., Loewenhaar-Blauweiss, A., & Adler, J. (2017). *Theresienstadt, 1941–1945: The face of a coerced community*. New York, NY: Cambridge University Press.

Adorno, T. W., & Rolf, T. (2003). *Can one live after Auschwitz? A philosophical reader*. Stanford, CA: Stanford University Press.

Alba, R. (1999). Immigration and the American realities of assimilation and multiculturalism. *Sociological Forum, 14*(1), 3–25. doi:10.1023/a:1021632626811.

Alba, R. D., & Nancy, F. (2015). *Strangers no more: Immigration and the challenges of integration in North America and Western Europe*. Princeton, NJ: Princeton University Press.

Alexander, J. C. (2009). *Remembering the Holocaust: A debate*. Oxford; New York, NY: Oxford University Press.

Alexander, J. C. (2016). Culture trauma, morality and solidarity: The social construction of 'Holocaust' and other mass murders. *Thesis Eleven, 132*(1), 3–16. doi:10.1177/0725513615625239.

Altman, A. (2012). Genocide and crimes against humanity: Dispelling the conceptual fog. *Social Philosophy and Policy, 29*(1), 280–308. doi:10.1017/s0265052511000033.

Ambrose, S. E. (1990). *Eisenhower: Soldier and president* (Rev. ed.). New York, NY: Simon and Schuster.

Anderson, E. (2011). *The cosmopolitan canopy: Race and civility in everyday life*. New York, NY: W. W. Norton & Company, Inc.

Anderson, E. (2012). The iconic Ghetto. *The Annals of the American Academy of Political and Social Science, 642*(1), 8–24. doi:10.1177/0002716212446299.

Anti-Defamation League (ADL), USC Shoah Foundation, & Yad Vashem. (2017). *Echoes and reflections video toolbox*. Retrieved from http://echoesandreflections.org/video_toolbox/.

Anti-Defamation League, USC Shoah Foundation, & Yad Vashem. (2014). *Echoes and reflections: Teacher's resource guide*. New York, NY: Anti-Defamation League.

Appelbaum, P. M. (2002). *Multicultural and diversity education: A reference handbook*. Santa Barbara, CA: ABC-CLIO.

Arad, Y., Gutman, I., & Abraham, M. (1999). *Documents on the Holocaust: Selected sources on the destruction of the Jews of Germany and Austria, Poland, and the Soviet Union* (8th, Bison Books ed.). Lincoln; Jerusalem: University of Nebraska Press.

Arendt, H. (1965). Eichmann in Jerusalem. A report on the banality of evil. *Revue Française de Sociologie*, 6(1), 100. doi:10.2307/3319667.
ASA Committee on Professional Ethics. 1999 (2008). *Code of ethics*. Washington, DC: American Sociological Association.
Auerbacher, I. (1993). *I am a star: Child of the Holocaust*. New York, NY: Puffin.
Auerbacher, I. (1995). *Beyond the yellow star to America*. Unionville; New York, NY: Royal Fireworks Press.
Auerbacher, I., & Gilbride, B. U. (2009). *Children of terror*. New York, NY: IUniverse.
Bardgett, S., & Cesarani, D. (2006). *Belsen 1945: New historical perspectives* (Vol. null). Edgware, Portland, OR: Vallentine Mitchell.
Baron, L. (2010). Film. In P. Hayes & J. K. Roth (Eds.), *The Oxford handbook of Holocaust studies*. Oxford: Oxford University Press.
Bartrop, P. R. (2016). *Resisting the Holocaust: Upstanders, partisans, and survivors*. Santa Barbara, CA: ABC-CLIO, An Imprint of ABC-CLIO, LLC.
Bastel, H., Matzka, C., & Miklas, H. (2010). Holocaust education in Austria: A (hi) story of complexity and ambivalence. *Prospects*, 40(1), 57–73. doi:10.1007/s11125-010-9147-5.
Bauer, Y. (1989). *Jewish reactions to the Holocaust*. Tel-Aviv: MOD Books.
Bauer, Y. (2001). *Rethinking the Holocaust*. New Haven, CT: Yale University Press.
Bauer, Y. (2010). Understanding the Holocaust: Some problems for educators. *Prospects*, 40(2), 183–188. doi:10.1007/s11125-010-9154-6.
Bauer, Y., & Keren, N. (2001). *A history of the Holocaust* (Rev. ed.). New York, NY: Franklin Watts.
Bauman, Z. (1989). *Modernity and the Holocaust*. Ithaca, NY: Cornell University Press.
Bazyler, M. J. (2016). *Holocaust, genocide, and the law: A quest for justice in a post-Holocaust world* (1st ed.). New York, NY: Oxford University Press.
Bazyler, M. J., & Roger, P. A. (2006). *Holocaust restitution: Perspectives on the litigation and its legacy*. New York, NY: New York University Press.
Bazyler, M. J., & Tuerkheimer, F. M. (2014). *Forgotten trials of the Holocaust*. New York, NY: New York University Press.
Beim, A., & Fine, G. A. (2007). Trust in testimony: The institutional embeddedness of Holocaust survivor narratives. *European Journal of Sociology/Archives Européennes de Sociologie*, 48(1), 55–75. doi:10.1017/S000397560700029X.
Belzberg, E. (2016). *Watchers of the sky*. San Francisco, CA: USA Music Box Films.
Ben-Bassat, N. (2000). Holocaust awareness and education in the United States. *Religious Education*, 95(4), 402–423. doi:10.1080/0034408000950404.
Berenbaum, M. (2010). Judaism. In P. Hayes & J. K. Roth (Eds.), *The Oxford handbook of Holocaust studies* (pp. 607–619). Oxford: Oxford University Press.
Berenbaum, M., & Museum United States Holocaust Memorial. (1993). *The world must know: The history of the Holocaust as told in the United States Holocaust memorial museum* (1st ed.). Boston, MA: Little, Brown.
Bergen, D. L. (2016). *War and genocide: A concise history of the Holocaust* (Vol. 3). Lanham, MD: Rowman & Littlefield Publishers, Inc.
Best, J. (2013). *Social problems* (2nd ed.). New York, NY: W. W. Norton & Company, Inc.
Bigsby, C. W. E. (2006). *Remembering and imagining the Holocaust: The chain of memory*. Cambridge, New York, NY: Cambridge University Press.

References

Block, G., & Drucker, M. (1992). *Rescuers: Portraits of moral courage in the Holocaust.* New York, NY: Holmes & Meier.
Bokova, I. (2014). Forward. In K. Fracapane & M. Hass (Eds.), *Holocaust education in a global context* (pp. 5–6). Paris: United Nations Educational, Scientific and Cultural Organization (UNESCO).
Bonilla-Silva, E. (2014). *Racism without racists: Color-blind racism and the persistence of racial inequality in America.* Lanham, MD: Rowman & Littlefield Publishers, Inc.
Bonilla-Silva, E. (2015). The structure of racism in color-blind, "post-racial" America. *American Behavioral Scientist, 59*(11), 1358–1376. doi:10.1177/0002764215586826.
Bonilla-Silva, E. (2018). *Racism without racists: Color-blind racism and the persistence of racial inequality in America* (5th ed.). Lanham, MD: Rowman & Littlefield Publishers, Inc.
Boyne, J. (2006). *The boy in the striped pajamas: A fable* (1st American ed.). New York, NY: David Fickling Books.
Brenner, R. F. (1997). *Writing as resistance: Four women confronting the Holocaust: Edith Stein, Simone Weil, Anne Frank, Etty Hillesum.* University Park, PA: Pennsylvania State University Press.
Brodkin, K. (1998). *How Jews became white folks and what that says about race in America.* New Brunswick, NJ: Rutgers University Press.
Bromley, P., & Russell, S. G. (2010). The Holocaust as history and human rights: A cross-national analysis of Holocaust education in social science textbooks, 1970–2008. *Prospects: Quarterly Review of Comparative Education, 40*(1), 153–173. doi:10.1007/s11125-010-9139-5.
Browning, C. R. (2000). *Nazi policy, Jewish workers, German killers.* New York, Cambridge: Cambridge University Press.
Buettner, A. (2009). Skeletal figures – presence and the unrepresentable in images of catastrophe. *Continuum, 23*(3), 351–366. doi:10.1080/10304310902862890.
Bukiet, M. J. (2002). *Nothing makes you free: Writings by descendants of Jewish Holocaust survivors* (1st ed.). New York, NY: W. W. Norton & Company, Inc.
Carini, P. F. (2001). *Starting strong: A different look at children, schools, and standards.* New York, NY: Teachers College Press.
Carrier, P., Fuchs, E., & Messinger, T. (2015). *International status of education about the Holocaust: A global mapping of textbooks and curricula.* Paris: UNESCO.
Celinscak, M. (2015). *Distance from the Belsen heap: Allied forces and the liberation of a Nazi concentration camp.* London: University of Toronto Press.
Cesarani, D. (2010). Adolf Eichmann: The making of a 'genocidaire'. *Teaching History,* (141), 40.
Cesarani, D. (2006). *Becoming Eichmann: Rethinking the life, crimes, and trial of a "desk murderer".* 1st Da Capo Press (Ed.). Cambridge, MA: Da Capo Press.
Cesarani, D. (2016). *Final solution: The fate of the Jews 1933–49.* London: Macmillan.
Cesarani, D., & Levine, P. A. (2002). *"Bystanders" to the Holocaust: A re-evaluation.* London; Portland, OR: Frank Cass.
Chang, G. H. (2001). *Asian Americans and politics: Perspectives, experiences, prospects.* Stanford, Calif; Washington, DC: Woodrow Wilson Center Press.
Chapman, A., & Rebecca, H. (2017). Understanding what young people know: Methodological and theoretical challenges in researching young people's knowledge and understanding of the Holocaust. *Holocaust Studies, 23*(3), 289–313. doi:10.1080/17504902.2017.1296067.

Chelsea, E. S., & Shaw Greg, M. (2009). Tolerance in the United States. *Public Opinion Quarterly, 73*(2), 404.

Cohen, A. (1994). *The gate of light: Janusz Korczak, the educator and writer who overcame the Holocaust.* Rutherford, NJ: Fairleigh Dickinson University Press.

Cohen, E. H. (2016). Teacher autonomy within a flexible national curriculum: Development of Shoah (Holocaust) education in Israeli state schools. *Journal of Curriculum Studies, 48*(2), 167–191. doi:10.1080/00220272.2015.1033464.

Cohen, J., Roth, I., Berenbaum, M., Arnold, M., Kopp, R., & Theater National Jewish. (2013). *Documentary: I will refuse to bubble.* London: Digital Theatre Plus.

Cohen, B., & Vazsonyi, A. (2013). *Israeli Holocaust research: Birth and evolution.* New York, NY; Abingdon: Routledge.

Cole, T. (2004). Nativization and nationalization: A comparative landscape study of Holocaust museums in Israel, the US and the UK. *Journal of Israeli History, 23*(1), 130–145. doi:10.1080/1353104042000241965.

Cole, T. (2011). *Traces of the Holocaust: Journeying in and out of the ghettos.* London; New York, NY: Continuum.

Colen, C. G., Ramey, D. M., Cooksey, E. C., & Williams, D. R. (2018). Racial disparities in health among nonpoor African Americans and Hispanics: The role of acute and chronic discrimination. *Social Science & Medicine, 199*, 167–180. doi: 10.1016/j.socscimed.2017.04.051.

Collins, P. H. (2012). Looking back, moving ahead: Scholarship in service to social justice. *Gender & Society, 26*(1), 14–22. doi:10.1177/0891243211434766.

Collins, P. H. (2015). *Intersectionality's definitional dilemmas.* In (pp. 1–20). Palo Alto, CA: Annual Reviews.

Collins, P. H. (2016). Toward a new vision: Race, class, and gender as categories of analysis and connection. In S. Ferguson (Ed.), *Race, gender, sexuality, social class: Dimensions of inequality.* Thousand Oaks, CA: SAGE Publications, Inc.

Collins, P. H., & Bilge, S. (2016). *Intersectionality.* Malden, MA; Cambridge: Polity Press.

Conot, R. E. (1983). *Justice at Nuremberg* (1st ed.). New York, NY: Harper & Row.

Cooper, J. (2008). *Raphael Lemkin and the struggle for the genocide convention.* New York, NY: Palgrave Macmillan.

Council on Foreign Relations (CFR), & National Geographic. (2016). *What college-aged students know about the world: A survey on global literacy.* Washington, DC: https://www.cfr.org/content/newsletter/files/CFR_NatGeo_ASurveyonGlobalLiteracy.pdf.

Cowan, P., & Henry, M. (2007). Does addressing prejudice and discrimination through Holocaust education produce better citizens? *Educational Review, 59*(2), 115–130. doi:10.1080/00131910701254858.

Cowan, P., & Henry, M. (2011). "We saw inhumanity close up." What is gained by school students from Scotland visiting Auschwitz? *Journal of Curriculum Studies, 43*(2), 163.

Cowan, P., & Henry, M. (2017). *Understanding and teaching Holocaust education.* Los Angeles, CA; London: SAGE Publications, Inc.

Curry, A. (2010). The 'blind space' that lies beyond the frame: Anne Provoost's *Falling* (1997) and John Boyne's *The Boy in the Striped Pyjamas* (2006). *International Research in Children's Literature, 3*(1), 61–74. doi:10.3366/ircl.2010.0006.

Davis, B. L., & Rubinstein-Avila, E. (2013). Holocaust education: Global forces shaping curricula integration and implementation. *Intercultural Education, 24*(1–2), 149.
Dawidowicz, L. S. (1976). *A Holocaust reader.* New York, NY: Behrman House.
Dean, M. C. (2010). *Ghettos.* Oxford: Oxford University Press.
Dean, M., & Hecker, M. (2012). *The United States Holocaust memorial museum encyclopedia of camps and ghettos, 1933–1945.* Bloomington, IN: Indiana University Press.
Des Pres, T. (1976). *The survivor: An anatomy of life in the death camps.* New York, NY: Oxford University Press.
Desmond, M., & Emirbayer, M. (2016). *Race in America.* New York, NY: W. W. Norton & Company, Inc.
Deutsch, N., Nurit, E. P., & Granot-Bein, Y. (2018). Six teaching orientations of Holocaust educators as reflections of teaching perspectives and meaning making processes. *Teaching and Teacher Education, 71,* 86–97. doi:10.1016/j.tate.2017.12.004.
Dewey, J. (1909). *Moral principles in education.* Breinigsville, PA: Merchant Books.
Docker, J. (2010). Raphael Lemkin, creator of the concept of genocide: A world history perspective. *Humanities Research, 16*(2), 49.
Dodd, C., & Bloom, L. (2007). *Letters from Nuremberg.* New York, NY: Crown.
Druker, J. (1994). Primo Levi's survival in Auschwitz and the drowned and the saved: From testimony to historical judgment. *Shofar: An Interdisciplinary Journal of Jewish Studies, 12*(4), 47–58. doi:10.1353/sho.1994.0101.
Duckworth, A. (2016). *Grit: The power of passion and perseverance* (First Scribner hardcover ed.). New York, NY: Scribner.
Durkheim, É., & Pickering, W. S. F. (1979). *Durkheim: Essays on morals and education.* London; Boston, MA: Routledge & Kegan Paul.
Dwork, D. (Ed.). (2002). *Voices & views: A history of the Holocaust.* New York, NY: Jewish Foundation for the Righteous.
Dwork, D. (2010). Rescuers. In P. Hayes & J. K. Roth (Eds.), *The Oxford handbook of Holocaust studies.* Oxford: Oxford University Press.
Dwork, D., & van Pelt, R. J. (2009). *Flight from the Reich: Refugee Jews, 1933–1946* (1st ed.). New York, NY: W. W. Norton & Company, Inc.
Eckmann, M. (2010). Exploring the relevance of Holocaust education for human rights education. *Prospects, 40*(1), 7–16. doi:10.1007/s11125-010-9140-z.
Epstein, H. (1979). *Children of the Holocaust: Conversations with sons and daughters of survivors.* New York, NY: Putnam.
Epstein, T. (2018). Constructing and questioning connections between history education and heritage education. *Theory & Research in Social Education, 46*(2), 325–329. doi:10.1080/00933104.2017.1386960.
Epstein, T., & Peck, C. L. (2018). *Teaching and learning difficult histories in international contexts: A critical sociocultural approach.* New York, NY: Routledge.
Evans, R. J. (2001). *Lying about Hitler: History, Holocaust, and the David Irving trial.* New York, NY: Basic Books.
Facing History and Ourselves. (2018). *Holocaust topics.* FHAO. Retrieved from https://www.facinghistory.org/topics/holocaust.

Fallace, T. D. (2006). The origins of Holocaust education in American public schools. *Holocaust and Genocide Studies, 20*(1), 80–102. doi:10.1093/hgs/dcj004.

Fallace, T. D. (2008). *The emergence of Holocaust education in American schools* (Vol. 1). New York, NY: Palgrave Macmillan.

Favez, J. -C. (1999). *The red cross and the Holocaust*. Cambridge, UK; New York, NY: Cambridge University Press.

Fein, H. (1979a). *Accounting for genocide: National responses and Jewish victimization during the Holocaust*. New York, NY: Free Press.

Fein, H. (1979b). Is sociology aware of genocide? Recognition of genocide in introductory sociology texts in the United States, 1947–1977. *Humanity & Society, 3*(3), 177–193.

Fein, H. (1990). Social recognition and criminalization of genocide. *Current Sociology, 38*(1), 1–7. doi:10.1177/001139290038001003.

Fein, H. (2000). Civil wars and genocide: Paths and circles. *Human Rights Review, 1*(3), 49–61. doi:10.1007/s12142-000-1021-z.

Fein, H. (2007). *Human rights and wrongs: Slavery, terror, genocide*. Boulder, CO: Paradigm Publishers.

Feinberg, S., & Totten, S. (2016). Foundational concerns: Developing historically accurate and pedagogically sound Holocaust lessons and units. In S. Totten & S. Feinberg (Eds.), *Essentials of Holocaust education: Fundamental issues and approaches* (pp. 1–17). New York, NY: Routledge.

Feingold, H. L. (1995). *Bearing witness: How America and its Jews responded to the Holocaust* (1st ed.). Syracuse, NY: Syracuse University Press.

Fermaglich, K. L., & Foundation Koret. (2006). *American dreams and Nazi nightmares: Early Holocaust consciousness and liberal America, 1957–1965*. Hanover; Waltham, MA: Brandeis University Press.

Flanzbaum, H. (1999). *The Americanization of the Holocaust*. Baltimore, MD: Johns Hopkins University Press.

Fogelman, E., Cohen, S. K., & Ofer, D. (2017). *Children in the Holocaust and its aftermath: Historical and psychological studies of the Kestenberg Archive*. New York, NY: Berghahn.

Foster, S., & Karayianni, E. (2017). Portrayals of the Holocaust in English history textbooks, 1991–2016: Continuities, challenges and concerns. *Holocaust Studies, 23*(3), 314–344. doi:10.1080/17504902.2017.1296087.

Foster, S. J., & Keith, C. (2006). *What shall we tell the children? International perspectives on school history textbooks*. Greenwich, CT: IAP- Information Age Pub. Inc.

Foster, S. J., Pettigrew, A., Pearce, A. R., Hale, R., Burgess, A., Paul, S., & Lenga, R. (2016). *What do students know and understand about the Holocaust? Evidence from English secondary schools*. London: Center for Holocaust Education, UCL.

Fracapane, K., & Hass, M. (2014). *Holocaust education in a global context*. Paris: United Nations Educational, Scientific and Cultural Organization (UNESCO).

Frank, A. (1993). *Anne Frank: The diary of a young girl*. New York, NY: Bantam Books.

Frank, A. W. (2013). *The wounded storyteller: Body, illness, and ethics* (2nd ed.). London; Chicago, IL: The University of Chicago Press.

Frank, A., Hardy, H. J. J., Barnouw, D., van der Stroom, G., Laboratorium Netherlands Gerechtelijk, & Oorlogsdocumentatie Rijksinstituut voor. (2003). *The diary of Anne Frank: The revised critical edition* (Rev. Critical ed.). New York, NY: Doubleday.

Frankl, V. E. (1992). *Man's search for meaning: An introduction to logotherapy* (4th ed.). Boston, MA: Beacon Press.

Freedman, R. (2014). Engaging with Holocaust education in post-apartheid South Africa. In K. Fracapane & M. Hass (Eds.), *Holocaust education in a global context* (pp. 134–142). Paris: United Nations Educational, Scientific and Cultural Organization (UNESCO).

Friedländer, S. (2003). *When memory comes*. Madison, WI: University of Wisconsin Press.

Frieze, D-L. (2013). New approaches to Raphael Lemkin. *Journal of Genocide Research, 15*(3), 247–252.

Gardner, H. (1999). *The disciplined mind: What all students should understand*. New York, NY: Simon & Schuster.

Garroutte, E. M. (2001). The racial formation of American Indians: Negotiating legitimate identities within tribal and federal law. *American Indian Quarterly, 25*(2), 224–239.

Gates, H. L., Jr., & West, C. (2000). *The African-American century: How black Americans have shaped our country*. New York, NY: Free Press.

Gebert, K. (2014). Conflicting memories: Poland and Jewish perceptions of the Shoah. In K. Fracapane & M. Hass (Eds.), *Holocaust education in a global context* (pp. 28–39). Paris: United Nations Educational, Scientific and Cultural Organization (UNESCO).

Gerber, D. A. (1986). *Anti-Semitism in American history*. Urbana, IL: University of Illinois Press.

Gilbert, M. (2000). *Never again: A history of the Holocaust*. New York, NY: Universe.

Goodman, S. (2018). *It's not about grit: Trauma, inequity, and the power of transformative teaching*. New York, NY: Teachers College Press.

Gray, M. (2014). *Contemporary debates in Holocaust education*. Basingstoke: Palgrave Macmillan.

Greenspan, H. (1999). Listening to Holocaust survivors: Interpreting a repeated story. *Shofar, 17*(4), 83–88.

Greenspan, H. (2010a). *On listening to Holocaust survivors: Beyond testimony* (2nd, Rev. & expand ed.). St. Paul, MN: Paragon House.

Greenspan, H. (2010b). Survivors' accounts. In P. Hayes & J. K. Roth (Eds.), *The Oxford handbook of Holocaust studies* (pp. 414–427). Oxford: Oxford University Press.

Grever, M. (2018). Teaching the war. In T. Epstein and C. L. Peck (Eds.), *Teaching and learning difficult histories in international contexts: A critical sociocultural approach* (pp. 30–44). New York, NY: Routledge.

Gross, M. H. (2013). To teach the Holocaust in Poland: Understanding teachers' motivations to engage the painful past. *Intercultural Education, 24*(1–2), 103.

Gutmann, A. (1999). *Democratic education: With a new preface and epilogue* (Rev. ed.). Princeton, NJ; Chichester: Princeton University Press.

Hass, A. (1990). *In the shadow of the Holocaust: The second generation*. Ithaca, NY: Cornell University Press.

Hayes, P. (2017). *Why? Explaining the Holocaust* (1st ed.). New York, NY: W. W. Norton & Company, Inc.

Hayes, P., & Roth, J. K. (2010). *The Oxford handbook of Holocaust studies*. Oxford: Oxford University Press.

Herzberg, D., Guarino, H., Mateu-Gelabert, P., & Bennett, A. S. (2016). Recurring epidemics of pharmaceutical drug abuse in America: Time for an all-drug strategy. *American Journal of Public Health, 106*(3), 408–410. doi:10.2105/AJPH.2015.302982.

Heyl, M. (2014). Historic sites as a framework for education. In K. Fracapane & M. Hass (Eds.), *Holocaust education in a global context* (pp. 87–92). Paris: United Nations Educational, Scientific and Cultural Organization (UNESCO).

Hilberg, R. (1978). *The destruction of the European Jews.* New York, NY: Octagon Books.

Hilberg, R. (1993). *Perpetrators victims bystanders: The Jewish catastrophe, 1933–1945* (1st HarperPerennial ed.). New York, NY: HarperPerennial.

Hilgartner, S., & Bosk, C. L. (1988). The rise and fall of social problems: A public arenas model. *American Journal of Sociology, 94*(1), 53–78.

Hinton, A. L. (2002). *Annihilating difference: The anthropology of genocide* (Vol. 3). Berkeley, CA: University of California Press.

Holder, N., Suris, A., Holliday, R., & North, C.S. (2017). Principles of mental health intervention for survivors of major disasters. *Psychiatric Annals, 47*(3), 124–127. doi:10.3928/00485713-20170202-01.

Horowitz, S. R. (2010). Literature. In P. Hayes & J. K. Roth (Eds.), *The Oxford handbook of Holocaust studies* (pp. 428–443). Oxford: Oxford University Press.

House of the Wannsee Conference Education Department. (2018). House of the Wannsee conference memorial. https://www.ghwk.de/en/. Accessed July.

Iceland, J. (2017). *Race and ethnicity in America* (Vol. 2, p. 2). Oakland, CA: University of California Press.

Imber, S. (2016). *Educational philosophy in teaching the Holocaust.* Jerusalem: Yad Vashem.

Imhoff, R., Bilewicz, M., Hanke, K., Kahn, D. T., Henkel-Guembel, N., Halabi, S., ... Hirschberger, G. (2017). Explaining the inexplicable: Differences in attributions for the Holocaust in Germany, Israel, and Poland. *Political Psychology, 38*(6), 907–924. doi:10.1111/pops.12348.

Jacobs, J. L. (2010). *Memorializing the Holocaust: Gender, genocide and collective memory.* London: I. B. Tauris.

Jacobson, S., Colón, E., & Frank, H. A. (2010). *Anne Frank: The Anne Frank House authorized graphic biography* (1st ed.). New York, NY: Hill and Wang.

Jay, M. (2009). *Allegories of evil: A response to Jeffrey Alexander.* Oxford; New York, NY: Oxford University Press.

Jedwab, J. (2010). Measuring Holocaust knowledge and its impact: A Canadian case study. *Prospects, 40*(2), 273–287.

Jensen, R. J. (2007). *Reagan at Bergen-Belsen and Bitburg* (1st ed.). College Station, TX: Texas A&M University Press.

John-Steiner, V. (1985). *Notebooks of the mind: Explorations of thinking* (1st ed.). Albuquerque, NM: University of New Mexico Press.

John-Steiner, V. (2000). *Creative collaboration.* New York, NY; Oxford: Oxford University Press.

Julius, A. (2010). *Trials of the diaspora: A history of anti-semitism in England.* Oxford; New York, NY: Oxford University Press.

Junger, S. (2016). *Tribe: On homecoming and belonging* (1st ed.). New York, NY: Twelve.

Kaiser, W. (2014). Teaching about perpetrators of the Holocaust in Germany. In K. Fracapane & M. Hass (Eds.), *Holocaust education in a global context* (pp. 20–27). Paris: United Nations Educational, Scientific and Cultural Organization (UNESCO).

Kapralski, S. (2018). The Holocaust: Commemorated but not remembered? Postcolonial and post-traumatic perspectives on the reception of the Holocaust memory discourse in Poland. *Journal of Historical Sociology*, *31*(1), e48–e65. doi:10.1111/johs.12165.

Kasinitz, P. (2008). *Inheriting the city: The children of immigrants come of age*. New York, NY; Cambridge, MA: Russell Sage Foundation.

Kelleway, E., Spillane, T., & Haydn, T. (2013). 'Never again'? Helping year 9 think about what happened after the Holocaust and learning lessons from genocides. *Teaching History*, (*153*), 38–44.

Kevles, D. J. (1985). *In the name of eugenics: Genetics and the uses of human heredity* (1st ed.). New York, NY: Alfred A. Knopf.

Kevles, D. J. (2016). The history of Eugenics. *Issues in Science and Technology*, *32*(3), 45–50.

King, M. L., Jr. (1963). *Letter from Birmingham city jail*. Philadelphia, PA: American Friends Service Committee.

King, M. L., Jr., & Honey, M. K. (2011). *All labor has dignity*. Boston, MA: Beacon Press.

Kingston, L. N. (2014). The rise of human rights education: Opportunities, challenges, and future possibilities. *Societies Without Borders*, *9*(2), 188–210.

Kolbert, J. (2001). *The worlds of Elie Wiesel: An overview of his career and his major themes*. London; Selinsgrove, PA: Susquehanna University Press.

Krysan, M. (2000). Prejudice, politics, and public opinion: Understanding the sources of racial policy attitudes. *Annual Review of Sociology*, *26*(1), 135–168. doi:10.1146/annurev.soc.26.1.135.

Kushner, T. (2017). The Holocaust in the British imagination: The official mind and beyond, 1945 to the present. *Holocaust Studies*, *23*(3), 364–384. doi:10.1080/17504902.2017.1296084.

Lake, R., & Connery, M. C. (Eds.). (2013). *Constructing a community of thought: Letters on the scholarship, teaching, and mentoring of Vera John-Steiner* (Vol. 22). New York, NY: Lang.

Lamont, M. (2018). Addressing recognition gaps: Destigmatization and the reduction of inequality. *American Sociological Review*, *83*(3), 419–444. doi:10.1177/0003122418773775.

Lang, B. (2010). Six questions on (or about) Holocaust Denial. *History and Theory*, *49*(2), 157–168.

Langer, L. L. (1983). *The Americanization of the Holocaust on stage and screen*. Bloomington, IN: Indiana University Press.

Langer, L. L. (1986). Holocaust testimonies and their audience. *Orim*, *1*(2), 96–110.

Langer, L. L. (1991). *Holocaust testimonies: The ruins of memory*. New Haven, CT: Yale University Press.

Lawson, T. (2017). Britain's promise to forget: Some historiographical reflections on what do students know and understand about the Holocaust? *Holocaust Studies*, *23*(3), 345–363. doi:10.1080/17504902.2017.1296086.

Lemkin, R. (1944). *Axis rule in occupied Europe: Laws of occupation, analysis of government, proposals for redress*. Washington, DC: Carnegie Endowment for International Peace, Division of International Law.

Lemkin, R. (1947). Genocide as a crime under international law. *The American Journal of International Law*, *41*(1), 145–151.

Lemkin, R. (1948). Genocide as a crime under international law. *United Nations Bulletin, 4*, 70–71.
Lemkin, R., & Jacobs, S. L. (2012). *Lemkin on genocide*. Lanham, MD: Lexington Books.
Lengyel, O. (1995). *Five chimneys*. Chicago, IL: Academy Chicago Publishers.
Levi, P. (1959). *If this is a man*. New York, NY: The Orion Press.
Levi, P. (1978). *Survival in Auschwitz: The Nazi assault on humanity*. New York, NY: Collier Books.
Levi, P. (1979). *If this is a man and the truce*. Harmondsworth: Penguin.
Levi, P. (1986). *Survival in Auschwitz: The Nazi assault on humanity*. New York, NY: Collier Books.
Levi, P. (1989a). *The drowned and the saved* (1st Vintage International ed.). New York, NY: Vintage International.
Levi, P. (1989b). *The mirror maker: Stories and essays* (1st American ed.). New York, NY: Schocken Books.
Levin, N. (1968). *The Holocaust: The destruction of European Jewry, 1933–1945*. New York, NY: T. Y. Crowell Co.
Levy, D., & Sznaider, N. (2002). Memory unbound: The Holocaust and the formation of cosmopolitan memory. *European Journal of Social Theory, 5*(1), 87–106. doi:10.1177/1368431002005001002.
Levy, D., & Sznaider, N. (2006). *The Holocaust and memory in the global age* (English ed.). Philadelphia, PA: Temple University.
Lewy, G. (1965). *The catholic church and Nazi Germany* (1st ed.). New York, NY: McGraw-Hill.
Lewy, G. (2017). *Perpetrators: The world of the Holocaust killers*. New York, NY: Oxford University Press.
Lindemann, A. S. (2000). *Anti-semitism before the Holocaust*. New York, NY; Harlow: Longman.
Lindemann, A. S., & Levy, R. S. (2010). *Antisemitism: A history*. New York, NY: Oxford University Press.
Lindquist, D. H. (2010). Complicating issues in Holocaust education. *Journal of Social Studies Research, 34*(1), 77–93.
Lindquist, D. H. (2013). Defining the Shoah: An opening lesson for a Holocaust unit. *Social Studies, 104*(1), 32–37. doi:10.1080/00377996.2012.660212.
Lipstadt, D. E. (1993). *Denying the Holocaust: The growing assault on truth and memory*. New York, NY; Toronto: Free Press.
Lipstadt, D. E., & David, H. (2016). *Denial: Holocaust history on trial*. First movie tie-in ed. New York, NY: Ecco, an imprint of HarperCollins.
Longerich, P. (2010). *Holocaust: The Nazi persecution and murder of the Jews* (Vol. [English ed.]). Oxford: OUP Oxford. Book.
Lower, W. (2017). *The Holocaust in the East: Local perpetrators and soviet responses*. London: SAGE Publications, Inc.
Luckert, S., Bachrach, S. D., & United States Holocaust Memorial Museum. (2009). *State of deception: The power of Nazi propaganda*. Washington, DC: United States Holocaust Memorial Museum.
Magid, S. (2012). The Holocaust and Jewish identity in America: Memory, the unique, and the universal. *Jewish Social Studies: History, Culture, Society, 18*(2), 100–135. doi:10.2979/jewisocistud.18.2.100.

Magilow, D. H., & Silverman, L. (2015). *Holocaust representations in history: An introduction*. London; New York, NY: Bloomsbury Academic.

Maitles, H. (2014). What type of citizenship education; what type of citizen? *UN Chronicle, 50*(4), 17–20. doi:10.18356/7295804a-en.

Majer, D., & Museum United States Holocaust Memorial. (2003). *"Non-Germans" under the Third Reich: The Nazi judicial and administrative system in Germany and occupied Eastern Europe with special regard to occupied Poland, 1939–1945*. Baltimore, MD: Johns Hopkins University Press.

Marceau, M. (2002). How I worked in the French resistance and created Bip as a figure of hope. *Michigan Quarterly Review (Univ. of Michigan, Ann Arbor), 41*(1), 114.

Marcus, K. L. (2015). *The definition of anti-semitism*. New York, NY: Oxford University Press.

Martin, D. (2014). Good education for all? Student race and identity development in the multicultural classroom. *International Journal of Intercultural Relations, 39*(0), 110–123.

Matthäus, J. (2009). *Approaching an Auschwitz survivor: Holocaust testimony and its transformations*. New York, NY; Oxford: Oxford University Press.

McGuire, S. Y., & McGuire, S. (2018). *Teach yourself how to learn: Strategies you can use to ace any course at any level* (1st ed.). Sterling, VA: Stylus Publishing, LLC.

McRainey, D. L., & Russick, J. (2010). *Connecting kids to history with museum exhibitions*. Walnut Creek, CA: Left Coast Press.

Milgram, S. (1963). Behavioral studies in obedience. *Journal of Abnormal Psychology, 67*.

Miller, K. D. (2012). *Martin Luther King's biblical epic: His final, great speech*. Jackson, MS: University Press of Mississippi.

Mills, C. W. (1966). *The sociological imagination*. New York, NY: Oxford University Press.

Mirel, J. (2002). The decline of civic education. *Daedalus, 131*(3), 49–55.

Mitchell, B. M., & Salsbury, R. E. (1999). *Encyclopedia of multicultural education*. Westport, CT: Greenwood Press.

Monroe, K. R., Lampros-Monroe, C., and Pellecchia, J. R. (2015). *A darkling plain: Stories of conflict and humanity during war*. New York, NY: Cambridge University Press.

Moore, D. D., & Inc ebrary. (2004). *GI Jews: How World War II changed a generation*. Cambridge, MA: Belknap Press of Harvard University Press.

Most, A., & Muse Project. (2013). *Theatrical liberalism: Jews and popular entertainment in America*. New York, NY: New York University Press.

Napolitano, D. C., Totten, S., Berenbaum, M., Imber, S., Budd Caplan, D., Levine, P., & Shulman, W. (2007). Holocaust: Education. In M. Berenbaum & F. Skolnik (Eds.), *Encyclopedia Judaica* (pp. 447–459). Detroit, MI: Macmillan Reference USA.

Ngai, M. M. (2004). *Impossible subjects: Illegal aliens and the making of modern America*. Princeton, NJ: Princeton University Press.

Ngai, M. M. (2010). *The lucky ones: One family and the extraordinary invention of Chinese America*. Boston, MA: Houghton Mifflin Harcourt.

Ngai, M. M., & Gjerde, J. (2013). *Major problems in American immigration history: Documents and essays* (2nd ed.). Boston, MA: Wadsworth, Cengage Learning.

Niemoller, M. (2007). I did not speak. *Earth Focus One Planet-One Community*, (32), 2.

North, C. S., & Betty, P. (2013). Mental health response to community disasters: A systematic review. *JAMA, 310*(5), 507–518. doi:10.1001/jama.2013.107799.

Novick, P. (1999). *The Holocaust in American life*. Boston, MA: Houghton Mifflin.

Olick, J. K., & Levy, D. (1997). Collective memory and cultural constraint: Holocaust myth and rationality in German politics. *American Sociological Review, 62*(6), 921–936.

Pakula, A. J., & Styron, W. (1982). *Sophie's choice: Screenplay*. Hollywood, CA: Script City.

Patterson, O. (1998). *Rituals of blood: Consequences of slavery in two American centuries*. New York, NY: Basic/Civitas Books.

Paynter, E. (2018). The liminal lives of Europe's transit migrants. *Contexts, 17*(2), 40–45. doi:10.1177/1536504218776959.

Pearce, A. (2008). The development of Holocaust consciousness in contemporary Britain, 1979–2001. *Holocaust Studies, 14*(2),71–94. doi:10.1080/17504902.2008.11087217.

Pearce, A. (2014). *Holocaust consciousness in contemporary Britain* (Vol. 27). New York, NY: Routledge.

Pearce, A., & Chapman, A. (2017). Holocaust education 25 years on: Challenges, issues, opportunities. *Holocaust Studies, 23*(3), 223–230. doi:10.1080/17504902.2017.1296082.

Penslar, D. J. (2013). *Jews and the military: A history*. Princeton, NJ: Princeton University Press.

Perl, S. (2004). *Writing the Holocaust: The transformative power of response journals*. New York, NY: Modern Language Association of America.

Pettigrew, A. (2017). Why teach or learn about the Holocaust? Teaching aims and student knowledge in English secondary schools. *Holocaust Studies, 23*(3), 263–288. doi:10.1080/17504902.2017.1296069.

Pingel, F. (2006). From evasion to a crucial tool of moral and political education: Teaching national socialism and the Holocaust in Germany. In S. J. Foster & K. Crawford (Eds.), *What shall we tell the children? International perspectives on school history textbooks* (pp. 131–154). Greenwich, CT: IAP- Information Age Pub. Inc.

Pingel, F. (2014). The Holocaust in textbooks: From a European to a global event. In K. Fracapane & M. Hass (Eds.), *Holocaust education in a global context* (pp. 77–86). Paris: United Nations Educational, Scientific and Cultural Organization (UNESCO).

Polgar, M. (2015). *Human rights education in Pennsylvania: Helping US remember*. ASA Annual Conference, Chicago, IL, 2015.

Portes, A., Fernández-Kelly, P., & Haller, W. (2009). The adaptation of the immigrant second generation in America: A theoretical overview and recent evidence. *Journal of Ethnic and Migration Studies, 35*(7), 1077–1104. doi:10.1080/13691830903006127.

Portes, A., & Rumbaut, R. G. (2014). *Immigrant America: A portrait* (4th ed.). Oakland, CA: University of California Press.

Potter, S. J. (2016). Reducing sexual assault on campus: Lessons from the movement to prevent drunk driving. *American Journal of Public Health, 106*(5), 822–829. doi: 10.2105/AJPH.2016.303082.

Power, S. (2002). *A problem from hell: America and the age of genocide* (Vol. 1st Perennial). New York, NY: Perennial.

President's Commission on the Holocaust Elie Wiesel – Chairman. (1979). *Report to the president*. Washington, DC: USGPO.

Prose, F. (2009). *Anne Frank: The book, the life, the afterlife* (1st ed.). New York, NY: Harper.

Rafter, N. H. (1992). Claims-making and socio-cultural context in the first U.S. Eugenics campaign. *Social Problems, 39*(1), 17–34. doi:10.2307/3096909.

Reilly, J. (1997). *Belsen in history and memory*. London: F. Cass, Routledge.

Reinherz, A. (2014, June 19). Legislators sign off on Holocaust education. *Jewish Chronicle*, 4.

Rice, C. (2010). *Extraordinary, ordinary people: A memoir of family* (1st ed.). New York, NY: Crown Archetype.

Rice, M. (2017). *"What! Still alive?!": Jewish survivors in Poland and Israel remember homecoming* (1st ed.). Syracuse, NY: Syracuse University Press.

Rittner, C., & Roth, J. K. (1997). *From the unthinkable to the unavoidable: American Christian and Jewish scholars encounter the Holocaust* (Vol. 48). Westport, CT: Greenwood Press.

Rohrlich, R. (1998). *Resisting the Holocaust*. New York, NY; Oxford: Berg.

Rosenbaum, A. S. (2009). *Is the Holocaust unique? Perspectives on comparative genocide* (3rd ed.). Boulder, CO: Westview Press.

Rosenberg, B. H., & Rozwaski, C. Z. (1999). *Contemplating the Holocaust*. Northvale, NJ: Jason Aronson.

Roth, I. (2016). *Holocaust survivor testimony*. TOLI Summer Seminar, New York, NY.

Roth, I., & Roth, E. (2004). *Bondi's brother*. Williston Park, NY: Shoah Educational Enterprise.

Rumbaut, R. G., & Alejandro, P. (2001). *Ethnicities: Children of immigrants in America*. Berkeley, CA: University of California Press.

Russell, L. (2006). *Teaching the Holocaust in school history*. London: Continuum.

Ryan, W. (1971). *Blaming the victim*. (Vol. 762). New York, NY: Vintage books.

Saidel, R. G. (1996). *Never too late to remember: The politics behind New York City's Holocaust museum*. New York, NY: Holmes & Meier.

Santayana, G., Wokeck, M. S., Coleman, M. A., & Gouinlock, J. (2011). *The life of reason, or, the phases of human progress* (Critical ed., Vol. 7). Cambridge, MA: MIT Press.

Sarna, J. D. (2004). *American Judaism: A history*. New Haven, CT: Yale University Press.

Schoen Consulting. (2018). *The Holocaust knowledge and awareness study*. Conference on Jewish Material Claims Against Germany.

Schweber, S. (2004). *Making sense of the Holocaust: Lessons from classroom practice*. New York, NY: Teachers College Press.

Schweber, S. (2008). "What happened to their pets?": Third graders encounter the Holocaust. *Teachers College Record, 110*(10), 2073–2115.

Schweber, S. (2010). Education. In P. Hayes & J. K. Roth (Eds.), *The Oxford handbook of Holocaust studies* (pp. 695–708). Oxford: Oxford University Press.
Schweber, S. (2011). Holocaust education. In (pp. 461–478). Dordrecht: Springer Netherlands.
Senesh, H. (2004). *Hannah Senesh: Her life and diary* (1st complete ed.). Woodstock, VT: Jewish Lights Pub.
Shamai, S., Yardeni, E., & Klages, B. (2004). Multicultural education: Israeli and German adolescents' knowledge and views regarding the Holocaust. *Adolescence, 39*(156), 765–778.
Shermer, M., & Grobman, A. (2000). *Denying history: Who says the Holocaust never happened and why do they say it?* Berkeley, CA: University of California Press.
Short, G. (1999). Antiracist education and moral behaviour: Lessons from the Holocaust. *Journal of Moral Education, 28*(1), 49–62. doi:10.1080/030572499 103304.
Short, G. (2003). Lessons of the Holocaust: A response to the critics. *Educational Review, 55*(3), 277–287. doi:10.1080/0013191032000118938.
Short, G., & Reed, C. A. (2004). *Issues in Holocaust education*. Burlington, VT: Ashgate.
Simon, R. I. (2006). The terrible gift: Museums and the possibility of hope without consolation. *Museum Management and Curatorship, 21*(3), 187–204.
Smith, T. W. (1995). *Holocaust denial: What the survey data reveal*. New York, NY: American Jewish Committee (AJC).
Smith, K. L., King, M. L., Jr., & Zepp, I. G. (1986). *Search for the beloved community: The thinking of Martin Luther King, Jr.* Lanham, MD: University Press of America.
Snider, C., Aichele, C., Glenn, S. D., & Wittig, L. (2017). *Report on instruction in the Holocaust, genocide and human rights violations*. US: Pennsylvania. Retrieved from http://www.stateboard.education.pa.gov/Documents/.
Snipp, C. M. (2003). Racial measurement in the American census: Past practices and implications for the future. *Annual Review of Sociology, 29*(1), 563–588. doi: 10.1146/annurev.soc.29.010202.100006.
Snipp, C. M. (2010). Defining race and ethnicity: The constitution, the Supreme Court, and the census. In H. Markus & P. Moya (Eds.), *Doing race* (pp. 105–122). New York, NY: W. W. Norton & Company, Inc.
Snyder, T. (2012). The causes of the Holocaust. *Contemporary European History, 21*(2), 149–168. doi:10.1017/S0960777312000094.
Snyder, T. (2015a). *Black earth: The Holocaust as history and warning* (1st ed.). New York, NY: Tim Duggan Books.
Snyder, T. (2015b). *The Holocaust as history and warning*. Washington, DC: USHMM.
Southern Poverty Law Center. (2017). *Teaching tolerance*. Montgomery, AL: Southern Poverty Law Center.
Spector, K. (2007). God on the gallows: Reading the Holocaust through narratives of redemption. *Research in the Teaching of English, 42*(1), 7–55.
Spiegelman, A. (1997). *Maus: A survivor's tale* (1st ed.). New York, NY: Pantheon Books.
Spiegelman, A. (2011). *Maus: A survivor's tale* (25th anniversary ed.). New York, NY: Pantheon Books.
Spinelli, J. (2003). *Milkweed: A novel* (1st ed.). New York, NY: Alfred A. Knopf.

Stefaniak, A., & Bilewicz, M. (2016). Contact with a multicultural past: A prejudice-reducing intervention. *International Journal of Intercultural Relations, 50*, 60–65. doi:10.1016/j.ijintrel.2015.11.004.

Stein, A. (2009). Trauma and origins: Post-Holocaust genealogists and the work of memory. *Qualitative Sociology, 32*(3), 293–309. doi:10.1007/s11133-009-9131-7.

Stein, A. (2014). *Reluctant witnesses: Survivors, their children, and the rise of Holocaust consciousness*. New York, NY: Oxford University Press.

Stevick, D. (2018). *How does education about the Holocaust advance global citizenship education?* Paris: UNESCO. Retrieved from http://unesdoc.unesco.org/images/0026/002619/261969e.pdf.

Stevick, D., & Gross, Z. (2014). Research in Holocaust education: Emerging themes. In K. Fracapane & M. Hass (Eds.), *Holocaust education in a global context* (pp. 59–76). Paris: United Nations Educational, Scientific and Cultural Organization (UNESCO).

Stevick, E. D., & Michaels, D. L. (2013). Holocaust education: Promise, practice, power, and potential [special issue]. *Intercultural Education, 24*(1–2), 1–179. doi:10.1080/14675986.2013.793025.

Stone, D. (2016). Distance from the Belsen heap: Allied forces and the liberation of a Nazi concentration camp by Mark Celinscak (review). *Holocaust and Genocide Studies, 30*(3), 551–553.

Stone, D. (2017). *Concentration camps: A short history* (1st ed.). Oxford: Oxford University Press.

Styron, W. (1999). *Sophie's choice* (Modern Library ed.). New York, NY: The Modern Library.

Svonkin, S. (1997). *Jews against prejudice: American Jews and the fight for civil liberties*. New York, NY: Columbia University Press.

Tec, N. (2003). *Resilience and courage: Women, men, and the Holocaust*. New Haven, CT: Yale University Press.

The Olga Lengyel Institute for Holocaust Education and Human Rights (TOLI). (2017). *The Olga Lengyel Institute (TOLI)*. New York, NY: TOLI. Retrieved from https://www.toli.us/.

The Olga Lengyel Institute (TOLI). (2018). *Reclaiming our humanity: Lessons of the Holocaust for today*. New York, NY: TOLI. Retrieved from https://www.toli.us/satellite-program/mississippi/.

Thomson, I. (2002). *Primo Levi*. London: Hutchinson.

Tinberg, H. (2005). Taking (and teaching) the Shoah personally. *College English, 68*(1), 72.

Tinberg, H., & Weisberger, R. (2014). Bystanders and agents. In (p. 51). Bloomington, IN: Indiana University Press.

Tinberg, H. B., Weisberger, R., & Muse, P. (2013). *Teaching, learning, and the Holocaust: An integrative approach*. Bloomington, IN: Indiana University Press.

Totten, S. (2002). *Holocaust education: Issues and approaches*. Boston, MA: Allyn and Bacon.

Totten, S. (2003). *Working to make a difference: The personal and pedagogical stories of Holocaust educators across the globe*. Lanham, MD; Boulder, CO; New York, NY: Lexington Books.

Totten, S., Bartrop, P. R., & Jacobs, S. L. (2004). *Teaching about the Holocaust: Essays by college and university teachers*. Westport, CT: Praeger.

Totten, S., & Feinberg, S. (2001). *Teaching and studying the Holocaust*. Boston, MA: Allyn and Bacon.

Totten, S., & Feinberg, S. (2016). *Essentials of Holocaust education: Fundamental issues and approaches* (Vol. 1). New York, NY: Routledge.

Totten, S., & Pedersen, J. E. (1997). *Social issues and service at the middle level*. Boston, MA: Allyn and Bacon.

Tumolo, M. W. (2015). *Just remembering: Rhetorics of genocide remembrance and sociopolitical judgment*. Madison, WI; Lanham, MD: Fairleigh Dickinson University Press.

Türk, V., Edwards, A., & Wouters, C. W. (2017). *In flight from conflict and violence: UNHCR's consultations on refugee status and other forms of international protection*. Cambridge: Cambridge University Press.

UNESCO: United Nations Educational Scientific and Cultural Organization, OSCE: Organization for Security and Co-operation in Europe. (2018). *Addressing antisemitism through education*. Poland: UNESCO. Retrieved from http://unesdoc.unesco.org/images/0026/002640/264042e.pdf.

United Nations. (2017 (Enacted 1948), 10 December 1948). *Universal declaration of human rights*. Retrieved from http://www.un.org/en/universal-declaration-human-rights/index.html.

United States Federal Bureau of Investigation (FBI). (2017). *Crime in the United States. (Journal, Electronic)*. Retrieved from https://ucr.fbi.gov/crime-in-the-u.s/2017.

United States Holocaust Memorial Museum. (2018). *Teaching about the Holocaust: Resources for educators*. Washington, DC: United States Holocaust Memorial Museum. Retrieved from http://www.ushmm.org/educators.

Universal Declaration of Human Rights. General Assembly resolution 217 A. 10 December, 1948.

USC Shoah Foundation. (2018). *iWitness: One voice at a time*. Los Angeles, CA: Institute for Multimedia Literacy at the USC School of Cinematic Arts.

Vági, Z., Csősz, L., & Kádár, G. (2013). *The Holocaust in Hungary: Evolution of a genocide* (Vol. 6, p. 6). Lanham, MD: AltaMira Press, (in association with the United States Holocaust Memorial Museum).

van Boxtel, C., Grever, M., & Klein, S. (2016). *Sensitive pasts: Questioning heritage in education*. New York, NY: Berghahn Books.

Vashem, Y. (1963). *Yad Vashem studies on the European Jewish catastrophe and resistance*. Jerusalem: Yad Vashem.

Venezia, S., & Prasquier, B. (2009). *Inside the gas chambers: Eight months in the Sonderkommando of Auschwitz* (English ed.). Cambridge: Polity.

Wachsmann, N. (2015). *KL: A history of the Nazi concentration camps* (1st ed.). New York, NY: Farrar, Straus and Giroux.

Warner, K. E. (2014). 50 years since the first surgeon general's report on smoking and health: A happy anniversary? *American Journal of Public Health, 104*(1), 5–5. doi: 10.2105/AJPH.2013.301722.

Waxman, Z. (2006). *Writing the Holocaust: Identity, testimony, representation*. Oxford; New York, NY: Oxford University Press.

Waxman, Z. (2017). *Women in the Holocaust: A feminist history* (1st ed.). Oxford: Oxford University Press.

Weiner, P., Weiner, K., & Dwork, D. (2012). *A boy in Terezín: The private diary of Pavel Weiner, April 1944–April 1945*. Evanston, IL: Northwestern University Press.

Weiss, H. (2013). *Helga's diary: A young girl's account of life in a concentration camp*. Penguin. New York, NY: W.W. Norton & Company, Inc.

Wiesel, E. (1995). *All rivers run to the sea: Memoirs* (1st American ed.). New York, NY: Alfred A. Knopf.

Wiesel, E. (1999). *And the sea is never full: Memoirs, 1969* (1st American ed.). New York, NY: Alfred A. Knopf.

Williams, D. R. (2012). Miles to go before we sleep: Racial inequities in health. *Journal of Health and Social Behavior, 53*(3), 279–295. doi:10.1177/0022146512455804.

Wronka, J. (1998). *Human rights and social policy in the 21st century*. Lanham, MD: University Press of America.

Wronka, J. (2017). *Human rights and social justice* (2nd ed.). Thousand Oaks, CA: SAGE Publications, Inc.

Wyman, M. (1989). *DP: Europe's displaced persons, 1945–1951*. London; Philadelphia, PA: Balch Institute Presses.

Wyman, D. S. (1998). *The abandonment of the Jews: America and the Holocaust, 1941–1945*. New York, NY: The New Press.

Yahil, L. (1990). *The Holocaust: The fate of European Jewry, 1932–1945*. New York, NY: Oxford University Press.

Zapruder, A. (2002). *Salvaged pages: Young writers' diaries of the Holocaust*. New Haven, CT: Yale University Press.

Zuberi, T. (2001). *Thicker than blood: How racial statistics lie*. Minneapolis, MN: University of Minnesota Press.

Zuberi, T., & Bonilla-Silva, E. (2008). *White logic, white methods: Racism and methodology*. Lanham, MD: Rowman & Littlefield Publishers, Inc.

Zweig, R. W. (2001). *German reparations and the Jewish world: A history of the claims conference* (2nd ed.). London; Portland, OR: Frank Cass.

Index

Abandonment, 2
Accounting, 100–101
Anti-Defamation League (ADL), 17, 73, 114
Antisemitism
  "antitype," 87
  chimeral antisemitism, 60
  global strategies, 116
  legal basis, 81
  Nazis, 81
  political, 82
  racialized anti-semitism, 50
  xenophobic antisemitism, 60
Association of Holocaust Organizations (AHO), 107, 115
Atrocities, 117

"Blind space," 90
Bloodlands, 24
Bystanders, 48

Camp survivors, 99
Catastrophe, 64–66
Categorical exclusion, 81
Chimeral antisemitism, 60
Claims conference, 13
Cognitive learning theory, 41
Convention against Genocide, 13
Cosmopolitan perspectives, 34
Crime, 99
Cultures
  appropriation, 49
  Holocaust education, 79–85
  misrepresentation, 86–89
  resilience, 86–89
  studies, 76–79
Curricular variety
  bloodlands, 40
  concentration camp, 37
  genocide of Jews, 37
  human rights, 37
  Israeli education, 36
  language, 41
  policy-makers, 37
  UNESCO, 36
  variation, 39

Dehumanizing, 56
Denialism
  expression/manifestation, 86
  spectrum, 88
Dignifying humans, 56
Dignity, 56–58
Directives, 118–122
Displaced persons (DPs), 41

Echoes and Reflections, 14, 97, 105
Emigrants, 74
Eugenic discrimination, 28
Eviction, 84
Extermination, 51

Facing History and Ourselves, 105
False Aryan stereotype, 103
Frankification, 63

Genocidal persecution, 6
Genocide
  antisemitic genocide, 127
  awareness, 114
  concept, 13
  crimes, 27–28
  definition, 13
  education, 33
  heinous international crime, 127

prevention, 13, 14, 114
stages, 117
supporting environment, 14
Genocide education
  antisemitism, 44
  barbarism, 42
  discriminatory mass, 43
  international laws, 43
  international military tribunal (IMT), 43
  racism, 44
German administrative documents, 5
German Holocaust education, 120
German military, 25
Global holocaust education, 111–128
Global perspectives, 34
Grand larceny, 5
Gray zones, 53

Holocaust amnesia, 14, 107
Holocaust and Human Rights Education (HHRE), 15, 86, 89, 126
Holocaust-based xenophobia, 79
Holocaust camp, 99
Holocaust denial, 86–89
Holocaust education
  Austria, 121
  barbarity, 14
  consciousness, 16–19
  curricula, 112, 113, 118
  destructive impact, 14
  economic reparations, 13
  genocide. *See* Genocide
  Germany, 120, 126
  Global. *See* Global holocaust education
  goals, 12
  Israeli, 119
  learning about/from, 38–42
  multicultural education, 79, 85
  pedagogical approaches, 12
  political interpretations, 37
  prevention, 13–16

reading, 47–51
redemption, 15–16
remembrance, 23–29
reparation, 13–16
representing, 47–51
responsibilities, 55–71
resilience, 23–29
respect, 23–29
sight and insight, 104–107
students improvement, 19–23
survivors. *See* Survivors
teachings about, 12
twenty-first century, 127–128
types, 32–36
writing, 47–51
Holocaust fatigue, 113
Holocaust generations, 97
Holocaust hesitation, 124–127
Holocaust memories, 97
Humanity, 56–58
Humanizing, 58–64
Human resilience, 75
Human rights, 45–47

Immigration policies, 2
Informed choices, 12
Innovation, 121
"Integrated history," 96
International assistance, 2
International community, 1
International Criminal Court (ICC), 13
International human rights law, 69–71
International military tribunal (IMT), 43
International Red Cross (IRC), 104
Intolerance, 34
Iron curtain, 25
Israeli Holocaust education, 119
iWitness, 97, 105

"Jewish councils," 84
"Jewish-free living," 82

Jews
  cultures, 125
  final solution, 7
  free of Jews, 58
  migration, 83
  museums, 115
  Nazi Germany, 82
  "race," 82
  sheep, 6
  social circumstances, 75
Judeo-Christian interpretations, 6

"Lagers," 102, 103
Liberation, 104
Location museums, 115

Maliciousness, 23–29
Mass crimes, 5
Mass murderers, 24
Memory, 66–69, 107–109, 127
Migrants, 74
Misrepresentations, 50
Multicultural holocaust education
  aspects, 78
  categorical exclusion, 81
  social problems, 80
Museum of Jewish Heritage in New
    York (MJH), 115
Museums
  connect kids, 113
  Jewish, 115
  location museums, 115
  memorial sites, 113
  resources, 115

Nazi crimes, 119
Nazi Germany
  "become white folks," 81
  Jewish, 82
  racism, 82
Nazi police, 1
Nazi rule, 120
Never again, 14, 60
"Non-Germans," 83
Nuremburg laws, 101

Olympics of suffering, 116
Onlookers, 48

Perpetrator perspectives, 89–92
Persecution, 5, 61
Planning, 5
Polish schools, 119
Political antisemitism, 82
Political interpretations, 37
Prisoners, 52
Problem-solvers, 5
Professional organizations, 71

Racial classification, 25
Racialized antisemitism, 50
Racism
  antisemitic racism, 83
  legalized, 82
  Nazi Germany, 82
  political antisemitism, 82
  science, 4
Reanimating, 65
Recounting, 100–101
Refugees, 6
  Jews, 42
  resettlement, 92
Resilience
  cultural resilience, 96
  inspirations, 92–93
  models, 92–93
  segregation, 101
  stigmatization, 101
  survivors, 101–104
Resisters, 75
Responsibilities
  catastrophe, 64–66
  dehumanizing, 56
  dignifying humans, 56
  dignity, 56–58
  free of Jews, 58
  genocide, 57
  humanity, 56–58
  humanizing, 58–64
  human rights, 57

international human rights law, 69–71
learning environments, 55
memory, 66–69
primary documents, 57
survivals, 66–69
victims of crimes, 57
"Revisionist history," 86
"Ruins of memory," 96

Second generation, 122
Secret operations, 2
Self-incrimination, 118
Socialism, 48
Social responsibilities, 28
Solutions, 5
Sonderkommando, 53
State-sanctioned immorality, 2
Students
  bridging metaphor, 23
  citizenship education, 21
  critical thinking, 21
  curricular resources, 21–22
  dehumanization, 20
  dehumanization problems, 20
  humanizing, 20
  inclusive and supportive pedagogy, 20
  populations persecution, 20
Survivals, 66–69
Surviving remnant, 2
Surviving war, 27–28
Survivors
  crime, 99
  descendants, 122–124
  documentaries and recordings, 113
  narratives, 95, 101
  navigating selections, 95
  recounting, 100
  resilience, 101–104
  syndrome, 3
  testimony, 106, 108, 112
  voices, 96, 97–100
  writings, 96

Tainted heritage, 123
Technologies, 113–115
Testimonies, 95, 96, 100, 106
The Olga Lengyel Institute (TOLI), 73
"Three Rs," 106
Transformation, 121

United Nations Declaration of Human Rights, 13
United Nations Educational Scientific and Cultural Organization (UNESCO), 37, 115–118
United States Holocaust Memorial and Museum (USHMM), 3, 14, 23, 86, 115
US Holocaust Museum, 111

Variations, 118–122
Victim groups, 7
Victims, 25, 49, 75
  crimes, 57
  Jewish, 117
  Nazi, 121
  persecution, 120

Wannsee conference in Munich Germany, 5
"War on prejudice," 79
World War I, 2

Xenophobia, 83
Xenophobic antisemitism, 60

Zionism, 48

www.ingramcontent.com/pod-product-compliance
Lightning Source LLC
Chambersburg PA
CBHW051615230426
43668CB00013B/2110